Publications
wan,
oad,
110002
32127
oo.com

6
25-6 (HB)

OR
ERVICES
hawan,
i Road,
i - 110002

by:
elhi,

Publishers, Delhi, India

KITCHE
AN

Published by
Rajiv Jain for Aman
LG-4A, Ganpati Bha
4675-B/21, Ansari R
Darya Ganj, Delhi -
PH: 23255012, 232
E-mail: sshjbs@yah

[The responsibility
entirely that of the
whatsoever.]

First Edition 200
ISBN-81-8204-0

SOLE DISTRIBU
JINDAL BOOK S
LG-4A, Ganpati B
4675-B/21, Ansa
Darya Ganj, Del

Laser Typesettin
S.M. Graphics, D

Printed by:
NCT Printers &

AMAN F
NEW

PREFACE

The kitchen has always been the nerve centre of the household, and never has the kitchen's central role been more important than it is today. Although the main function of a kitchen is cooking, it can be the centre of other activities as well, especially within homes, depending on its size, furnishing, and equipment. In kitchen, numerous independent systems works in harmony to minimise the energy required to prepare meals and clean up afterwards. A successful kitchen designer creates a pleasant atmosphere while solving problems of storage capacity, accessibility, functionality, ventilation, lighting, safety, and durability.

A kitchen without utensils is unthinkable and a well-equipped kitchen is every cook's dream. But since cooks are also individuals, a list of kitchen equipment and utensils which may suit one may not suit another. However there are certain essential items that every cook needs and as such are identified by the number of times they are used. A modern kitchen can be equipped with many efficient labour-saving devices. These machines make tasks such as chopping, shredding and pureeing easier and less time consuming. Kitchen appliances are major investment, not only in the initial purchase cost but also in the use, care, energy consumption, and maintenance for the lifetime of the appliance. So while setting up a new kitchen, one has to spend certain amount of time and thought in choosing and buying equipments and utensils where utmost importance should be given to quality.

This book offers an established set of kitchen design guidelines accepted as the norm for the industry and provides valuable information of some of the most useful equipments in the modern kitchen. It will be an indispensable tool and an essential addition to the professional libraries of architects, interior designers, and anyone interested to make their kitchen more comfortable.

Contents

1

INTRODUCTION

A kitchen is a separate room or other space set aside for the cooking or preparation of meals. When cooking first moved indoors, it was performed, with other domestic labours, in the common room, where the fire burned on the hearth, or—even earlier, before chimneys were known—on the floor in the centre of the room. With the building of larger houses, the kitchen became a separate room.

Little is known of the culinary arrangements of antiquity. Excavations at Pompeii show separate rooms fitted with the simple equipment still used in some Asian cooking. A large brazier, or metal basket on legs, held burning charcoal over which a single basin could be simmered. In homes of wealthy Romans a bench of brick or masonry contained several holes, so that a number of dishes could be cooked at once. Water was kept in jars and heated in large caldrons.

Although the peoples of North Europe used stoves from ancient times for heating, they cooked over open fires and baked in outdoor ovens. In the Middle Ages, many of the finest kitchens were in the monasteries; the kitchens were in separate buildings and were equipped for cooking, brewing, and baking on a large scale. In North American colonial and pioneer days the kitchen was large enough to accommodate the operations of spinning, weaving, sewing, knitting, and harness mending as well as cooking. Early American manor houses, especially in the South, usually had separate kitchens, often connected with the house by a covered way or porch. Many farmhouses, before the use of gas or electricity, had a separate summer kitchen, where canning or preserving and the preparation of meals for harvest workers could be carried on without heating the house.

Kitchens remain places for cooking as well as hubs of family life. In addition to a sink, cabinets, stove, and refrigerator, many have a dishwasher, trash compactor, garbage disposal, and smaller appliances, such as food processors and microwave ovens. Microwave ovens, usually smaller than conventional ovens and used as adjuncts, heat foods quickly without drying them out, but also without browning, and can be used to quickly defrost frozen food.

Figure 1. A modern kitchen

A modern kitchen is typically equipped with a stove or microwave oven and has a sink with water on tap for cleaning food and dishwashing. Modern kitchens often also feature a dishwasher. Some installations to store food usually also are present, either in the form of an adjacent pantry or more commonly cabinets and a refrigerator.

Although the main function of a kitchen is cooking, it can be the centre of other activities as well, especially within homes, depending on its size, furnishing, and equipment. If a washing machine is present, washing and drying laundry is also done in the kitchen. The kitchen may also be the place where the family eats, provided it is large enough. Sometimes, it is the most comforting room in a house, where family and visitors tend to congregate.

Development of the Kitchen

The development of the kitchen has been intricately and intrinsically linked with the development of the cooking range or stove. Until the 18th century, open fire was the sole means of heating food, and the architecture of the kitchen reflected this. When technical advances brought new ways to heat food in the 18th and 19th centuries, architects took advantage of newly-gained flexibility to bring fundamental changes to the kitchen. Water on tap only became gradually available during industrialisation; before, water had to be collected from the nearest well and heated in the kitchen.

Early History

The houses in Ancient Greece were commonly of the atrium-type: the rooms were arranged around a central courtyard. In many such homes, a covered but otherwise open patio served as the kitchen. Homes of the wealthy had the kitchen as a separate room, usually next to a bathroom (so that both rooms could be heated by the kitchen fire), both rooms being accessible from the court. In such houses, there was often a separate small storage room in the back of the kitchen used for storing food and kitchen utensils.

In the Roman Empire, common folk in cities often had no kitchen of their own; they did their cooking in large public kitchens. Some had small mobile bronze stoves, on which a fire could be lit for cooking. Wealthy Romans had relatively well-equipped kitchens. In a Roman villa, the kitchen was typically integrated into the main building as a separate room, set apart for practical reasons of smoke and sociological reasons of the kitchen being operated by slaves. The fireplace was typically on the floor, placed at a wall—sometimes raised a little bit--such that one had to kneel to cook. There were no chimneys.

Early medieval European longhouses had an open fire under the highest point of the building. The "kitchen area" was between the entrance and the fireplace. In place of a chimney, these early buildings had a hole in the roof through which some of the smoke could escape. Besides cooking, the fire also served as a source of heat and light to the single-room building. A similar design can be found in the Iroquois longhouses of North America.

In the larger homesteads of European nobles, the kitchen was sometimes in a separate sunken floor building to keep the main building, which served social and official purposes, free from smoke.

The first known stoves in Japan date from about the same time. The earliest findings are from the Kofun period (3rd to 6th century). These stoves, called *kamado,* were typically made of clay and mortar; they were fired with wood or charcoal through a hole in the front and had a hole in the top, into which a pot could be hanged by its rim. This type of stove remained in use for centuries to come, with only minor modifications. Like in Europe, the wealthier homes had a separate building which served for cooking. A kind of open fire pit fired with charcoal, called *irori,* remained in use as the secondary stove in most homes until the Edo period (17th to 19th century). A kamado was used to cook the staple food, for instance rice, while irori served both to cook side dishes and as a heat source.

The kitchen remained largely unaffected by architectural advances throughout the middle ages; open fire remained the only method of heating food. European medieval kitchens were dark, smokey, and sooty places, whence their name "smoke kitchen".

In European medieval cities around the 10th to 12th centuries, the kitchen still used an open fire hearth in the middle of the room. In wealthy homes, the ground floor was often used as a stable while the kitchen was located on the floor above, like the bedroom and the hall. In Japanese homes, the kitchen started to become a separate room within the main building at that time.

In castles and monasteries, the living and working areas were separated; the kitchen was moved to a separate building, and thus couldn't serve anymore to heat the living rooms.

With the advent of the chimney, the hearth moved from the centre of the room to one wall, and the first brick-and-mortar hearths were built. The fire was lit on top of the construction; a vault underneath served to store wood. Pots made of iron, bronze, or copper started to replace the pottery used earlier. The temperature was controlled by hanging the pot higher or lower over the fire, or placing it on a trivet or directly on the hot ashes.

Leonardo da Vinci invented an automated system for a rotating spit for spit-roasting: a propeller in the chimney made the spit turn all by itself. This kind of system was widely used in wealthier homes.

Using open fire for cooking and heating was risky; fires devastating whole cities occurred frequently.

Beginning in the late middle ages, kitchens in Europe lost their home-heating function even more and were increasingly moved from the living area into a separate room. The living room was now heated by tiled stoves, operated from the kitchen, which offered the huge advantage of not filling the room with smoke. Freed from smoke and dirt, the living room thus could become to serve as an area for social functions and increasingly became a showcase for the owner's wealth and was sometimes prestigiously furnished. In the upper classes, cooking and the kitchen were the domain of the servants, and the kitchen was set apart from the living rooms, sometimes even far from the dining room. Poorer homes often did not have a separate kitchen yet; they kept the one-room arrangement where all activities took place, or at the most had the kitchen in the entrance hall.

The medieval smoke kitchen remained common, especially in rural farmhouses and generally in poorer homes, until much later. In a few European farmhouses, the smoke kitchen was in regular use until the middle of the 20th century. These houses often had no chimney, but only a smoke hood above the fireplace, made of wood and covered with clay, and used to smoke meat. The smoke then rose more or less freely, warming the upstairs rooms and protecting the woodwork from vermin.

Characteristics of Colonial American Kitchens

In the Colonial American kitchen, the same distinction as for the medieval European kitchen is visible. The early settlers in the north often had no separate kitchen; a fireplace in a corner of the cabin served as the kitchen space. Later, the kitchen did become a separate room, but remained within the building.

The development in the southern states was quite different, but then, so were the climate and sociological conditions. In southern estates, the kitchen was often relegated to an outhouse, separated from the mansion, for much of the same reasons as in the feudal kitchen in medieval Europe: the kitchen was operated by slaves, and their working place had to be separated from the living area of the masters by the social standards of the time. In addition, the area's warm climate made operating a kitchen quite unpleasant, especially in the summer.

Completely separated summer kitchens also developed on larger farms further north to avoid that the main house was heated by the preparation of the meals for the harvest workers or tasks like canning.

Impacts of Industrialisation

Technological advances during industrialisation brought major changes to the kitchen. Iron stoves, which enclosed the fire completely and were more efficient, appeared. Early models included the Franklin stove around 1740, which was a furnace stove intended for heating, not for cooking. Benjamin Thompson in England designed his "Rumford stove" around 1800. This stove was much more energy efficient than earlier stoves; it used one fire to heat several pots, which were hung into holes on top of the stove and were thus heated from all sides instead of just from the bottom. However, his stove was designed for large kitchens; it was too big for domestic use.

The "Oberlin stove" was a refinement of the technique that resulted in a size reduction; it was patented in the U.S. in 1834 and became a commercial success with some 90,000 units sold over the next 30 years. These stoves were still fired with wood or coal. Although the first gas street lamps were installed in Paris, London, and Berlin at the beginning of the 1820s and the first U.S. patent on a gas stove was granted in 1825, it wasn't until the late 19th century that using gas for lighting and cooking became commonplace in urban areas.

The urbanisation in the second half of the 19th century induced other significant changes that ultimately would also change the kitchen. Out of sheer necessity, cities began planning and building water distribution pipes into homes, and built canalisations to deal with the waste water. Gas pipes were laid; gas was used first for lighting purposes, but once the network had grown sufficiently, it became available also for heating and cooking on gas stoves.

At the turn of the 20th century, electricity had been mastered well enough to become a commercially viable alternative to gas and slowly started replacing the latter. But like the gas stove, the electrical stove had a slow start. The first electrical stove had been presented in 1893 at the Chicago world fair, but it wasn't until the 1930s that the technology was stable enough and began to take off.

Industrialisation also caused social changes. The new factory working class in the cities was housed under generally poor conditions. Whole families lived in small one or two-room apartments in tenement buildings up to six stories high, badly aired and with insufficient lighting. Sometimes, they shared apartments with "night sleepers", unmarried men that paid for a bed at night. The kitchen in such an apartment was often used as a living and sleeping room, and even as a bathroom. Water had to be fetched from wells and heated on the stove. Water pipes were laid only towards the end of the 19th century, and then often only with one tap per building or per story. Brick-and-mortar stoves fired with coal remained the norm until well into the second half of the century. Pots and kitchenware typically were stored on open shelves, and parts of the room could be separated from the rest using simple curtains.

In contrast, there were no dramatic changes for the upper classes. The kitchen, located in the basement or the ground floor, continued to be operated by servants. In some houses, water pumps were installed, and some even had kitchen sinks and drains (but no water on tap yet, except for some feudal kitchens in castles). The kitchen became a much cleaner space with the advent of "cooking machines", closed stoves made of iron plates and fired by wood and increasingly charcoal or coal, and that had flue pipes connected to the chimney.

For the servants the kitchen continued to serve also as a sleeping room; they slept either on the floor, or later in narrow spaces above a lowered ceiling, for the new stoves with their smoke outlet no longer required a high ceiling in the kitchen. The kitchen floors were tiled; kitchenware was neatly stored in cupboards to protect them from dust and steam. A large table served as a workbench; there were at least as many chairs as there were servants, for the table in the kitchen also doubled as the eating place for the servants.

The middle class tried to imitate the luxurious dining styles of the upper class as best as it could. Living in smaller apartments, the kitchen was the main room-here, the family lived. The study or living room was saved for special occasions such as an occasional dinner invitation. Because of this, these middle-class kitchens often were more homely than those of the upper class, where the kitchen was a work-only room occupied only by the servants. Besides a cupboard to store the kitchenware, there were a table and chairs, where the family would dine, and sometimes-if space allowed-even a fauteuil or a couch.

Gas pipes were laid only in the late 19th century, and gas stoves started to replace the older coal-fired stoves. Gas was more expensive than coal, though, and thus the new technology first was installed in the wealthier homes.

Where workers' apartments were equipped with a gas stove, gas distribution would go through a coin meter.

In rural areas, the older technology using coal or wood stoves or even brick-and-mortar open fireplaces remained common throughout. Gas and water pipes were first installed in the big cities; small villages were connected only much later.

Impact of Rationalisation

The trend to increasing gasification and electrification continued at the turn of the 20th century. In industry, it was the phase of rationalisation, where work processes were attempted to be streamlined. Taylorism was born, and time-motion studies were used to optimise processes. These ideas also spilled over into domestic kitchen architecture due to a growing trend that called for a professionalisation of household work, started in the mid-19th century by Catharine Beecher and amplified by Christine Frederick's publications in the 1910s.

Working class women frequently worked in factories to ensure the family's survival, as the men's wages often did not suffice. Social housing projects led to the next milestone: the "Frankfurt kitchen". Born in 1926, this kitchen measured 1.9m by 3.4m, with a standard layout. It was built for two purposes: to optimise kitchen work to reduce cooking time (so that women would have more time for the factory) and to lower the cost of building decently-equipped kitchens. The design, created by Margarete Schutte-Lihotzky, was the result of detailed time-motion studies and heavily influenced by the railway dining car kitchens of the period. It was built in some 10000 apartments in a social housing project of architect Ernst May in Frankfurt.

The initial reception was heavily critical: people were not accustomed to the changed processes also designed by Schütte-Lihotzky; it was so small that only one person could work in it; some storage spaces intended for raw loose food ingredients such as flour were reachable by children.

Figure 2. The Frankfurt kitchen

But the Frankfurt kitchen embodied a standard for the rest of the 20th century in rental apartments: the "work kitchen". Too small to live or dine in, it was soon criticised as "exiling the women in the kitchen", but the post-World War II conservatism coupled with economic reasons prevailed. The kitchen once more was seen as a work place that needed to be separated from the living areas. Practical reasons also played a role in this development: just as in the bourgeois homes of the past, one reason for separating the kitchen was to keep the steam and smells of cooking out of the living room.

Impact of Technicalisation

The idea of standardised dimensions and layout developed for the Frankfurt kitchen took hold. The equipment used remained a standard for years to come: hot and cold water on tap and a kitchen sink and an electrical or gas stove and oven. Not much later, the refrigerator was added as a standard item. The concept was refined in the "Swedish kitchen" using unit furniture with wooden fronts for the kitchen cabinets. Soon the concept was amended by the use of smooth synthetic door and drawer fronts, first in white, recalling a sense of cleanliness and alluding to sterile lab or hospital settings, but soon after in lively, friendly colours, too.

A trend began in the 1940s in the United States to equip the kitchen with electrified small and large kitchen appliances such as blenders, toasters, and later also microwave ovens. Following the end of World War II, massive demand in Europe for low-price, high-tech consumer goods led to Western European kitchens being designed to accommodate new appliances such as refrigerators and electric/gas cookers. Parallel to this development in tenement buildings went the evolution of the kitchen in homeowner's houses. There, the kitchens usually were somewhat larger, suitable for everyday use as a dining room, but otherwise the ongoing technicalisation was the same, and the use of unit furniture became a standard also in this market sector.

General technocentric enthusiasm even led some designers to take the "work kitchen" approach even further, culminating in futuristic designs like Luigi Colani's "kitchen satellite" (1969, commissioned by the German high-end kitchen manufacturer Poggenpohl for an exhibit), in which the room was reduced to a ball with a chair in the middle and all appliances at arm's length, an optimal arrangement maybe for "applying heat to food", but not necessarily for actual cooking. Such extravaganzas remained outside the norm, though.

In the former Eastern bloc countries, the official doctrine viewed cooking as a mere necessity, and women should work "for the society" in factories, not at home. Also, housing had to be built at low costs and quickly, which led directly to the standardised apartment block using prefabricated slabs. The kitchen was reduced to the max and the "work kitchen" paradigm taken to its extremes: in East Germany for instance, the standard tenement block of the model "P2" had tiny 4 m^2 kitchens in the inside of the building (no windows), connected to the dining and living room of the 55 m^2 apartment and separated from the latter by a pass-through or a window.

Open Kitchens

Starting in the 1980s, the perfection of the extractor hood allowed an open kitchen again, integrated more or less with the living room without causing the whole apartment or house to smell. Before that, only a few earlier experiments, typically in newly built upper middle class family homes, had open kitchens. Examples are Frank Lloyd Wright's *House Willey* (1934) and *House Jacobs* (1936). Both had open kitchens, with high ceilings (up to the roof) and were aired by skylights. The extractor hood made it possible to build open kitchens in apartments, too, where both high ceilings and skylights were not possible.

The re-integration of the kitchen and the living area went hand in hand with a change in the perception of cooking: increasingly, cooking was seen as a creative and sometimes social act instead of work, especially in upper social classes. Besides, many families also appreciated the trend towards open kitchens, as it made it easier for the parents to supervise the kids while cooking. The enhanced status of cooking also made the kitchen a prestige object for showing off one's wealth or cooking professionalism. Some architects have capitalised on this "object" aspect of the kitchen by designing freestanding "kitchen objects". However, like their precursor, Colani's "kitchen satellite", such futuristic designs are exceptions.

Another reason for the trend back to open kitchens (and a foundation of the "kitchen object" philosophy) is also to be found in the changes in the food alimentation. Whereas in the 1950s most cooking started out with raw ingredients and a meal had to be prepared for real, the advent of frozen meals and pre-prepared convenience food has changed the cooking habits of many people, who consequently used the kitchen less and less. For others, who followed the "cooking as a social act" trend, the open kitchen had the advantage that they could be with their guests while cooking, and for the "creative cooks" it might even become a stage for their cooking performance.

Types of Kitchen

Domestic kitchen design *per se* is a relatively recent discipline. The first ideas to optimise the work in the kitchen go back to Catherine Beecher's *A Treatise on Domestic Economy* (1843, revised and republished together with her sister Harriet Beecher Stowe as The American Woman's Home in 1869). Beecher's "model kitchen" propagated for the first time a systematic design based on early ergonomics. The design included regular shelves on the walls, ample work space, and dedicated storage areas for various food items. Beecher even separated the functions of preparing food and cooking it all-together by moving the stove into a compartment adjacent to the kitchen.

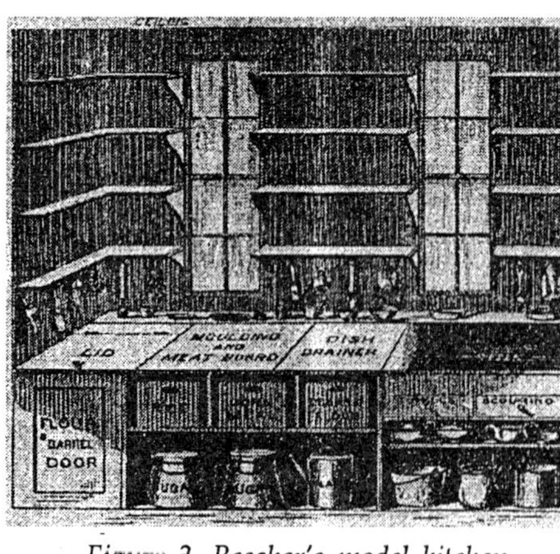

Figure 3. Beecher's model kitchen

Christine Frederick published from 1913 a series of articles on "New Household Management" in which she analysed the kitchen following Taylorist principles, presented detailed time-motion studies, and derived a kitchen design from them. Her ideas were taken up in the 1920s by architects in Germany and Austria, most notably Bruno Taut, Erna Meyer, and Margarete Schutte-Lihotzky. A social housing project in Frankfurt realised in 1927/28 was the breakthrough for her Frankfurt kitchen, which embodied this new notion of efficiency in the kitchen.

While this "work kitchen" and variants derived from it were a great success for tenement buildings, home owners had different demands and didn't want to be constrained by a 6.4 m^2 kitchen. Nevertheless, kitchen design was mostly ad-hoc following the whims of the architect. In the U.S., the "Small Homes Council", since 1993 the "Building Research Council", of the School of Architecture of the University of Illinois at Urbana-Champaign was founded in 1944 with the goal to improve the state of the art in home building, originally with an emphasis on standardisation for cost reduction.

It was there that the notion of the "kitchen work triangle" was formalised: the three main functions in a kitchen are storage, preparation, and cooking, and the places for these functions should be arranged in the kitchen in such a way that work at one place does not interfere with work at another place, the distance between these places is not unnecessarily large, and no obstacles are in the way. A natural arrangement is a triangle, with the refrigerator, the sink, and the stove at a vertex each. This observation led to a few common kitchen forms, commonly characterised by the arrangement of the kitchen cabinets and sink, stove, and refrigerator:

— A single file kitchen has all of these along one wall; the work triangle degenerates to a line. This is not optimal, but often the only solution if space is restricted.

— The double file kitchen has two rows of cabinets at opposite walls, one containing the stove and the sink, the other the refrigerator. This is the classical work kitchen.

— In the L-kitchen, the cabinets occupy two adjacent walls. Again, the work triangle is preserved, and there may even be space for an additional table at a third wall, provided it doesn't intersect the triangle.

— A U-kitchen has cabinets along three walls, typically with the sink at the base of the "U". This is a typical work kitchen, too, unless the two other cabinet rows are short enough to place a table at the fourth wall.

— The block kitchen is a more recent development, typically found in open kitchens. Here, the stove or both the stove and the sink are placed where an L or U kitchen would have a table, in a freestanding "island", separated from the other cabinets. In a closed room, this doesn't make much sense, but in an open kitchen, it makes the stove accessible from all sides such that two persons can cook together, and allows for contact with guests or the rest of the family, for the cook doesn't face the wall anymore.

Modern kitchens often have enough informal space to allow for people to eat in it without having to use the formal dining room. Such areas are called "breakfast areas", "breakfast nooks" or "breakfast bars" if the space is integrated into a kitchen counter. Kitchens with enough space to eat in are sometimes called "eat-in kitchens".

Restaurant and canteen kitchens found in hotels, hospitals, army barracks and similar establishments are generally subject to public health laws. They are inspected periodically by public-health officials, and forced to close if they don't meet hygienic requirements mandated by law.

Canteen kitchens (and castle kitchens) were often the places where new technology was used first. For instance, Benjamin Thompson's "energy saving stove", an early 19th century fully-closed iron stove using one fire to heat several pots, was designed for large kitchens; another thirty years passed before they were adapted for domestic use.

Today's western restaurant kitchens typically have tiled walls and floors and use stainless steel for other surfaces (workbench, but also door and drawer fronts) because these materials are durable and easy to clean. Professional kitchens are often equipped with gas stoves, as these allow cooks to regulate the heat quicker and more finely than electrical stoves. Some special appliances are typical for professional kitchens, such as large installed deep fryers, steamers, or a Bain Marie.

The fast food and convenience food trends have also changed the way restaurant kitchens operate. There is a trend for restaurants to only "finish" delivered convenience food or even just re-heat completely prepared meals, maybe at the utmost grilling a hamburger or a steak.

The kitchens in railway dining cars present special challenges: space is constrained, and nevertheless the personnel must be able to serve a great number of meals quickly. Especially in the early history of the railway this required flawless organisation of processes; in modern times, the microwave oven and prepared meals have made this task a lot easier.

Galleys are kitchens aboard ships. On yachts, galleys are often cramped, with one or two gas burners fuelled by a gas bottle, but kitchens on cruise ships or large warships are comparable in every respect with restaurants or canteen kitchens. On passenger airplanes, the kitchen is reduced to a mere pantry, the only function reminiscent of a kitchen is the heating of in-flight meals (where they haven't been "optimised" away altogether) delivered by a catering company. An extreme form of the kitchen occurs in space, e.g. aboard a Space Shuttle (where it is also called the "galley") or the International Space Station. The astronauts' food is generally completely prepared, dehydrated, and sealed in plastic pouches, and the kitchen is reduced to a rehydration and heating module.

Outdoor areas in which food is prepared are generally not considered to be kitchens, although an outdoor area set up for regular food preparation, for instance when camping, might be called an "outdoor kitchen". Military camps and similar temporary settlements of nomads may have dedicated kitchen tents.

In schools where food technology is taught, there will be a series of kitchens with multiple equipment (similar in some respects to laboratories) solely for the purpose of teaching. These will consist of between 6 and 12 workstations, each with their own oven, sink and kitchen utensils.

Equipment in a Modern Kitchen

A kitchen without utensils is unthinkable and a well-equipped kitchen is every cook's dream. But since cooks are also individuals, a list of kitchen equipment and utensils which may suit one may not suit another. However there are certain essential items that every cook needs and as such are identified by the number of times they are used. For example, items used often, such as knives, spoons, pans etc. fall in this category.

Different pieces of cooking equipment exist for every purpose. While setting up a new kitchen, certain amount of time and thought has to be given in choosing and buying equipment and utensils where utmost importance should be given to quality.

A kitchen can, today, be equipped with many efficient labour-saving devices. Machines make tasks such as chopping, shredding and pureeing easier and less time consuming. The housewives and the cooks no longer need to spend the day in the kitchen stirring food and soups, as the modern and efficient equipment helps them to do the work much faster.

A kitchen appliance is a major investment, not only in the initial purchase cost but also in the use, care, energy consumption, and maintenance for the lifetime of the appliance. Most major household appliances have a relatively long life expectancy. Therefore, a poor choice can be both irritating and costly, especially if the appliance must be replaced early because of high energy and repair costs or failure.

Most of today's appliances use less energy than those made just 10 years ago. When comparing refrigerators from 1972 to 1984, an energy-efficient refrigerator can save, on the average, $47 per year in reduced energy costs. An energy-efficient dishwasher can save, on the average, $35 per year. Ranges are not required to have energy guide labels; therefore, their energy use has not been calculated.

Some of the appliances needed in a kitchen are listed below.

1. *Blenders and Mixers.* They simplify and cut the time for various culinary techniques such as creaming, whisking, etc.
2. *Cooking Range.* Used in the conventional cooking method, it can be electric or gas operated.
3. *Food Processors.* Are the high-tech kitchen appliances, combining the capabilities of electric mixers and blenders and operate at various speed. Used for mincing, chopping, creaming, etc.

4. *Pressure Cooker.* A combination of a saucepan and a steamer. Normally made of aluminium as it helps to spread heat more evenly.
5. *Pulveriser.* A heavy duty electrical grinding machine with a very high speed for grinding and breaking down of ingredients.
6. *Refrigerator.* A must for any modern kitchen; not only stores and keeps the things fresh but has become an integral part of cooking too.
7. *Ovens.* A must for baking and roasting purposes. *Microwave oven* is a revolutionary piece of kitchen equipment which helps food to cook faster - in minutes and seconds rather than hours.
8. *Toaster.* Mainly used for toasting breads.
9. *Griller.* Comes in different sizes and shapes for different purposes like grilling of sandwich or grilling of chicken etc.
10. *Oven-Toaster-Griller Combine.* As the name suggests does the three functions in the space of one.
11. *Hand Blender.* Does light mixing and whipping work.
12. *Coffee Machine.* Comes in various types: Filter coffee, Cona coffee etc.
13. *Water Purifier.* For filtering water of various impurities.
14. *Geyser.* Required for supply of hot water mainly for dish washing.
15. *Dish Washer.* Finishes dishwashing efficiently and quickly.

Cooking Utensils

There are pots and pans to suit each method of cooking. However many of them are versatile enough to fulfil several functions. Listed below are some of the most commonly used cooking utensils and cooking aids.

1. *Chakla & Belan.* Chakla is a small marble or wooden platform and belan the rolling pin, usually made of wood. They are used for rolling dough to make various Indian breads.
2. *Baking Trays.* Large and small, aluminium/stainless steel trays used for baking purposes.
3. *Bamboo Broom.* A normal short broom of bamboo sticks, widely used in Chinese kitchens to clean the wok.
4. *Chimta.* In simple term, tongs, meant for holding a hot cooking object while frying, griddle cooking etc.
5. *Chopping Board.* Made of food grade fibre, comes in different shapes, sizes, thickness and colours used for the purpose of cutting and chopping food items on it.

2

KITCHEN LAYOUT AND DESIGN

Good kitchen design starts early, even as early as locating the room within the house. If you're lucky enough to be able to choose which direction your kitchen will face, consider orienting it toward the east or southeast, where morning sun will fill it with light. Before investing in pricey new features for your kitchen, consider carefully what you want your renovation to achieve.

The design phase of a successful kitchen takes at least as long as the construction phase. This adds to the cost, but paying a design professional to help you develop and build the right design for your house and family is far cheaper than building the wrong kitchen. Paper and pencils are cheap; cabinets, plaster and plumbing are dear.

Before consulting an architect or designer,. take time to sketch out several versions of your kitchen ideas. At this point you can start conceptualising the design yourself, before consulting an architect or designer. Get some graph paper and, using a scale of 6 inches to the square, draw the outline of the kitchen. Pencil in walls, doors and windows in their current locations. Cut out pieces of paper or cardboard to scale to represent the refrigerator, sink and cook top, and begin arranging them into a work triangle that meets your needs. Locate the rest of the major kitchen elements-counters, cabinets, tables, islands and whatever else you think your kitchen should have. Then place a sheet of tracing paper over the graph and draw the floor plan in bold lines so that you can see it. Most likely, as you work on this floor plan you'll start to see alternatives. Draw each variation on tracing paper and number them. To help free up your thinking, try developing a radically different floor plan, and explore its variations as you did with your initial floor plan.

Architects work directly for the client, either for a flat fee or at an hourly rate, and earn no commissions by selling particular products. This gives architects the freedom to recommend whatever they think best suits the project's needs. You can bring them the design you've worked out yourself, or rely on them to come up with the ideas.

Finding the right architect or designer is a bit like finding the right barber or psychiatrist. The one that's right for you is the one that's right for you. Peruse books and periodicals for designs that catch your eye. Architects who are just beginning to win recognition are not necessarily more expensive than those who are little known. But the best method is word of mouth. Ask friends, business associates and neighbours who have recently undergone kitchen renovations.

Kitchen design stores, cabinet shops, contractors and carpenters can also be good people to talk to during the design phase of your project. But be sure to get only the information they're best able to provide. A carpenter is an excellent person to ask about construction possibilities such as removing bearing walls, but may not be the person to ask about the actual kitchen layout. A contractor can organise the job and quote a price, but for designing the room you are better off with an architect.

Successful renovations are inspired by limitations of budget, space, design and construction timetables. These constraints inspire the architect, contractor and client to focus on the essentials and disregard the superfluous. Good design is also the best way to control renovation costs up front.

Kitchen Layout

There are three stages to planning a kitchen:

- — Measuring up and noting the position of the existing services, windows and doors.
- — Working out the plan to get the appliances, work tops and cupboards where you want them.
- — Deciding on any changes to the services you need.

This section is intended to help you with the actual planning, but they are only suggestions and will not be practical in all situations, you will often have to compromise. The golden rule is - keep it simple - and remember that the kitchen is one of the main selling points for a house.

The principal activity zones in the kitchen are generally recognised as being - food preparation, cooking and serving, and finally washing up. Each activity zone needs to include the worktop(s) and appliances required for that activity, also the zone will require the storage space for the utensils, ingredient etc. required for it.

In addition to the three zones, it is important to arrange the appliances and worktops in the correct order i.e. worktop - appliance - worktop. A work triangle is formed between the three zones. For the greatest efficiency the total length of the three sides of the triangle should be between 3600mm and 6600mm, and as far as possible, the work triangle should be uninterrupted by through traffic.

The 4 basic layouts are:

Corridor Layout

In a long, narrow area with doors at each end you have little choice other than two facing rows of appliances and storage units. You should allow at least 1200mm between two rows for a safe walk-through corridor and to allow comfortable access to front loading appliances. In really narrow rooms, the fittings might need to be restricted to one side of the room.

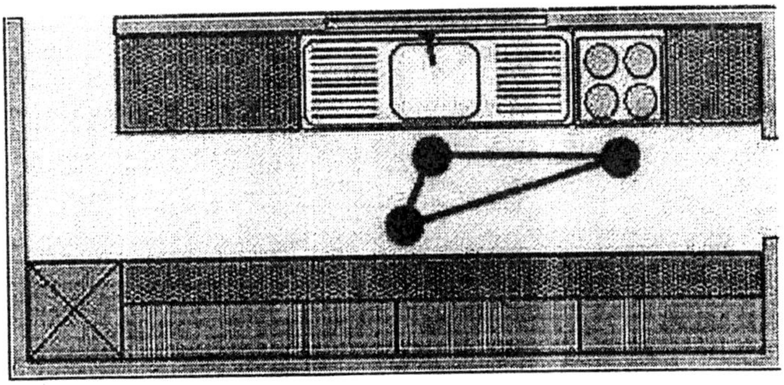

Figure 1. Corridor layout

L-shaped Layout

This is often the best solution where the kitchen can fit into a corner. Where space is not sufficient for a straight-

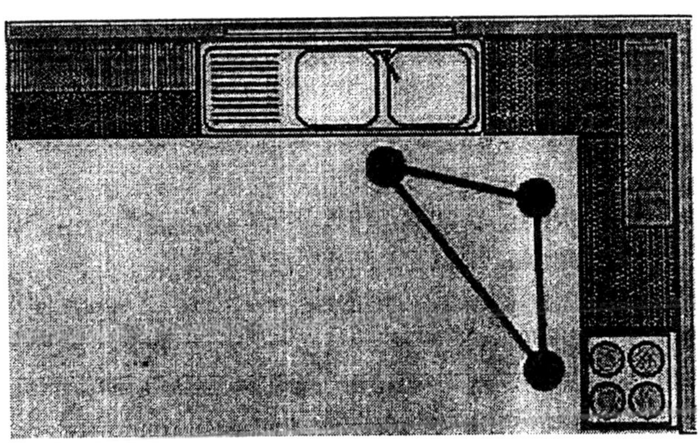

Figure 2. L-shaped layout

line or parallel arrangement, the L-shaped kitchen design is well suited to access several groups of equipment, and is adaptable for table service restaurants. It gives you the ability to place more equipment in a smaller space. You'll often find an L-shaped design in dishwashing areas, with the dish machine placed at the center corner of the L.

U-shaped Layout

This layout is convenient as all working areas are within easy reach. It may be the only choice for small rooms although it can also be used with effect where a kitchen area needs to be fitted at one end of a larger room. Try to allow for 1200mm between the parallel sides of the U.

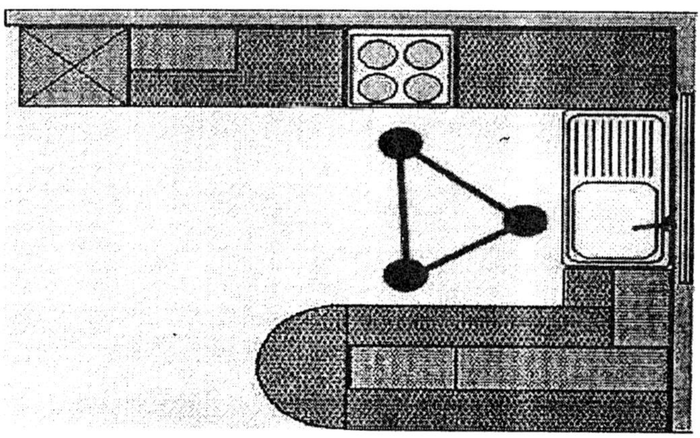

Figure 3. U-shaped layout

Island Layout

Often thought of as a luxury, the island layout needs a fairly large room, however in such a room, it does reduce the amount of walking you need to do. Try to allow for 1200mm between the island and any other cupboard/ obstruction etc. Although the design shown has the cooking hob on the island, the island could be used for the food preparation area.

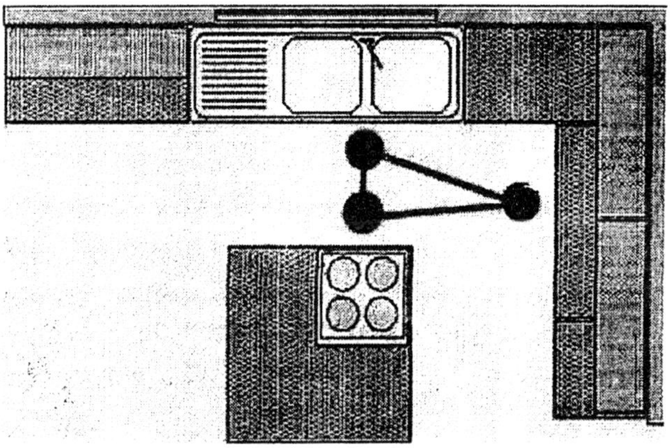

Figure 4. Island layout

Planning the Layout

Designing a new kitchen layout — remember there are no absolute rules, after all it is your kitchen but...

1. First of all, list the floor/wall mounted appliances you want to include in your kitchen — see choice of appliances below for the most likely ones you will want to include. Likely appliances required in a kitchen include:

   — Cooker or hob and oven

   — Extractor hood for cooker/hob

   — Washing machine

   — Dish washer

   — Tumble dryer

   — Fridge/freezer

   — Room air extractor

2. Measure your kitchen at floor level and at about 900mm from the floor - use the smaller measurement for your floor plan.

3. Draw a scale plan, using squared paper makes things easier.

4. Mark on the plan the services as they currently exist - hot and cold water, drains, electric points, gas points, any existing extractor vents in the walls.
5. Cut out paper or card scale footprints for each appliance and sink you want to include. Write the name of each appliance on its respective piece of paper/card.
6. Most kitchens need three 'work areas'. Preparation, cooking and washing-up, each area should include all the appliances required and a suitable sized work area around it.
7. Roughly position the scale footprints of the appliances in their most logical position with respect to the existing position of the services. Do not worry if you need more services, it just indicated that you will need to add some.
8. Look at the free area between the appliances and decide how many base units you need or can fit. Cut out paper/card footprints for these units.
9. Position the base unit footprints on your plan.
10. You now need to think if there is enough work top surface around each work zone — a lot of the appliances are sized to fit under work surfaces so you should not lose too much. Try to avoid having work surfaces less than 1 metre in length.
11. If you cannot fit in all the appliances or base units you have select or you think the room is already too full, ask yourself if you can relocate any appliance in another room — i.e. move the washing machine to the garage.
12. Think how you can rearrange the kitchen to make it easier to use, begin to think about relocating the position of the existing services. Remember that in addition to the floor mounted appliances, you will also

need electric points for the smaller, moveable appliances which you get out of the cupboard each time you want to use them. All services and window/doors can be repositioned — it is just that additional work is involved; the rough order from easiest to most difficult is - electricity, gas, water supplies, drains (above floor), blocking up doors/windows, drains below floor and moving doors/windows. But remember that you may need professional assistance to move doors/windows and you will need a registered gas fitter to move a gas point.

13. Bearing all this in mind, 'play' with the layout to achieve your dream kitchen — then look at any relocation of services required — are you happy with the amount of work involved? You will often that you have to compromise.

14. When you are happy with a basic floor arrangement, think about the wall area and where you can fit wall units, these tend to be needed in the food preparation area. Try and keep the wall units inline with the base units below them.

15. You should now be in the position to list:
    - The number and style of floor units you require.
    - The number and style of wall units you require.
    - The appliances to be fitted.
    - The work you need to do to add or reposition the services.

Basic Design Principles

Kitchen design is highly specialised and complex. An authorised designer is imperative, in conjunction with an architect or alone. Kitchen designers understand how a kitchen works. If you've retained an architect and/or an interior designer, insist on working with a kitchen designer as well, particularly if you're planning to use a custom cabinet manufacturer, to ensure a well-planned, well-executed design. Once you get the kitchen oriented, there are some basic design principles that will help you with the layout:

Traffic

— A house is not an island; it requires frequent contact with the outside world, much of which is accomplished by car. An attached garage closely adjoining the kitchen or a back door opening on the driveway can reduce the burden of carrying groceries in and the trash out.

— A mud room can reduce kitchen traffic by acting as a staging area for trips into and out of the house. It offers a buffer from cold air, storage space for coats, hats and boots and even pantry shelves for items you won't be using immediately. Taking all this activity out of the kitchen provides more room for cooking and eating, which are, after all, a kitchen's main events.

The Work Triangle

For most of the 20th century, kitchens were organised around what's known as the work triangle — the geometry determined by sink, range and refrigerator. Since most kitchen work is a dance among the three appliances, a good design will make the distances between them comfortable. If they're too short, the work area will be cramped; if too far, the cook will become worn out trotting between them. The rule of thumb is that the three legs of the triangle should add up to between 12 and 26 feet.

There are three basic layouts for the work triangle: u-shaped, l-shaped and galley. In the u-shaped kitchen, there's a triangular path from the sink on one wall to the range on another, to the refrigerator on a third. In an l-shaped kitchen, one element of the work triangle is against one wall with the other two along another. In very tight circumstances, all three points are arranged along the same wall, like the cooking facilities on-board ship, thus the name galley kitchen.

Ideally no traffic should pass through the work triangle. Nothing is more irritating than having people crash into you when you're trying to cook. If there's going to be an island or table in the room, place it where it will neither obstruct the work triangle nor be too far to be a useful work station itself.

Keep in mind that people not directly involved in cooking often need access to the kitchen, particularly the refrigerator. Of the three components of the work triangle, the refrigerator should be located at the triangle's outer corner for easy access. The sink should be accessible as well, but the cooking surface ought to be as protected as possible, and therefore at the most remote point of the work triangle.

Necessary Gadgets

— To function well, the sink, cook top and refrigerator each need to be surrounded with a certain amount of floor and counter space. The refrigerator door needs a clear swing and, if possible, enough room for two people to reach in simultaneously. The doors of any cabinets around the fridge should not conflict with its door. And the refrigerator also needs an 18-inch run of counter as a staging area for foods going into or coming out of it.

— By custom, the sink is placed beneath a window, both to provide daylight for chores done there and to give one a view outdoors. Working at a sink with a window is still much more pleasant than working at a sink without one. Designers often place the sink first and lay out the rest of the work triangle from there.

— Minimum counter lengths are considered to be 36 inches on one side of the sink and 24 on the other, which gives you a staging area for dirty dishes on one side and a drying area on the other. It seems logical to locate the greatest expanse of counter on the side of the sink closest to the cook top, since that is where most foods prepared at the sink are destined.

— The optimum location for the cook top is along an exterior wall, rather than on an island or peninsula. With a stove on an outside wall, it's easy to install an effective hood and ventilation system, essential to expel grease, smoke and combustion gases. The stove or cook top needs a 21- to 30-inch overhead clearance so cooks can readily see and access rear burners and the ventilation system can do its work efficiently.

— If you plan to install a dishwasher, place it close to the sink. Where you choose to put it might depend on whether you're right- or left-handed and on the path dishes are likely to take when cleared from the table. Also consider the choreography of two people loading and unloading the machine.

Storage Areas

— Glassware and dishes should be stored in cabinets or shelves near the sink. Frequently used pots and pans could be stowed between the sink and cook top or from a hanging rack.

— Consider locating your silverware drawers close to the drying rack or dishwasher but out of the primary work triangle so that someone can set the table without interrupting the cook.

— Professional cooks, who spend a great deal of time in their kitchens, prefer to have their utensils within easy reach.

— Shelves or cabinets above the cook top can hold foods that aren't affected by warmth, such as pasta, rice, and cereal. A shelf just below these cabinets but above the cook top can transform the space into a cooking workshop, providing a handy resting place for timers, spices, cooking supplies and implements.

— A large volume of kitchen goods can be stowed in a pantry, an efficient, relatively inexpensive means of storage. Since a pantry is essentially a closet lined with shelves, it's easy on the budget. Also plan to reserve part of the pantry as a utility closet, where mops, brooms and cleaning supplies can be easily stored.

Eating In

— Islands can serve as tables for informal meals. If it's the height of conventional counters — 36 inches — you'll need stools and an ample overhang of about 12 inches to comfortably accommodate sitters' knees.

— If you're thinking about placing a table in your kitchen, here are some basic parameters: A rectangular table with a seating capacity of four to six should measure 2 1/2 feet by 5 to 5 1/2 feet. You'll need 2 1/2 to 3 feet of clearance all around for chairs and adequate circulation. A round table takes up less space but can accommodate more people if need be. Remember that a small increase in radius makes for a big increase in the circumference of the table and therefore the floor space it will take up.

TRENDS IN KITCHEN DESIGN

Industry professionals say now more than ever, kitchen

design is driven by consumer demands and economic factors. The fact is, we are seeing smaller and more efficient kitchens. Experts see this trend as the result of three things: a shortage of qualified labour, an ever—increasing battle for space in general for business uses, and budget constraints, including the demand for an increased return on investment. Following are some examples of what's in vogue in the commercial kitchen world.

Display Kitchen

A display kitchen is where much of the food preparation is done in full view of customers. Being able to watch a busy kitchen staff at work really is interesting to most of us. It whets the appetite and gives the feeling that the guest is being catered to, with a meal that is freshly prepared as he or she looks on. For today's more sophisticated diner, the perceptions of quality, freshness, and presentation are just as important as how the food tastes.

A well—functioning display kitchen also accentuates the sense of showmanship that certainly is part of the culinary arts. It enhances the total dining experience by being part of the atmosphere and the evening's entertainment value. It presents opportunities for the culinary staff to interact with guests. Of course, this may impact the type of person you hire as a staff member! Not everyone is good at, or comfortable with, conveying such a "public" image. But for chefs who enjoy the limelight, something magical happens when they can see the patrons, and vice versa.

One nice design detail is to install half—walls, in what is sometimes called a semi—open kitchen. The staff can be seen preparing food "from the waist up," without a view of the inevitably messy and unsightly aspects of cooking—soiled pots and pans, stacks of plates, the dirty floor, and so on. Nothing should go on in a display area that indicates any type of "volume cooking." The emphasis is on individually prepared dishes. Food preparation in view of the guests also addresses another modern-day concern: food safety.

Most guests believe that when food is prepared in full view, the staff is more conscious of safe food handling practices than they would be closeted away at a prep station in the back of the house. Today, as the cost of restaurant space keeps climbing, there is some financial urgency behind such a multitask environment. The modern restaurateur must maximise profit per square foot of space, and risks failure by using space extravagantly and having to pay the higher costs of heating, cooling, and insuring it.

Combining at least part of the kitchen with the dining area is one way to conserve space. On the other way, the display kitchen is generally more expensive. When it is in public view, everything from equipment to walls to preparation surfaces has to look good. A final word about display or semi-open kitchens: They should only be considered as an option when the menu and food preparation techniques actually lend themselves to display—pizza dough being twirled overhead, steaks being flame-broiled over an open grill, the intricacy of sushi preparation.

Appliances "on Display": In terms of equipment, we've noticed massive brick wood-burning ovens (or gas-fired counterparts) as display kitchen staples. They're not exactly portable, weighing up to 3,000 pounds, but they're attractive, energy-efficient, and quite functional—they can turn out a pizza in three to five minutes. Induction range tops have found their way into display kitchens, since they are sleek-looking, easy to clean, and are speedy and energy efficient.

Induction cooking works by creating an electromagnetic field, which causes the molecules (in this case, of a pan) to move so rapidly that the pan not the Tange top-heats up, in turn cooking the food inside. The magnetic field only prompts other magnetic items (i.e., metal cookware) to heat, while its ceramic surface stays cool to the touch. Not every metal pan is well suited to induction cooking, but there are specific, multiply metal pans made for this purpose.

Cleanup is as simple as wiping off the cooktop surface; there are no spills seeping into burners, and no baked on messes. A 2.5-kilowatt induction burner puts out the equivalent cooking power of the 20,000 BTU burner on a typical saute range. Yet another display kitchen requirement is the rotisserie oven or grill. We usually think of whole chickens, browning perfectly in a glass-front rotisserie cabinet, but there are now attachments that allow you to bake pasta, casseroles, fish, vegetables, and more. From countertop units no more than 30 inches wide, to floor models six feet in width, rotisseries may be purchased as gas, electric, or wood-fired. Ease of cleaning should be a consideration when choosing a rotisserie unit, because they are in view of patrons.

The cooking suite is a real boon to today's hard-working "chef on display". A cooking suite (or cooking island) is a freestanding, custom—built unit into which just about any combination of kitchen equipment can be installed. Instead of a battery of heavy-duty appliances against a wall, a cooking suite allows workers to mart bath sides of the island. It is a way to effectively concentrate the cooking activities, improving communication because appliances and personnel are centrally located. Often, a cooking suite requires less floor space than a conventional hot line, with shorter electrical and plumbing connection lines.

Marche Kitchen

If you can walk up to a stand-alone counter, place an order, and get fresh food, cooked to order, as you wait, you are in a Marche kitchen (pronounced mar-SHAY). A display-style retail concept with European origins, this is different than a display kitchen, since the diners stand and, watch the action instead of being seated and waited on. The novelty and excitement comes from the combination of freshness and the commercial equipment moved from back of the house, right up front!

It's almost as though the wall between dining room and kitchen has been peeled away, and you're practically standing inside a clean, attractive, well-lit kitchen full of griddles, fryers, broilers, refrigerators, steam jacketed kettles, and all the trappings of "big deal cooking." Food is prepped, cooked, and served in one place, which saves steps for the workers and doesn't require the heavy hauling of ingredients from kitchen to serving line. Most Marche kitchens are designed with some flair-blonde wood, tiled pedestals and warmer trays, faux finishes on ventilation hoods and equipment to make them more attractive. In some of them, customers pay for each course separately as they receive it on the serving line.

Technologically Superior Kitchen

Another idea taking hold today is simply a small kitchen with carefully orchestrated work centres, all designed with ergonomics and efficient labour utilisation in mind. It is created to use the fewest possible number of people to perform each task, and out fitted with the highest-quality equipment to minimise downtime. Greater use of technology improves customer service and saves time. Commonsense touches trash receptacles built into the counters, compact storage for individual areas to minimise wasted steps having to go fetch supplies—all mean the crew is able to work smarter, not harder. "Plug and use" (portable) equipment combinations (steamer/ovens; refrigerated space beneath range tops) that are easy to service, with surfaces that are easy to clean, also are popular.

Banquet Kitchens

If your restaurant plans include space for private dining-meeting rooms or separate catering are as you may also need a banquet kitchen to properly service these areas. This kitchen will probably not see daily use, but when it is needed, it is a labour-intensive, production-oriented place that requires powerful, reliable, and multifunctional equipment. If your banquet and special events business becomes successful, you will stretch your main kitchen resources awfully thin without an "extra" banquet kitchen, and you'll run your wait staff ragged if the meeting rooms are located far from the main kitchen.

Banquet kitchens are sometimes called service kitchens. Think of your service kitchen as an extension of your main kitchen. The purpose of the banquet kitchen is to make only the final food preparation before serving to the banquet or meeting crowd. Only modest, one-day storage is needed here and—since most foods will be delivered partly or completely prepared, directly from the main kitchen—there is no need for separate prep areas in the banquet kitchen. All cleaning, peeling, slicing, and butchering can take place in the main kitchen.

You do not need a separate dishwashing area, either. If you make the financial commitment to a service kitchen, it is true that it is making money only when it is in operation. However, don't think of it as a waste if it is not constantly busy. Remember, when the lights are out and nobody's using it, it is still depreciating as an asset, not actively costing operating dollars or shrinking your bottom line. How much space will you need for these additional kitchen facilities? It depends mostly on how many people you can seat in your banquet rooms.

A service kitchen of 75 square feet can accommodate seating of 50 to 100; for 1000 seats, you'll need as much as 500 square feet of kitchen space. The general rule is 50 square feet of kitchen space for every 75 to 100 seats. In addition, you will need about 1/2 square foot per seat for storage of banquet tables and chairs when they are not in use. In designing a layout for your service kitchen, look at portable equipment you can use to hold and serve food. It will be the most adaptable.

If the banquet rooms are close to the main kitchen, you may be able to assign a certain amount of main kitchen space as your "banquet area." At its simplest, it could be a few stainless steel tables on which banquet food is plated for wait staff to pick up and deliver. This area may also include a separate beverage dispenser and ice machine, so waiters from banquet and main dining areas won't trip over each other using the same facilities. Think carefully about traffic flow for busy times of day.

Depending on how busy your banquet/catering business becomes, there may be a need for additional cooking equipment on the main hot line or perhaps expansion of other stations to meet the demands. Although this does enable you to keep the food preparation all in one space, it has a downside. The additional equipment is needed only when there is a banquet. At other times, it either sits idle or is used by the staff simply because it's sitting there, which is an inefficient way to use your appliances. The real solution is to separate the service kitchen from the main kitchen from the start.

Kitchen Budget

Deciding how much money to spend on design,

construction, and equipment is a crucial first step—not just a total figure, but an estimate of how funds are to be allocated and how much time each step will take. First, does the design budget realistically match the concept in size and scope. The budget should reflect the type of market in which the finished restaurant will operate. There's a tendency to overspend at the front end of a project, so much so that the finished facility can't be profitable for many months while construction and design costs are being paid off.

So early on, set your ego aside and, likewise, refuse to accept grandiose plans from consultants who may have good ideas but don't seem to be thinking about your cost parameters. In fact, the lack of early budgeting and planning is the undoing of many a promising concept. It's true that it is difficult to decide months in advance what to spend on design, construction, decor, furniture, fixtures, equipment, china, flatware, glassware, table linens, smallware, publicity, and other preopening expenses, but a good budget should include all of these and more, plus a contingency amount of about 20 percent to cover any cost overruns.

For renovations or adaptive reuse projects in older structures, the contingency amount may even be higher than 20 percent, since problems often crop up that were not anticipated due to the ages or conditions of buildings, utilities, and fixtures, as well as the special care and additional permits often required to refurbish them. It is also more difficult to budget for a restaurant that is part of a larger project—say, a hotel restaurant—than a freestanding restaurant, because you are often bound by the design decisions of others.

Underestimating your budget will not impress your banker or your investors. It is more likely to compromise your concept and misrepresent your ideas to the contractors you hire to work with you. All your costs will vary widely, and will depend on many factors in your market: economic conditions, location, the type of restaurant you want, and so on. The key to controlling them is planning.

Let's take an equipment purchase as an example. Invest some time with the salespeople or manufacturers' representatives. Pay attention during their equipment demonstrations. Don't order something that is more, or bigger, than what you need. Price new equipment before you look at used—that way, you have an idea of what is truly a "good deal." Look for equipment that can perform more than one function—a combi oven, for instance, can hold, bake, or steam. If you order it custom-made, give the manufacturer enough time to do it right. Then, well before it arrives, be sure the preliminary utility connections (called rough-ins) are in the correct places.

Check widths of doors and the intended space where the equipment will be installed to be certain they are wide enough. These are all small steps, and many of them don't specifically have to do with budgeting. But they all add up to one huge factor: making a smart investment that you can live with. In creating a budget, it is reasonable to expect cost estimates up front from any designer, architect, or consultant you may hire, after they have received enough information from you to prepare their own fee estimates. And remember, "costs" and "fees" are different animals.

One factor that has major cost implications is time. If work crews don't show up on schedule or materials you've ordered don't arrive promptly, the delays can become costly. Contractors may charge expensive overtime, and there'll be no time to dispute any details you may not be satisfied with. In some cases, you may have to delay your opening. So, along with your budget, you must develop a time line, which will help you pinpoint when you have to spend certain amounts.

If your concept is fully developed and you've already obtained the site for your foodservice facility, it is reasonable to assume:

— The design phase should take no more than 16 to 18 weeks. This includes the time to get necessary permits from authorities and the bidding process to hire contractors.

— The construction and/or remodel process should not take more than 16 to 24 weeks.

Having to make "change orders"—requests to alter your requirements after the initial agreements with contractors can increase costs. However, there are situations in which modifications are needed that were not anticipated. In this case, the details should be presented (by you, in writing) to the contractor. To whom should you turn for assistance with kitchen design? You can rely on the advice of consultants or the expertise of equipment manufacturers. Either way, you should take the following steps:

— In addition to defining the concept itself, define the goals you expect to achieve from it. Decide on your menu before the design process begins.

— Be very clear on how much money you intend to spend. Trust the professionals who pay attention to your budget, not the ones who consistently try to talk you into spending "just a little bit extra."

— Make a commitment to yourself to choose the most energy-efficient equipment in your price range.

— Consider future growth that may require additional space and utilities.

— Consider equipment and work spaces (tables, shelves) that are movable. Think "maximum flexibility."

— Separate the stages of food production so that raw materials can be prepared well in advance.

— Look for equipment that has a good reputation and a proven performance record. As much as possible, each piece should be multifunctional, simple to operate, easy to maintain, and energy efficient.

— Control costs where the customers won't notice and the kitchen crew won't be affected.

— Some experts suggest that the overall cost of your kitchen equipment should not exceed one-third of the total investment for the entire facility.

Placement of the Kitchen

Kitchen placement is the first critical step in the constructiuon of building. Kitchen as the "heart" of the house. Like a human heart, its job is to pump and circulate life-giving blood throughout the rest of the operation. Kitchen placement will affect the quality of the food, the number of guests who can dine at any particular time of day, the roles of the servers, utility costs, and even the atmosphere of the dining area. Consider each of these factors for a moment.

A poorly designed kitchen can make food preparation and service more difficult than it should be, and it can even undermine the morale of the staff. So, if a new restaurateur has little cash to spend on professional designers, that cash is probably best spent planning the location and design of the kitchen—the one area where equipment, ventilation, plumbing, and general construction costs combine for a major investment. We can also learn to plan wisely by thinking of the restaurant kitchen as a manufacturing plant: With a combination of labour and raw materials, it turns out product.

The unique aspect of foodservice is that this finished product is sold in an outlet that is attached to the factory! Like any other type of manufacturing plant, productivity is highest when the assembly lines and machinery are arranged in a logical, sequential order to put the components together. In foodservice, this includes everything from tossing a salad to turning in orders so that no guest is left waiting too long for a meal.

SERVICE SYSTEM

A major issue that must be addressed before deciding on a kitchen design is the way in which food will be delivered to guests. This is known as the service system. A large operation, such as a hotel, can have more than one service system at work simultaneously: elegant tableside service, room service, and casual bar service. At the other end of the spectrum, quick-service restaurants employ service systems that emphasize speed and convenience, including takeout service and the fast-food option of standing at the same counter to order, pay for, and wait for a meal served within minutes.

Each service system has subsystems; together, they encompass every aspect of the progression of food from kitchen, to table, and back to the dishwashing area. This progression is called flow, much like the traffic flow of a busy street grid. There are two types of flow to consider when planning your kitchen design:

a) Product flow, and

b) Traffic flow.

Product flow is the movement of all food items, from their arrival at the receiving area, through the kitchen, to the guests.

Traffic flow is the movement of employees through the building as they go about their duties. The ideal, in both types of flow systems, is to minimise backtracking and crossovers-again, to make sure the "streets" don't get clogged.

There are three basic flow patterns in every foodservice operation:

1. The raw materials to create each dish have a "back to front to back" flow pattern. They arrive at the "back" of the restaurant, in the kitchen, where they are prepared.
2. Next, they travel to the "front" of the restaurant, to be served in the dining area.
3. Finally, they return to the "back" again, as waste. The movements are so predictable that they can be charted.

Within the kitchen, there is also a flow unique to each cooking section. It could be a pattern of steps the chefs follow to put each dish together or the methodical way the dishwashers scrape, sort, and wash dishes and dispose of waste. The third type of traffic pattern is the flow of the service staff as waiters pick up food, deliver it to the guests, and clear the tables. On a busy night, the whole system really does resemble a busy freeway. So, as you might imagine, there's always the possibility of disaster if somebody makes a wrong turn.

The key to managing these three types of flow is that each should not interfere with the others. The service systems and flow patterns of your business should guide your kitchen design. An operation with huge numbers to feed in short time periods will differ from one that also feeds large numbers but in a longer time period. Can you see how? The distance from the kitchen to the dining area is one important consideration, and kitchen designers have devised numerous strategies to cope with it. You may have noticed that, at some restaurants, the waiters are expected to do quite a few food—related tasks outside the kitchen, at wait stations closer to the guests. They might slice and serve bread, ladle soup, arrange and dress salads, or pour beverages themselves.

The idea is to speed service and preserve the (sometimes inadequate) kitchen space for actual cooking tasks. Another critical decision to be made early in the design process: Should the wait staff come into the kitchen to pick up food, or should it be handed to them through a pass window between kitchen and dining area? Although the pass window is considered more informal, it can still be used in a fancier restaurant, perhaps masked from public view by a wall or partition. Each of these items—distance and kitchen access—help determine your flow patterns.

In a perfect world, flow patterns would all be straight lines that do not intersect. However, this ideal is rarely achieved. One simple rule is that the faster you want your service to be, the more important it is that your flow patterns do not cross. In a fast-service scenario, the flow lines must be short and straight.

The next time you're standing at a fast-food counter, notice how few steps most of the workers have to take to pour your soft drink, pick up your burger, and bag your fries. Speed is the desired outcome. The reverse is true in a fine-dining establishment, where the work may all be done in the kitchen specifically to enhance the feeling of a leisurely dining experience. No clattering plates, no bustling wait stations here.

Now that we've looked at the flow of people as they perform their restaurant duties, let's follow the food flow line: the path of raw materials from the time they enter the building to the time they become leftovers. The receiving area is where the food is unloaded from delivery trucks and brought into the building. Most restaurants locate their receiving areas close to the back door. The next stop is storage—dry storage, refrigerated storage, or freezer storage—where large quantities of food are held at the proper temperatures until needed.

Food that emerges from storage goes to one of several preparation or "prep" areas for vegetables, meats, or salad items. Slicing and dicing take place here, to prepare the food for its next stop: the production area. The size and function of the prep area varies widely, depending mostly on the style of service and type of kitchen. When most people think of a restaurant kitchen, what they imagine is the production line. Here, the food is given its final form prior to serving: boiling, sauteing, frying, baking, broiling, and steaming are the major activities of this area. The food is plated and garnished before it heads out the door on a serving tray And that's the end of the typical food flow line.

There are several kitchen work centres that are not included in the typical food flow sequence, but are closely tied to it. For instance, storage areas should be in close proximity to the preparation area, to minimise employees' walking back and forth. In some kitchens, there is a separate ingredient room, where everything needed for one recipe is organised, to be picked up or delivered to a specific workstation. Storage is much more useful when it's placed near the prep area than near the receiving area, saving steps for busy workers.

The bakery is usually placed between the dry storage and cooking areas, because mixers and ovens can be shared with the cooking area. A meat-cutting area is also essential. It should be in close proximity to both refrigerators and sinks for safety and sanitation reasons, as well as for ease of cleanup. Remember, however, that some kitchens are simply not big enough to accommodate separate, specialised work centres. Kitchen space planning becomes a matter of juggling priorities, and it is a continuous compromise.

If work centres are adjacent to one another, without being cramped, you save time and energy, and if people who work in more than one area have handy, unobstructed paths between those areas, they can work more efficiently. One work centre that is often misplaced is the pot sink, which always seems to be relegated to the most obscure back corner of the kitchen. True, it's not the most attractive area, but think of the many other work centres that depend on it!

The typical kitchen generates an overflow of pots and pans. Why isn't the pot sink placed closer to the production line to deal with the mess? And, speaking of pots, think carefully about where to store them. Both clean and dirty, they take up, a lot of space and require creative storage solutions. Often, pot/pan racks can hang directly above the sink area, giving dishwashers a handy place to store clean pots directly from the drain board.

3

KITCHEN AREAS

The kitchen is the one room where members of a family can be found eating, working on homework, talking on the phone or just hanging out with friends. The kitchen has always been the nerve centre of the household, and never has the kitchen's central role been more important than it is today. As the centrepiece of the home, there are some interesting alternatives for kitchen that go well beyond the norm.

Almost all modern food service establishments will have the following working areas in its' kitchen.

— Service areas,

— Preparation areas,

— Production areas,

— Bakery area,

— Warewashing area,

— Storage areas: dry, refrigerated, cleaning supplies, dishes and utensils,

— Receiving area,

— Office,

— Employee locker rooms, toilets.

SERVICE AREAS

These are probably the most difficult areas to describe, since there are as many types of service areas as there are different restaurants! The service area is the busy zone between the kitchen and the guests, in which the food production staff and wait staff use the most efficient means to get food out of the kitchen and to the customers. The teamwork on both sides of the pass window evolved into today's service area. At a small tableservice restaurant, it may be an area no larger than 4 to 6 feet long that houses the pass window.

Many eateries hire people called expediters to stand on either side of the window and facilitate ordering and order delivery. An expediter may organise incoming and outgoing orders for speed, check each tray for completeness and accuracy of the order before it's delivered, and even do a bit of last-minute garnishing as plates are finished. When standing in the kitchen to do this, the person is sometimes known as a wheel person or ticket person.

In quick-service establishments, the service areas are the counters, clearly visible to incoming customers. A recent innovation is the separation of beverages and condiments from prepared foods. Nowadays, customers fill their own drink cups, dispense their own mustard or ketchup, and so on. In some restaurants, the wait station and service area are one and the same. A common problem in this area is that usually no one remembers to plan for plenty of flat space for the wait staff to rest trays or set up tray holders. Generally, no matter what it is called, this area is viewed with apprehension by many restaurant designers. And no wonder. It is actually an extension of the back of the house that happens to be located in the front of the house.

Wait Station

The wait station typically has no inherent "eye appeal," and yet it is an absolutely necessary component of an efficient service system and must be stocked with everything the wait staff uses regularly. A likely list will include bread and butter, bread baskets, all coffee-making and serving paraphernalia, assorted garnishes, salad dressings and condiments, dishes and flatware, water pitchers and glasses, ice, linen napkins and tablecloths, bins for soiled linens, tray holders, credit card imprinters, computers, calculators, counter space, and so forth. Get the idea—Things are always hopping here. If your service area is immediately adjacent to your kitchen, a few simple design precautions will make the space safer for employees and provide a better flow pattern for your service traffic.

Many of these areas have swinging doors that link them to the kitchen. If possible, choose double doors, 42 inches in width, with clear, unbreakable plastic windows in each door that should be no smaller than 18 inches high and 24 inches wide. Each door should be installed to swing only one way and clearly marked "in" or "out." There should be at least 2 feet separating the doors. When refrigerators are located in the service area, glass doors will help save energy by allowing servers to see the contents without opening the door. Also, consider sliding doors instead of doors that swing open.

The floor is another important consideration. Make it nonskid, just like the kitchen floor. And, because there's always the possibility of a spill, be sure there are adequate floor drains. Finally, because of the intense use of this space and the interaction of your servers and production line people, this area should be well lit, like the kitchen. There are two distinct schools of thought about whether wait stations should also be the repositories for some prepared foods: soups, salads, precut pies and cakes, and so on.

While one group says it makes service of these items faster, another insists it also increases pilferage by staff members—and, therefore, increases costs. Where should your wait station (s) be located? The shorter the distance between wait station and kitchen, the better off you'll be. Long hikes between the two actually increase labour costs, as waiters spend their time going back and forth. It is also harder to keep items at proper temperatures if they must be carried for longer distances.

If space does not permit your wait station to be adjacent to your kitchen, there are a couple of options. The use of metal plate covers will keep food warm for an additional two to four minutes as it is delivered to guests. Or purchase lowerators, spring—loaded plate holders that can be temperature controlled to provide preheated plates. In so many situations, food is now prepared in full view of the guests. Therefore, it is more important than ever that designers create work centres that are well organised and can be kept looking clean.

Take advantage of undercounter storage space to minimise messiness. Provide a hand sink for hand washing and a utility sink to rinse kitchen tools and utensils, right at the work center. Select surfaces that are easy to clean, from wall paints to countertop materials. Think carefully about where to dispose of waste. Ventilation should receive professional attention, to minimise the grease buildup that naturally comes with cooking and to avoid the possibility of smoke wafting into the dining room.

Cafeteria Dining

For large group-feeding facilities-cafeterias, hospitals, prisons—the service area takes on a complexity rarely seen in a table-service or fast-food eatery. An institutional kitchen may need as much as 2000 to 3000 square feet of service area, since this is where serving lines are set up in a multitude of combinations:

1. The straight serving line
2. The shopping center system
3. The scramble (or free-flow) system

The straight line is exactly what its name implies. In terms of speeding customers through the food line, it is the slowest-moving arrangement, since most guests are reluctant to pass slower ones in front of them. However, single or double straight lines are still the most common design in commercial cafeterias, because they take up the least space and the average guest is comfortable with the arrangement.

Since customers must walk by all the food choices, they are, also more likely to make an impulse purchase. The shopping center (also called a bypass line) is a variation of the straight line. Instead of being perfectly straight, sections of the line are indented, separating salads from hot foods and so on. This makes it easier for guests to bypass one section. In serving lines where burgers, omelets, or sandwiches are prepared to individual order, the bypass arrangement keeps things moving.

The free flow or scramble system is designed so that each guest can go directly to the areas he or she is interested in. (Once in a while, you'll hear it referred to as a hollow-square system.) Food stations may be laid out in a giant U-shape, a square with islands in the middle, or just about any shape the room size will permit. It can be attractive but is often confusing for first-time customers. So you're most likely to find this layout in an industrial cafeteria, where employees eat every day and soon become familiar with it.

Scramble systems offer fast service and minimal waiting. They also allow for some types of exhibition cooking, including items grilled, stirfried, or sliced to order. Airline foodservice kitchens seem to have the largest and most complex service areas. Several dozen workers line a system of conveyor belts, assembling meal trays for as many as 70,000 passengers a day. To produce this kind of quantity, the prepared food is held in hot carts, and much of the preparation is done ahead of time to make the assembly process go quickly.

Preparation Areas

The term preparation areas are used to refer to food preparation. After all, a lot more activities than cooking are crammed into most kitchens! Here are some of the major work sections.

Fabrication

This is where raw (or processed) foods begin their journey to their final destination—the guest's plate. Sometimes referred to as pre prep, it is here that we break down prime cuts of beef, clean and fillet fish, cut up chickens, open crates of fresh produce, and decide what gets stored and what gets sent on to the other parts of the preparation area. In planning for each area, start with a flowchart to determine which functions should be included. If the restaurant plans to handle its own meat-cutting duties, you'll need room for a sink, a heavy cutting board, portion scales, meat saws, grinders, and slicers. Some can be placed on mobile carts and shared with other areas of the kitchen.

Preparation

Here, foods are sorted further into individual or batch servings. The loin we trimmed in the fabrication area is cut into steaks, lettuce and tomatoes are diced for salad assembly, shrimp is battered or peeled. Ingredients are also mixed-meat loaves, salad dressings, casseroles. Salad and vegetable prep areas are found in almost every foodservice setting. They are busy places, and their focus must be on efficiency.

When designing the layout, remember the need for worktables, compartment sinks, refrigerators, and mechanical equipment. Order some worktables with food and condiment "wells" that are cooled from beneath with ice, allowing easy accessibility. A prep area with unique requirements is the garde manger, a term that encompasses both food preparation and decoration or garnish.

The garde manger area is the source of cold foods—chilled appetizers, hors d'oeuvres, salads, pates, sandwiches, and so on. Obviously, refrigeration is of paramount importance here, as are knife storage and room for handheld and small appliances: ricers, salad spinners, graters, portable mixers, blenders, juicers. Colour-coded bowls, cutting boards, knives, scrub brushes and even kitchen towels all help to avoid cross-contamination among different types of raw foods.

Production

It's finally time to do some cooking, in the production area! This is divided into hot-food preparation, usually known as the hot tine, and cold-food preparation, called the pantry. Production is the heart of the kitchen, and all the other areas are meant to support it.

Holding

As its name suggests, this is the area in which either hot or cold foods are held until they are needed. The holding area takes on different degrees of importance in different types of foodservice operations. Basically, the larger the quantity of meals produced, the more critical the need for holding space. For banquet service and in cafeterias and hospitals, food must be prepared well in advance and stored at proper temperatures. In fast-food restaurants, the need is not as great but it still exists.

Assembly

The final activity of the preparation area is assembly of each item in an order. At a fastfood place, the worktable is where hamburgers are dressed and wrapped and fries are bagged. At an a la carte restaurant, the cook's side of the pass window is where steak and baked potato are put on the same plate and garnished. Again, in large-scale foodservice operations, grandscale assembly takes up more room. The menu and type of cooking you do will determine the makeup of your production area. Will you need a fabrication area at all, if yours is a fast-food franchise that uses mostly prepackaged convenience foods?

Conversely, cooking "from scratch" will probably require a lot of space for preparation, baking, and storage. Batch cooking, or preparing several servings at a time, will also affect your space allocation. Finally, the number of meals served in a given time period should be a factor in—planning your space. Your kitchen must be able to operate at peak capacity with plenty of room for everyone to work efficiently. For a hotel with banquet facilities or for an intimate 75-seat bistro, this means very different things.

Production Areas

There are two major ways to cook food: "dry heat" methods (saute, broil, roast, fry, bake) and "moist heat" methods (braise, boil, steam). The difference is, of course, the use of liquid in the cooking process. A kitchen that is well laid out may position its volume cooking at the back and its to—order cooking at the front. In large volume food production, deck ovens, steam jacketed kettles, and tilting braising pans will be found together.

In smaller (batch or a la carte) kitchens, fryers, broilers, open-burner ranges, and steam equipment are grouped together. In kitchens that require both types of cooking (large and small batches), the large-volume, slowercooking equipment is placed behind a half-wall under an exhaust hood. On the other side, or in front of the wall, is the equipment used for smaller-volume or quick-cooking dishes. Because the smaller dishes require more attention, putting this equipment at the front of the wall allows them to be watched more carefully.

In most communities, it is a law that all heat- and/or moisture-producing equipment must be located under ventilating hoods. Also, all surface cooking equipment (range tops, broilers) must be located so that the automatic fire-extinguishing (sprinkler) system can reach them. Ventilating hoods are very expensive, so the tendency is to crowd a lot of cooking equipment into the small space beneath them. Following are some of the "stations," or sections, of the typical hot line.

Broiler Station

A single or double-deck broiler is found here.

Griddle Station

The width of the griddle determines its capacity. It can be either a floor-standing model or a tabletop griddle that sits atop a counter. The tabletop model is a smart use of the space below it, where the cook can store supplies. There are even refrigerated drawers, so that meats can be kept chilled until they are ready to be cooked.

Saute Station

Here, we find three types of ranges: the flat-top sectional range, with individual heat controls for each section; the ring-top range, with rings of various sizes that can be removed to bring flames into direct contact with the saute pan; and the open-top range, also sectional, with two burners per section. Ovens can be placed tabletop in this area or they can be installed below the range. Above the range is often a mini-broiler known as a salamander, used for quick duties like melting butter or as a holding area.

Sauce Station

Not every kitchen has room for this station, where soups, sauces, and casseroles are prepared on range tops or in steam jacketed kettles.

Holding Station

Once again, we have an area designated for holding finished food before it is assembled on plates or put onto trays. Any of the individual stations can have their own holding areas or there can be one central area. Either way, they often include a dry or wet steam table or hot-water baths for keeping sauces warm.

Utility Distribution Center

In high-volume production kitchens, such as banquet and catering operations, the installation of a utility distribution system is recommended. A utility distribution system is designed to provide all the necessary services (gas, electricity, hot and cold water, and steam) to the cooking equipment placed under the exhaust canopy. Connected directly to the canopy, it's like having a huge fuse box that controls all the utilities, with a single connection for each of them, plus emergency shutoffs and inspection panels to allow quick access to (and easy cleaning of) all components.

As cooking equipment is added, or moved, the system can be adapted, rearranged, or expanded. Most systems are shaped like a big H. The two vertical, upright posts are called risers. The larger one, which houses the main utility connections, is called the primary riser; the smaller one is the secondary riser, which serves mostly for balance. The horizontal section between them is known as the raceway.

Pantry

The pantry is where cold foods are prepared for serving. Preparation responsibilities here may include salads, sandwiches, cold appetizers and entrees, and desserts. Sometimes it is referred to as the "cold kitchen." A two-compartment sink is a must for this area, since salad greens must be washed and drained here. Worktables with cutting boards should be adjacent to the sink, and it is helpful if the sink itself has corrugated drain boards.

Refrigeration is also necessary, since cold storage is required for many ingredients, as well as a holding area for cold prepared foods. In restaurants, this could be a pass-through setup, with sliding glass doors on both sides so that pantry employees can slide finished items into the refrigerator and servers can remove them as needed from the other side. In banquet or other high-volume foodservice operations, a walk-in refrigerator may be more appropriate. Inside the walk-in, mobile carts can store finished trays of plated salads for easy access.

If reach-in carts, are used, make sure they have tray slides on them that will hold large sheet pans. For sandwich-making, the pantry needs slicers and other types of cutting machines, as well as mixers for making dressings. Because these are often items that are shared with the fabrication area, the equipment should be placed on rolling carts. Another unique need is keeping breads enclosed so they do not dry out. And, if recipes require toasted bread, at least one commercial toaster is needed.

When the pantry is also the site of dessert preparation, additional refrigeration and counter space are needed. You must find room for a freezer and an ice cream chest with its special water well to store scoops. The latter must meet local health ordinance requirements. Soft-serve machines may also be needed. Again, mobile carts equipped with shelf slides can be helpful, both to store and to transport products.

Bakery Area

We use the term "baking" to refer to foods that start as batter or dough. Breads, desserts, and pastries are the output of the typical restaurant bakery area, which has its own unique characteristics and needs. Before designing a bakery area, ask yourself:

— What baked goods will we prepare here, and what baked goods will we purchase from outside sources?

— Will we bake "from scratch" or use premixed items and/or frozen doughs?

Often, to bake or not to bake on site is strictly a business decision, since it does require additional room, equipment, and skilled personnel. There are dozens of hybrid arrangements in foodservice: A restaurant may decide to purchase all breads but make desserts in house, or vice versa. Pizza operations must do baking on site, but other than that, there are lots of variations.

Within the kitchen, a bakery generally takes on one of two basic forms. It is either a compact area located next to the hot line, or it is a distinct area of its own. When it is a compact area, the setup may be as simple as a baker's table with storage bins beneath, which shares ovens and mixers with other areas. A larger, stand-alone baking area has other, unique attributes.

Mixing Station

Here, you'll find an array of large floor or tabletop mixers and their accessories. This, of course, requires electrical power and a generous amount of storage space. Here, you'll also find a table with scales, where ingredients are weighed, measured, and mixed.

Proofing Station

This is where the mixed dough is held to rise, with controlled temperature and humidity. Proofing boxes (enclosed cabinets for this purpose) require electricity, a water source, and drainage capability. Mobile racks also roll around in this section, storing sheet pans and dough.

Forming Area

This is where dough is shaped into rolls, pies and cakes are put in pans; and so forth. In small kitchens, the mixing station must sometimes double as the forming area. The tasks performed here require bakers' tables with tops approved by local health authorities, and mechanical dough dividers and shapers. The same mobile racks from the proofing station can stop here on their way to the oven.

Baking Station

Ovens and exhaust hoods take up most of the space here. The types of ovens depend entirely on what's being baked. If there is only one type of product, in large quantities, a carousel or reel oven is preferable. The combination steamer/oven can add moisture to the baking process to make harder crusts for some types of bread. Deck ovens are stacked on top of each other, each individually temperature controlled, for baking two types of products at once. Convection ovens circulate hot air inside the ovens during the baking process-good for breads but not so great for some types of pastries and cheesecakes. So there are many options, depending on your menu needs.

Finishing Station

A baker's worktable is a requirement here, where pastries and breads are given their final form prior to serving. This includes slicing, decorating, glazing, and so forth. You'll need room to stand the mobile racks, so that product can be rolled in and out of this station.

In creating a bakery area, also remember that baked goods require a variety of storage environments, ranging from room temperature with good air circulation to constant refrigeration. If this is also the general dessert-making area, leave room for the ice cream chest, freezer, and soft-serve machine. What can a bakery area share with other parts of the kitchen? Refrigerator space might be shared with the pantry or the service area.

Mixers can be shared with the preparation area, especially if they're tabletop models on rolling carts. The bakery should be located near the pot sinks, since baking generates a lot of dirty dishes. Some bakery areas have their own pot sinks, as well as hand sinks, too. It's also handy to be close to the dry storage and walk-in refrigerator areas, since that is where the raw materials come from. Worktable space should be no less than 6 feet per employee, and adequate lighting is important because of the delicate kinds of work done here, such as cake decorating.

Landing space for baked goods is needed, especially in front of the ovens. There should be plenty of room for sheet pans, which measure 18 by 26 inches. Proofing boxes should also be placed near the ovens. In preparation of fillings and syrups, a portable tilting steam jacketed kettle may be needed near the ovens. Another special requirement may be a range top burner to melt sugar or heat sauces.

Warewashing Area

Warewashing is the term for collecting soiled dishes, glasses, flatware, pots, and pans and scraping, rinsing, sanitising, and drying them. It is by far the most necessary, and least exciting, part of the foodservice business. Whether dishes are done by hand or by machine; or a combination of both, it's a messy job with high temperatures, high humidity, and slippery floors that require constant caution: For the restaurant owner, this is also one of the most costly areas to operate. Labour (and high turnover), utilities, and equipment are all expensive, and breakage can account for 10 to 15 percent of dish room expenses. Cost is not the only reason warewashing is of major importance.

Quite simply, it has a direct impact on public health. Done poorly, you jeopardize your business on a daily basis. For now, let's cover the way bussing and washing impact the size and location of the dish room. First, the dirty dishes have to get there. Some restaurants have bus persons or wait staff bring the dishes directly to the warewashing area; others try to save some steps by stacking the dishes in bus tubs on carts located throughout the dining room and bringing them to be washed only when the cart is full.

Quick-service and cafeteria-style restaurants may opt to have customers bus their own tables, depositing waste and trays at receptacles near the doors as they leave. Emphasis should be on designing a system to make sure every plate, cup, or fork has its own flow pattern, to get it in and out of service quickly and efficiently. A smooth, short flow pattern from dining room to dish room will keep breakage to a minimum and lower labour costs.

You'll need to find the shortest route that minimises the natural noise and clatter of working with dishes, and also keeps them out of sight of the guests as much as possible. In institutional settings, the dish room should be placed in the flow pattern of outgoing guests, so as not to interfere with the incoming ones. A convey or belt or placement of walls or partitions can minimise contact with dish room sights and sounds. Dishes must be scraped and stacked when they arrive at the warewashing area.

Sometimes, the scraping and stacking is the responsibility of the bus persons or waiters who bring in the dishes. This method is known as decoying, and it allows the dishwashers to concentrate on rinsing the dishes and loading them into machines. No matter who scrapes, you'd better figure out where the scrapings are going to end up. A trash can with plastic liner—A garbage disposal—Glasses and flatware have special sanitation needs. As used flatware is taken off a table, it should be placed immediately into a presoaking solution—either in a sink or a bus tub.

When heading into the dishwasher, flatware should be placed, facing up, in perforated, round containers, much like those you're familiar with in home dishwashers. Glasses and cups are arranged face down an special racks, not placed on regular dish racks along with the plates. If stemware is used, like tall wine or water glasses, there are special racks with individual, high compartments to prevent chipping the glass bases. There must be adequate room for storage of these specialised containers, both full and empty.

Neither flatware nor glassware should be towel-dried upon removal from the dishwasher. Instead, place flatware on large, absorbent towels and sort it as it dries; allow glasses to air-dry before removing them from racks. Again, this requires space. Most restaurants store their glasses in the racks until they're used again, which saves storage space and time. There are a number of ways to organise the dish room. In most cases, you will set your equipment in a straight line, an L-shape, or a hollow square, with the equipment making the sides of the square and employees standing inside.

In determining the size of your dish room, consider the size of the dining room. Remember that each person served will generate six to eight dirty dish items. Calculate how many full dish racks your dish machine can process in one hour. Finally, realise that the best dish rooms are, on average, working at 70 percent efficiency. Inside the dish room, scraping, spraying, lifting, and carrying mean greater labour costs and the potential for disaster without special attention to safety. Nonslip floors and adequate drainage are necessities. Usually, city ordinances also specify lighting requirements and govern the ventilation system.

Dish machines generate so much heat and humidity that proper ventilation is necessary for employee comfort; as a bonus, ventilation also helps clean dishes dry faster. Acoustical tile for walls and ceilings is important in this area, to keep dish room noise from spilling into the dining area. Another item that must be carefully chosen is the type of door that links the warewashing area to the rest of the facility.

4

Cabinets, Counter Tops and Kitchen Floor

Cabinets

Cabinets might be the most important part of your kitchen design. It is important that they fit well in the room/house they are built it in. The cabinets should fit well with the color patterns. You can use cabinets in coordination with wall and floor colours to set the tone for the whole room. The cabinets should fit well with the style of the house. Make sure to match the cabinets with the style of the house.

Cabinets are also the most visual and hands-on element in the kitchen, so it's no wonder replacing them is an important factor in any kitchen renovation. Your kitchen cabinets will set the tone for the whole room. In dark areas, you can select soft colours to offset the lack of natural light. Your choice of wood will have the most impact on the cabinet's ultimate look. If you want a light look, you could start with a light wood like ash, beech, birch, oak, maple, or chestnut. In the mid-range, consider cherry with a natural finish.

If you're renovating a kitchen, don't skimp on the one thing that will make or break your experience and potentially your kitchen — a professional kitchen design. The newest trend in cabinets is not just exterior looks, but personalised storage. Whether you're looking for open shelves, a built-in wine rack, china displays, or a wall of cubby holes, cabinet makers are producing an ever-increasing number of options based on consumer wants and needs. Now should be the time to select cabinets that make more efficient use of space. Roll-out trays, lid holders, bread boxes, and other concealed features promote efficiency and provide for a more user-friendly cooking space.

Installing New Kitchen Cabinets

Whenever installing stock cabinets, accurate measurements are critical to assure a snug fit. Custom made cabinetry is usually sold with a warranty conditional on having the cabinets installed by the dealer. In fact, the dealer will probably send someone out to make their own measurements.

Most ready-made cabinets come with a scribe allowance at the edges to allow you to adapt them to irregular walls. Scribing simply involves running a strip of masking tape along the side to be scribed; then, positioning the cabinet. Set the points of a pencil compass to the width of the widest gap between the side of the cabinet and the wall. Run the compass down the wall and the irregularities will be pencil marked on the tape. Now you can plane or sand down to the line so the cabinet will rest flush against the wall. If the scribe edge is not included on your cabinets or if your cabinets go all the way to the ceiling, plan on trimming the edges with a small piece of molding. It is easier to install the upper wall cabinets first because you have room to work with them. Since they will hang from the wall, you must make certain they are securely attached.

Before installing any of new cabinets, remove all the drawers, doors and hardware and label them as to their original locations for quick reassembly. This will make the units much lighter and more manageable.

1. Use a chalk line to mark the position of the wall studs on the walls from ceiling to floor.
2. Measure the height of the base cabinets. If your floor is not level, measure from the highest point.
3. Measure to another point above the line to where the bottom of the upper cabinet will rest (usually 18' to 19" above your 1st line) and draw another horizontal line across the wall. This line (approximately 54 inches above the floor) should also be made with a level to assure it is true horizontal and parallel to the line for the counter top.
4. Nail a temporary 1 x 2 ledger board to the wall so that the top of the board is even with the line for the upper cabinets. Be sure you are nailing into the studs. Now mark the cabinet widths along the length of the ledger strip.
5. You will need to make a few temporary jacks to support the wall cabinets while you attach them to

the wall. The total length of the jack should reach from the floor to the bottom of the upper cabinets. Wide blocks of wood nailed to both ends of a 2 x 4 work well for this purpose. Put the jacks into position near the ledger.

6. When readying the cabinets for installation, we recommend you first prepare those cabinets that will house a hood/vent, ducts and plumbing: Place the cabinet upside down on the floor with the hood in position upside down on the (bottom of the) cabinet. Trace the outline of the vent hole onto the base of the cabinet. Drill a starter hole for your sabre saw, then, cut around the outline and remove the cutout, Next, make a paper template of the ceiling or wall where the cabinet will be placed that shows where the end of the duct will enter. Place the template into position on the cabinet top or back and outline the duct hole. Again, drill a starter hole and cut out the circle with your sabre saw. Mark the location of the Wall studs on each cabinet's hanging cleats; then, drill pilot holes for screws at these points. Self-drilling bugle head screws can also be used. These require no pre-drilling, except when using at face frames. With the doors removed, lift the first cabinet into position onto the ledger board and the temporary jacks. Check to see that the cabinet is both level and plumb in position and, if needed, add shims at the back of the cabinet to bring it into a plumb position.

7. Screw the 2-1/2 inch No. 8 flathead wood screws through the cleat at the back of the cabinet and into the wall studs - two at the top and two at the bottom. Use longer screws if needed to assure at least 1 -1/4" to 1-3/4" penetration into the studs. Each unit should be attached to a minimum of two studs. If only one stud is located behind a unit, add a toggle bolt as an additional fastener.

8. Attach each of the upper cabinets in this manner. Then, go back and screw the adjacent units together. When connecting adjoining cabinets, it may be necessary to loosen wall screws to allow the faces of the cabinet to be attached flush to each other. Use hand screws or a C clamp with soft wood screws between the jaws of the clamp and the face frame often cabinet to hold the units flush while you screw them together.
9. Recheck all for level and plumb.
10. Remove the jacks and the ledger board and repair any holes in the wall.
11. If your lower cabinets have freestanding bases, set the bases in position and level them, shimming if necessary. Also, use a framing square to square them where your base cabinets meet in a comer. When placing shim material, place a block of wood between the shim and the hammer so as not to damage the flooring. Then anchor them to the floor and place the cabinet units on top of them. Those cabinets without freestanding bases must be levelled and anchored in position as a unit. As you set the base cabinets in place, measure and leave room for the appliances, adding a 1/4 inch for clearance - more if you will be adding end panels. Check the position of your base units against the line on the wall, making certain the tops are equally below the line by the thickness of your counter top.
12. Attach the cabinet units together so that the faces are flush. Slide a level down the entire length of the cabinets, adding a shim where there is a gap or to bring it up to level. Place your level front to back on the top of the cabinet to check for plumb - a again shimming if necessary.

13. Island cabinets must have the individual units screwed together and laced into position before levelling and plumbing on all four sides. If the base is separate, level and plumb it. Then, fasten it to the floor With toe nails or angle brackets. Place and anchor the cabinets to the base. When installing an island unit, it is important to square it to the cabinets along the wall and to the wall itself, as well as lining it up properly with the overhead fixtures. Measure off on both ceiling and floor to determine the exact location.

Counter Tops

Countertops are made from materials that are durable and, in most cases, easy to maintain. Most combine a base of plywood or particleboard that spans across the top of a cabinet and the finish surface material. If you are looking to buy new countertops, the material you choose will depend on your budget and the appearance and serviceable qualities you want. Natural stone, such as granite, is considered to be the height of elegance and will last longer than most kitchens. Stone, however, is very expensive and requires some care. Choices such as granite, marble and soapstone can also be installed on counterops in 12" square tiles and grouted. This can give you the beauty of natural stone for less expense than installing a solid piece. Another advantage is that individual tiles can be easily changed if damaged, so be sure to keep a few extra pieces from the original lot in case you need to replace any in the future.

Unusual colours and materials are the usual vogue in countertop design. While ceramic tile is still a charming and timeless option for your counter, its special care requirements have encouraged remodellers to look for alternatives. Solid surface countertops are becoming increasingly popular, and are used in most professionally designed kitchens because of the ease of cleaning and ability to hold up in the kitchen's high-traffic area. These countertops are easily repairable, and won't chip or crack. Another popular choice is granite, an option known for its durability and dramatic looks. Though granite can be rather pricey, there are also a number of solid surfacing options that imitate the look of granite at a lower cost.

When you choose your countertop, select a colour and texture that compliments your cabinetry, floor or paint selection. Don't be afraid to combine two or more countertop materials in one kitchen. Complimentary colours or textures on adjacent surfaces can create visual interest. Remember also that it pays to select a material that will withstand years of use without extraordinary maintenance requirements and is easily repairable should an accident occur.

When selecting a countertop, consumers look for strength, stain resistance, burn proof, long lasting, and elegance many reasons why a natural stone countertop would be an attractive feature in a kitchen. When selecting a natural stone countertop, consumers can look at the different types, finishes, appearances, thickness, and textures, which make up the beauty of natural stones. One great thing about natural stone is that no two stones are alike making every single kitchen one of a kind. There are many forms of natural stone that consumer can choose from: granite, marble, soapstone, slate, and Jerusalem stone.

Granite is hard as a rock. Though costly, when buffed to a shine it creates a smashing look for kitchen counters. It is also riding a crest of popular style that began over 10 years ago. With granite tops, the experience and expertise of the fabricator is vitally important. Granite, marble, and limestone, all popular for countertops, are beautiful natural materials. In most areas, you'll find a great selection of colours and figures.

The quality of the countertop edge treatment is important. As an example, a solid surface counter is easy to clean and repair and will take years of use. It might look terrific with a wood edge to match the cabinets, but the wood will not withstand constant exposure to water and household chemicals like the solid surface material. Restrict the wood edge to an area such as a freestanding hutch and use matching or contrasting solid surface material for the front edge.

Consider combining quality decorative materials such as tile, granite or marble with solid surface. Many fabricators can create custom designs for a spectacular visual effect without compromising durability and easy maintenance. When there are budget constraints, it makes sense to use the highest quality material for the counter areas that will sustain the greatest amount of use, specifying other materials to less often used areas.

Considered second to diamonds in hardness, granite is the more popular choice. Granite is chosen for durability and its rich composition of quartz crystals, mica, and feldspar trapped within. With granite, consumers wouldn't have to be afraid placing a hot pot due to it being heat resistant and wouldn't have to fear of scratching it, since only granite or diamond can scratch it. Granite is also resistant to the acidic products found in every kitchen. Because all stones are porous, a special sealant is required.

Chosen for its smoothness and vein like textures, marble is added to a section of a whole countertop by those who like to bake. Because marble is a softer stone, it is more porous which makes it susceptible to scratches and stains, requiring frequent sealing. Both granite and marble give off different appearances compared to other natural stone products, which is why they are popular.

Soapstone, known as "original stone countertop," is becoming just as popular as granite. Soapstone is quarried just like marble and granite with components of magnesite, dolomite, chlorite, and talc. Many people are attracted to having soapstone as a countertop because of its soft feel, however it can easily scratch. Soapstone won't etch from acids; stains can be rubbed out easily. Comes in colours of blue, green and gray, if mineral oil is applied consistently it will bring out a charcoal-gray color making it look older and much more elegant.

Slate countertops are liked because of their high resistance to heat, but are highly susceptible to scratches. Composed of seabed, slate stone reflects hues of dark green, blue, and black. Just like soapstone, if mineral oils are applied to it, the colours will be enhanced to a darker glowing hue.

A new countertop in the market is Jerusalem Stone, which resembles the sandy tones of limestone, but not as porous and soft and it's quarried from areas around Jerusalem. Many people like Jerusalem stone because of its durability, which is like granite and its smoothness like marble.

One reason, why natural stone is a favourite for a countertop, are that the finishes applied add on to the beauty and durability. Some popular natural stone finishes are polished, honed, flamed, and tumbled. Polished natural stone countertops have a high gloss surfaced that gives off a mirror like reflection. Honed finish is a hard surface with a smooth, matte look to it. This finish is very soft to touch with a fuzzy reflection. When a flamed finish is applied to the stone, it is exposed to intense heat creating a texture on the surface. To make a natural stone appear worn and old a tumbled finish is applied. There are other finishes to choose from, but it's all about what the consumer prefers and the uses of the countertop.

New to the countertop market and put into the same category of natural stone is engineered quartz. Many manufacturers are challenging the market share of natural stone by combining 93 percent of natural quartz with 7 percent resin to create a highly durable material that is twice as strong as granite. This product has been around for 15 years in Europe and just recently has been marketed in North America. Engineered quartz offers a countertop that is nonporous and stain resistant. The slabs being manufactured have colours and patterns that are all uniform making it easier for consumers to know that they will get what they want.

Unlike granite, engineered quartz doesn't require a sealant, just a cleaning on a regular basis. The only drawback with this type of countertop is that a hot pad or trivet is required when placing a hot pan on it and it is as expensive as granite about $70 - $300 per square foot. While natural stone looks very attractive, when installed in solid pieces it is highly expensive, about $50-$300 per square foot. The money invested is worth the quality, value, and the durability these countertops will have. An option that many consumers take to save money is having the natural stone cut into pieces and placing them like tiles. Another affordable option is placing a slab over an existing countertop.

Both natural stone and engineered quartz require the proper maintenance to avoid any discoloration, scratches, or any other costly damages. Natural stones require special sealants about every six months to a year. Always avoid acidic cleaners or solutions to prevent severe damage to the countertop. Although engineered quartz doesn't need to be sealed, special cleaning products must be used according to the manufacturer.

Countertops are the most looked at for a kitchen-remodelling project to bring out the beauty and elegance of kitchen. Countertops can take a moderate looking kitchen and turn it to a kitchen out of a magazine or from a remodelling show. For many consumers, having a countertop that will be long lasting, durable, and elegant such as natural stone is worth the cost.

Installing Pre-Formed Kitchen Counter Tops

The two common types of countertops are pre-formed and self-rimmed. Pre-formed tops come assembled from the manufacturer while self-rimmed tops are built at the jobsite using raw materials.

Preformed counter tops are available only in standard sizes so you'll generally purchase one a little longer than you need and cut it to length.

1. To measure for the size counter you will need, add the counter overhang and add it to the dimensions of your cabinet.
2. If an end splash is to be included, subtract 3/4 inch from the length of the counter top on that side. Plan your cut for an end which will have an end cap or end splash. Cut the excess off with a handsaw; but first, mark the cut line with some masking tape to protect against chipping. Smooth the edges of the cut with a file or sandpaper
3. The end splash will be screwed directly onto the edge of the counter top or into wood batons previously attached to the edge. Apply silicone sealant to all surfaces to be joined and hold the end splash in place with C-clamps while driving in the screws.
4. An end cap is a pre-shaped strip of matching laminate which will be glued to the end of the counter top.
5. U- and L-shaped counter tops will need to be ordered mitered or cut to order as it is difficult to accurately miter these sections at home. These pre-mitered sections should have small slots for draw bolts cut into the bottom edges. Again, coat the edges with silicone sealant before aligning the edges and tightening the bolts.

6. Fasten the adjoining backsplashes together with wood screws.
7. As with the cabinets, counter tops rarely fit perfectly against the back or side walls. Often, they come with a scribing strip that can be trimmed to the exact contours of your irregular walls. Scribing simply involves running a strip of masking tape along the edge to be scribed then positioning the counter top. Set the points of a pencil compass to the width of the widest gap between the counter top and the wall. Run the compass along the wall and the irregularities will be pencil marked on the tape. Now you can plane or and down to the line so the counter top will rest flush against the wall. Follow the same technique for scribing as explained in the section on cabinets.
8. Once your contours are correct, position the counter top on the cabinet base. Check that all is level and shim where needed. Check also that drawers and doors may be opened freely.
9. Fasten down the counter top by running screws up from below through the top frame and corners. If there are no corner brackets, install them on the base units. This will allow you to install the counter to easily. Again, self-drilling bugle head screws are great for it's job. Round head screws work best here because they will not be seen so do not have to be counter sunk and they bear more weight in this position. Use screws that will be long enough to reach 1/2 inch into the counter core.

Installing Self Rimmed Kitchen Counter Tops

Self rimmed plastic laminate counter tops are both handsome and durable for the hardworking kitchen, and they are not all that difficult to install. The sheets of 1/16" thickness are stocked with most dealers in 4 x 8 foot sheets but can be special ordered in a range from 2 to 5 foot widths and from 6 to 12 foot lengths. The laminate should be stored in your kitchen for at least 48 hours prior to installation to have time to adjust to the temperature and humidity. Make certain that the surface upon which you will be applying the laminate is even and smooth. If you will be topping an existing laminate counter, repair any gouges or loose edges and be sure the existing laminate is glued firmly. If the counter is rimmed with a metal band, remove it and fill any holes with wood dough.

Kitchen Floor

When exposed long hours of sunshine, your tile floor will collect heat and keep a gorgeous warmth. However, most of the time, you tile floor is not exposed to the sun and remains unbearably cold. In a kitchen, ceramic tile is a premium product, but it is always too cold. In the wintertime, you will dread walking barefoot on the cold tile floor, and you should not let your kids play on the floor, unless you want them to get real cold real fast.

Electric floor warming is easy to install and you can simply program a thermostat to keep the floor warm any time of the day, when you and your family need it. You don't have to worry about your little ones playing on the floor anymore. Tactile sensations are very important in a floor because feet are very sensitive. Walk on a thick carpet and you will feel a sense of comfort. Walk on cold tiles and you will feel very cold. Walk on warm tiles and you will feel comfortable and warm. You will be suprised to see how nice it is to walk barefoot on a heated surface.

Floor Covering Options

Your flooring choice is important because it will set the tone for the whole kitchen. The textural quality of the floor appeal to eye and has a radical effect on how we perceive the room as a whole. In kitchens, the two most elegant floors are tiles/stones and laminated or hardwood floors. Ceramic tile is a premium product for a kitchen and as such represents an impressive upgrade over any other floor. The only disadvantage is the cold feel.

Your kitchen is the heart of the home. That's where you gather with your family and friends, and your children play on the kitchen's floor. Floors can act as heat stores: when exposed long hours of sunshine through a south-facing window, they collect heat during the day and keep a gorgeous warmth through the night.

You can also warm your tile floor with an electric floor warming system to keep it warm any time of the day, when you and your family need it. Find out how you can add floor warming to your kitchen. It's not only about visuals, tactile sensations are very important in a floor because feet are very sensitive. Walk on a thick carpet and you will feel a sense of comfort. Walk on cold tiles and you will feel very cold. Walk on warm tiles and you will feel comfortable and warm.

Laminated Floors

Despite all the alternatives available today, genuine hardwood and laminate continue to attract admirers with its timeless appeal and warmth. At one time, choices in hardwood floors were fairly limited. Homeowners had only a handful of options. But that has changed dramatically. Recognising the increase in demand, flooring manufacturers have broadened their product lines to reflect the diversity in tastes and budgets.

For example, today's homeowners can choose whether they want plank, strip or parquet hardwood flooring, and in what width or thickness. They can determine whether they prefer solid wood or engineered wood. Of course, homeowners must also select the species they want, and what grade. Grade is generally determined by how clear or variegated the appearance of the wood is. Most types of hardwood are available either pre-finished or unfinished. Special "hand scraping" techniques are also available to give floors an aged look and feel.

5

KITCHEN REMODELLING

Nothing is more disruptive in a family's lifestyle than a major kitchen renovation project. Most family members spend a great deal of their time at home in the kitchen. This important room is used to prepare meals, for informal eating, and as a casual gathering place for family and friends. People soon realise how important the room is when its torn apart during renovations, even the simple task of making a cup of coffee becomes a major undertaking without a kitchen. It is therefore critically important that tear out and new installation are coordinated during the design phase to minimise down time. Most experts agree that a kitchen renovation project will return almost 100% on investment when the property is sold. Surveys by the real estate industry show that a kitchen is one, if not the most, important feature with potential purchasers.

Kitchen design is very subjective, there are few hard and fast rules. A feature or layout that is perfect for one person is far from perfect for another. The issue of lifestyle and how it revolves around the kitchen is very unique to each family. In most cases, the family, usually the prime user of the kitchen space, will have very definite ideas on what is needed and what the end result has to be to meet their needs. Often they have been looking through magazines, drawing rough floor plans, measuring, and dreaming about their ideal kitchen for quite some time.

During the initial look at your existing kitchen, research all of the information about new products and features on the market. Ask yourself questions about your requirements and put ideas on paper. Combine your notes and rough drawings along with accurate measurements and attempt to come up with two or three floor plans.

There are a few issues you should address during your initial look at the kitchen. Ask questions so that you understand all the needs. Discuss the existing kitchen space and layout with all the primary users of the kitchen in your household, listing the good and bad points of the design. Investigate the traffic patterns in and through the kitchen. Analyse the day to day meal preparation tasks. Try to formulate a normal daily meal preparation routine. Questions should be asked about your family's desire to do more in the kitchen. Is there a hobby or area of interest, such as baking, that you would like to do more of if the added space or facilities were available.

Discuss your family's wish list. If space or money was no object, what would you like to have in your dream kitchen? Discuss topics such as lighting, both area and task illumination, kitchen seating needs, as well as appliance upgrade needs. There are other areas that can be discussed which may surface during your investigation.

Two design "rules" that seem to true in every case deal with colour and illumination. Light colour or natural wood cabinets tend to brighten and visually enlarge a space. Improved general and task lighting always enhances the project. Older kitchens seemed to have dark cabinets and poor illumination which gave you the impression you were in a cave. Yesterday's kitchen was simply a place to prepare the meal, clean up and leave the room. Today's lifestyle is very much focused on the kitchen as a gathering place for a wide and varied number of activities, the room has to be bright, seem large, be functional, and adapt to many of those activities. Take your time and investigate all the alternatives as the planning stage is a very important process of any kitchen renovation project.

If you feel intimidated by the kitchen design process you may want to investigate the possibility enrolling in design courses that are offered by some community colleges in your area. Investigate the possibility of seminars offered by local, provincial, state, and federal trade associations. There is a good living to be made with a great deal of satisfaction in the kitchen renovation field. However, like all specialised trades, knowledge comes from learning and the greatest teacher is experience. Read books, attend seminar and training programs, and analyse every kitchen you come across for ideas and techniques. There are certain accepted standards associated with kitchen cabinetmaking.

Counter height, space allowance between base and upper cabinets, cabinet depth, as well as the space required for refrigerators and stoves. These dimensions are not cast in stone but are generally accepted in the industry particularly by accessory and appliance manufacturers. The width of the majority of stoves is thirty inches and most refrigerators require thirty-three inches for proper installation. Normally, a thirty-one inch space is designed into the plan for stove installation. This gives us one half inch on each side of the stove so that it can be easily removed and replaced during cleaning or repair.

Removing the Old Kitchen

More in the kitchen than in any other room in the house, the kitchen remodeller must be on the lookout for design and structural traps. For example, work put in by amateurs is often overengineered (and hard to remove) and often ignores codes and standard practices. The main thing to remember is to work carefully. The goal is to remove the old kitchen with as little damage to the surrounding areas as possible, to minimise unintended reconstruction work.

Appliances and fixtures removing: The kitchen is dismantled in the opposite order in which it is assembled. The first items to remove are the appliances and fixtures. Before beginning, locate the water and gas shutoffs, as well as the electric service panel. Locate the circuit breakers for each of the appliances and turn them off. Be sure to test each individual appliance to verify that the electricity is off before you begin working on it. Shut off the gas at the fixture supply or at the main, and shut off the water to the sink and dishwasher; either at the shutoffs under the sink or at the main shutoff valve.

Verify that the water and gas are off before continuing. Shutting off a supplied service may require notifying the utility providing that service, such as a gas company. Most appliances are installed in roughly the same manner, although may be some variation from brand to brand. In most cases, procedures can be reversed to remove the unit.

— *Ovens*: are attached with four or more flathead screws through the front of the oven case on either side of the oven cavity into the surrounding wood of the cabinets. Remove the screws, and slide the unit out gain access to the power cable or gas line. Disconnect the line, then remove the oven.

— *Drop-in Cooktop*: A drop-in cooktop is usually held in place with two or more thumbscrews. If the unit has a lid that lifts up, these thumbscrews are usually located inside, at the two side edges. If there is no lid, look inside the cabinet against the bottom of the countertop. Loosen the screws until they swing out of the way, or remove them completely. Disconnect the power cable or gas line and remove the unit.

— *Drop-in Range*: To remove a typical drop-in range, remove any screws that through the oven into the cabinet. Lift the lid around the burners, and remove any screws or thumbscrews that are securing the unit against the counter Slide the unit out of the opening and place it on the floor. Remove the gas line or flexible metal electrical cable.

— *Freestanding range*: If the range is freestanding, simply slide the unit away' from the wall, then locate and remove the plug from the large wall socket.

Removing the plumbing: The first step is to remove the plumbing under the sink, either by disconnecting, the fittings or cutting the lines. You need to disconnect the hot and cold water, lines and the drain lines and trap. The sink itself is held in by one of four methods:

— Stainless steel sinks have a channel welded to the underside of the sink rim, with clips and screws that hold the sink tight against the counter. Loosen the screws and remove or swing the clips aside, then pry up the sink.

— Many tiled-in sinks are set on the countertop decking and then held in place with tile. You need to chip off the old tile to completely expose the rim of the sink; then pry the sink up.

— Sinks with sink rims are similar to stainless-steel sinks, except that the rim is a separate piece. The screws and clips hold the sink, the rim, and the counter all sandwiched together. Simply remove the screws and clips.

— Self-rimming sinks have a smooth, rounded edge and no sink rim. Nothing holds them in place except a bead of sealant between the under-side of the sink rim and the counter, plus their own weight. To remove them, just pry up.

Cabinets and countertops removing: Once they are empty, and all doors and drawers have been removed, cabinets and countertops can be removed fairly easily. Be certain that the water was turned off at the shutoff valves. The appliances and plumbing fixtures should have been disconnected and removed. Usually it is most efficient to remove the upper cabinets first. If the cabinets are modular, you will find they are screwed together through the edges of the face frame. These should be the first screws to be removed. Next, any screws holding the cabinets to the wall must be removed.

In some cases, nails are used instead of screws. Use a nail pulley to get under the head and raise the nail; then remove the nail with a hammer. If salvaging them, be careful to avoid damage to the cabinets. Always take caution to avoid damage to the surface of the wall. Once all of the upper cabinets have been removed, the countertops are next. In some cases you may find that screws have been driven up through cleats on the top of the base cabinets into the underside of the counters. Simply remove the screws.

Remove any screws or brackets holding the countertops to the cabinets, and unscrew the take-up bolts on mitered countertops. A utility knife can be used to cut caulk beads along the edge of the countertop and back-splash. Remove trim moldings at the edges and tops of cabinets with a flat pry bar or putty knife. Use a flat pry bar to lift the countertop away from the base cabinets, as well as to remove base shoe moldings and baseboards. If the countertop cannot be pried up, use a reciprocating saw or jigsaw with a coarse wood-cutting blade to cut the countertop into manageable pieces for removal. Be careful not to cut into the base cabinets.

To remove ceramic tile, chisel the tile away from the base with a ball peen hammer and masonry chisel. A tile countertop that has a mortar bed can be cut into pieces with a circular saw and abrasive masonry-cutting blade. It is imperative to always remember to wear eye protection and heavy gloves when breaking tile. When the counters have been removed, the base cabinets can be taken out. Unscrew them as you did with the upper cabinets, remove the doors, take out the screws from the face frame, and then remove the screws from the wall.

Some older styles of cabinets were built on site when the house was constructed. These cabinets, in many cases, have no backs, and there is little to be done to salvage them. Begin by unscrewing and removing the doors. Using a hammer from the inside of the cabinet, knock the face frame free of the shelves. Depending on how the cabinets were originally built, either remove the sides to completely free up the shelves or pry the entire cabinet off the wall or off the cleats. Beware that these types of cabinets were assembled with a number of finishing nails. Built-in cabinets should be cut into pieces and discarded. Old cabinets can be salvaged if they are modular units that were installed with screws.

Remove trim moldings at the edges and tops of cabinets with a flat pry bar or putty knife. Remove vinyl base trim. Work a pry bar or putty knife underneath to peel off the vinyl, as well as to remove base shoe moldings and baseboards. During this removal process, wall surfaces can be protected with scraps of wood. Keep in mind while removing valances that some are attached to cabinets or soffits with screws, while others are nailed and must be pried loose. Any screws holding the cabinets to the wall must be removed. Cabinets can be taken apart piece by piece with a hammer and pry bar or cut into manageable pieces with a reciprocating saw. Once the old counters and cabinets are removed, remove them from the work area.

Removing Flooring: With any new kitchen, replacing the flooring is almost inevitable. If the old flooring is in good condition and adheres well to the floor, you may be able to lay the new flooring right over it. In most cases, a better overall finish is achieved by removing the old flooring. If you find an instance in which the cabinets were installed first, followed by underlayment, and then flooring, you will find large gaps in the underlayment when the cabinets are removed. The best thing to do in this situation is to simply remove the underlayment, flooring, and all.

To remove resilient sheet goods, slit them with a utility knife, work a spade underneath, and then peel up the flooring. Old resilient floor coverings that are embossed or cushioned should be removed or covered with plywood underlayment before installing new flooring. Be sure to remove the felt backing entirely by moistening the glued felt with soapy water and with a floor scraper or drywall knife. Ceramic tile that is damaged or loose must be removed by breaking the tiles with a heavy hammer or sledgehammer and prying up the pieces with a cold chisel. Remove baseboards and base shoe with a drywall knife and pry bar. Kitchen carpeting is almost always glued down. It must be scraped off completely to prepare for the new flooring.

When all of the appliances, cabinets, countertops, and flooring have been removed, study the proposed layout to prepare for what else needs to be removed. If the walls need to be opened up do as much of this as possible now. Finally, completely clean the kitchen, sweep up all of the debris, and remove all of the old items to their proper designated area.

When planning to remodel an old kitchen, problems commonly arise. Even if the home is only a few years old, it always seems like the windows are never quite where they ought to be, or the chimney flue forms a jutting corner right where your client wants you to add a cabinet. And, just about as common are problems that are already in the wall. That is, plumbing lines, wiring, and doors never seem to be where they should be. Electrical lines and outlets can be moved or added with little trouble, but reworking existing piping and ductwork involves more complicated solutions.

Be certain that you had a preliminary inspection. As a result of this inspection, you should have discussed with the client the cost of the desired changes. Inform your client of the expense of taking out and putting in new fixtures. Replacing fixtures also means renovating the electrical, plumbing, and heating lines that serve the kitchen. Before you begin work, it is extremely important to analyse the house structural system.

Architectural drawings generally show only schematic layouts, with locations and, hopefully, sizes of pipe to be used. The routing is left to be done "in the field. If the design does not provide the required structural support, immediately notify the architect, dealer, or designer so he or she can modify the plans and the client can be made aware of the additional working costs.

Frame Work Construction

Before you begin any framing work, have your plan worked out, to scale, on paper. Since most of the other interior work depends on the framing, it is crucial that you get the planning and framing work done properly. Existing floor and ceiling structural members can present problems. Floor joists and subflooring could be rotted. Repairing damaged framing generally is not a big deal, but it is extremely important that the existing joists be strong enough to handle the live load of the planned space.

The term "wall framing" includes primarily the vertical studs and horizontal members of interior and exterior walls that support ceilings, upper floors, and the roof. The wall framing also serves as a nailing base for wall-covering materials. The wall framing members used in conventional construction are generally nominal 2-by-4-inch (5-by-10 cm) studs spaced 16 inches (41 cm) on center. Depending on the thickness of the covering material and the purpose of the wall, 24-inch (61-cm) spacing is sometimes used. Top plates and sole plates are also nominal 2 by 4 inches (5 by 10 cm) in size.

Headers over doors or windows in load-bearing walls consist of doubled 2-by-6-inch (5-by-15-cm) and deeper members, depending on the span of the opening. Ceiling height for the first floor is 8 feet (244 cm) under most conditions. It is common practice to rough-frame the wall (subfloor to top of upper plate) to a height of 8 feet 1 ½ inches (248 cm). In most construction, precut studs are often supplied to a length of 7 feet 8 ⅝ inches (236 cm) for plate thickness of 1 ⅝, inches (4.13 cm). When dimension material is 1 ½, inches (3.8 cm) thick, precut studs would be 7 feet 9 inches (236 cm) long. This height allows the use of 8-foot (236-cm)-high drywall sheets and still provides clearance for floor and ceiling finish or for plaster grounds at the floor line. You are likely to encounter three types of framing systems: platform-frame construction, post-and-beam construction, and balloon-frame construction. Each system has its own set of unique characteristics that makes it generally easy to identify. While the platform method is more often used because of its simplicity, you may encounter any one of these systems when remodelling a home.

Platform-frame construction

The wall framing in platform construction is erected above the subfloor, which extends to all edges of the structure. A combination of platform construction for the first-floor sidewalk and full-length studs for end walls extending to end rafters of the gable ends is commonly used in single-story houses. One common method of framing is the horizontal assembly or "tilt-up" of wall sections. This system involves laying out precut studs, window and door headers, cripple studs, and window sills. Top plates and sole plates are then nailed to all vertical members and adjoining studs to headers and sills with 16-penny (16d) nails. Let-in corner bracing should be provided when required. The entire section is then erected, plumbed, and braced.

Post-and-beam construction

The post-and-beam form of building can be seen in historical structures dating back to the earliest European influence. Gaining popularity in current rural structures, it presents a different set of circumstances for the remodeller. Massive wood members carry the loads, leaving open spaces in the wall normally taken up by the wall studs. These open areas between the beams and posts, referred to as glazed areas, are free to be remodelled without weakening the wall, although side loads require diagonal bracing.

Braces may be diagonal wood members. Bracing may also be achieved by using sheathed framed walls or solid masonry in the glazed areas. These braces must not be removed. Areas below interior beams within the house can remain open or can be closed in. In post-and-beam houses, all of the building's loads are carried on heavy lumber posts. This type of construction, while not adaptable to many styles of architecture, is simple and straightforward.

Today, specialists in timber framing can combine post-and-beam construction with panels filled with insulation. Many panels have drywall on the inside and siding on the outside. The insulating values of these nonbearing panels is very good. Without making any structural changes to the house, these panels can be removed. Historical buildings used pegs or other wooden attachments to join the members. Current modern methods of steel angle and straps and plate systems ease assembly or reconstruction for today's carpenters.

Balloon-frame construction

The main difference between platform and balloon framing is at the floor lines. The balloon wall studs extend from the sill of the first floor to the top plate or end rafter of the second floor, whereas the platform-framed wall is complete for each floor. Balloon-frame construction uses wood studs rather than posts. Because the studs extend continuously from the top of the foundation to the roof, the stud cavity makes it easy to pull new wiring or reroute plumbing supply lines.

The use of firestops, however, creates blockages that may be in areas difficult to see and penetrate for new wiring or plumbing. In most areas, building codes require that firestops be used in balloon framing to prevent the spread of fire through the open wall passages. These firestops are ordinarily 2-by-4-inch blocking placed between the studs or as required by local regulations. In balloon-frame construction, both the wall studs and the floor joists rest on the anchored sill. The studs and joists are toenailed to the sill with 8d nails and nailed to each other with at least three 10d nails. The ends of the second-floor joists bear on a 2-by-4-inch ribbon that has been let into the studs. In addition, the joists are nailed with four 10d nails to the studs at these connections. The end joists parallel to the exterior on both the first and second connections. The end joists parallel to the exterior on both the first and second floors are also nailed to each stud.

Wall Preparation

Frequently, you'll run into the problem of a wall not being where it should be in the new plan. Before starting demolition, check the wall carefully. It may be a loadbearing one. Loadbearing walls carry the weight of the roof or upper floor down to the foundation. The entire stability of the house is dependent on these bearing walls. Any bearing wall must be replaced with a beam at ceiling level supported at the side walls or alternative support system.

Nonbearing walls are independent of the structural system and some serve merely as partitions separating interior spaces. They are relatively easy and inexpensive to remove, provided they don't carry drain and vent lines. About the only visible difference between a bearing and nonbearing wall is that the bearing wall has a double top plate. It can be identified by drilling a small hole in the wall a few inches from the point where it meets the ceiling.

Even better, go to the basement or attic and note the direction the floor joists run. Nonbearing walls usually run parallel to joists; bearing walls always run perpendicular to joists. Double joists or extra members built into a floor under a wall indicate that it is load-bearing. Any openings to exterior walls that are loadbearing, have structural framing above them. Headers distribute weight from above to the vertical framing at either side of these openings.

In some cases, a wall may need to be added. Doing so is quite simple and can be accomplished by following standard construction procedures. In a remodelling job, a few walls might need to be torn out. In most cases, tearout is not too difficult, but some circumstances can make the removal of walls a bit more challenging. Finding animals, such as a colony of honey bees, snakes, or rats can give you major complications when tearing out walls. Beware of electrical wires, plumbing, or heating piping, which are usually located in interior walls. It is always best to open walls with a hammer rather than a saw. If you rip into a wall with a reciprocating saw, you might wind up shocking yourself. Turn off the circuit breaker for that area and test the out-lets and lights. Other areas may be affected by that circuit. Hitting a wire with the face of a hammer is not likely to electrocute you.

Plumbing pipes can also be hidden in existing walls. Cutting through a water pipe can really cause severe problems. If a drain or vent pipe runs through a wall you want to remove, the pipe must be relocated. As with electrical wires, using a hammer to open existing walls is a lot safer than a saw when working around plumbing pipes. Heating, ventilation, and air-conditioning (HVAC) ducts can also present a challenge when remodelling a kitchen. Electrical wires are fairly easy to relocate. Plumbing is tougher to move than electrical wires, but it is easier to relocate plumbing than the heating and air-conditioning ducts. When involved with a large remodelling project, you are probably going to be rearranging most of the mechanical systems.

Removing drywall or plaster: You can usually tell the difference between drywall and plaster by knocking on the wall. Drywall has a hollow sound between the studs; plaster is more solid. Removing plaster requires a slightly different procedure than removing drywall. Tearing out either type of wall is a messy job. Be sure to move any furniture, protect the floor by covering it with drop cloths, and hang plastic or damp sheets in all doorways. Always wear a filter mask, goggles, gloves, and head protection when you take out a wall. Cut out the drywall between the studs with a circular saw, reciprocating saw, or handsaw. Expect to make lots of dust at this point. Cut the studs in half and wrench out the pieces.

For plaster over metal lath, use a metal-cutting blade or simply batter the plaster with a crowbar or sledge hammer until it falls off the wall in chunks, then pry away the lath. Use caution in removing metal lath and nails. It is usually corroded, and sharp edges result from cutting them.

Removing interior partitions and load-bearing walls : Removing interior partitions is a basic procedure. Once you get around the mechanical obstacles, ripping out nonload-bearing walls is easy. A reciprocating saw, a hammer, and a nail puller make the job simple. Load-bearing walls present more complications than simple partition walls. Structural walls can be removed, but some concessions must be made. You might have to install an I-beam or some other form of support. Instead of removing a wall, consider opening it up using a beam and using portions of the existing wall to support the load.

When opening a load-bearing wall, you must reinforce it to support the weight bearing on it. A temporary support on both sides of the wall is erected with studs and top and bottom plates. It should be slightly higher than the existing wall and wedged up to raise the joists and relieve the load. Shut off the circuit breaker that supplies the wiring. In addition, shut off the water supply valves. Plan ahead to rewire or change piping while this wall is open. Have all supplies on hand. Cut away the existing wall and ceiling surface, being careful not to damage wiring or piping inside the framework.

Remove the unwanted studs by cutting them at midspan and twisting the halves while using a pry bar. The top plate must remain intact. Rewire or move pipe. The beam members should be sized by an architect to sufficiently support the load. Double studs at the corners are cut to fit and nailed to the existing sole plate. Cut away the unused soleplate. If the span is wide, support the beam with extra pairs of studs by extending the beam further into the wall. Finish the wall with drywall.

Before you start removing support walls, talk with an engineer, architect, or contractor. Experienced carpenters can do a good job designing support systems, but this approach may be risky. If a problem shows up later, the indi-vidual who made the decision on what to use as a replacement for bearing walls can be held responsible. Therefore, it is most important to consult an engineer or architect.

If the kitchen installation includes the removal and replacement of wall finishes, check the insulation in the walls. Because the designer or architect has not had the opportunity to look inside the walls, you should report your findings so the designer or architect can determine if additional insulation is warranted. Wall insulation is manufactured in several R-values, or insulating values, corresponding to the thickness of the wall studs. Walls with 2-by-4-inch studs can accommodate R-11 batt insulation and, in some cases, R-13 or R-15, while 2-by-6-inch stud walls can accommodate R-19 batt insulation.

Blanket insulation is sold in rolls of widths made to fit between wall studs of either 16 or 24 inches between centers. The rolls are fitted with allowance for the studs. The installer only cuts it in lengths to fit from floor to ceiling. It comes in thicknesses of 1½ inches, 2 inches, or 3 inches for 2-by-4-inch studded walls. Thicker widths are available for 2-by-6-inch studded walls, although attempting to compress thicker insulation of higher "R" value into a 2-by-4-inch wall does not yield that higher "R" value.

The rolls usually have instructions printed on the backing to ease installation. Blanket facings have a paper "flange" that when scored, folded, and stapled, fits into the studs with a dead air space and vapour barrier. Batt insulation is sized to fill the space between studs spaced 16 or 24 inches on center and can be purchased faced or unfaced. It is sold in pre-cut lengths of 4 or 8 feet. Faced insulation has a vapour barrier installed on the warm side of the wall, and it can be stapled to the face of the studs.

Unfaced insulation is stuffed between the studs, but a separate vapour barrier, such as a sheet of polyethylene, must be installed over this insulation on the warm side of the wall. Insulation should be installed in all new wall construction. Even when not required for structural reasons, many homes are now being constructed with 2-by-6-inch studs to accommodate R-19 wall insulation to meet more-stringent energy codes. When reviewing installation plans, check the wall sections to verify the size of the studs being used in the exterior walls. In existing homes with no insulation, blown-in loose fill insulation is an option if the wall finishes are not being removed.

Rigid-foam or Styrofoam insulation can be used to insulate the interior side of a concrete or concrete block wall. The sheets are mechanically fastened to the wall, and studs or furring strips provide a means to install a fireproof layer of drywall over the insulation. Rigid-foam insulation sheets may be used on frame walls; some have a foil facing. This facing, placed adjacent to a dead-air space towards the living area, provides further insulation. Rigid insulation is available as an exterior sheathing material and adds 'R' value to a wall, but because it has little structural value it must be supplemented by diagonal bracing at the corners of walls. Diagonal braces at the corners of the walls must be cut and nailed into the studs, or a sheet of plywood is used on each side of the corner instead of the insulation sheet.

Doors, Windows, and Skylights

Doors, windows and skylights can turn a dull kitchen into a bright, cheerful place to live, work, and play. Kitchens almost always benefit from more natural light. Surveys have indicated that homebuyers are favourably impressed by rooms that have an abundance of natural light. To some extent, the existing construction of the kitchen can affect the options, but most buildings can be adapted to accept a wide variety of windows, doors, skylights, and roof windows.

Adding a lot of natural light to a small kitchen can make it appear larger and more appealing. Unfortunately, a tall window cannot be installed in an average kitchen, and wide windows won't fit between wall cabinets, but there are alternative solutions. If wall space is at a premium because of the kitchen cabinets or counters, and there is attic space or just a roof above the kitchen, skylights can be installed. Another option to suggest to your client is to consider a garden window. These big windows are shaped in a way that allows them to fit nicely in most kitchens without consuming unnecessary wall space. Another way to get extra light into a kitchen might be the use of a nine-light glazed door, a terrace door, or a sliding-glass door.

When installing a new kitchen or remodelling an existing one, additional interior doors, exterior doors, or moving or closing up an existing door may be required. Almost every modern door has a vertical stile and horizontal rail framework. This construction helps counteract wood's tendency to shrink, swell, and warp with humidity changes.

— *Solid panel doors*: With a solid panel door, you can see the framing. Spaces between frame members can be panelled with wood, louvred slats, or glass.

— *Flush doors*: Flush doors (hollow-core or solid-core), which have no panels, hide their framing beneath two or three layers of veneer. Alternating the direction of the veneer minimises warping.

— *Hollow-core doors*: A hollow-core door, usually $1\frac{3}{8}$ inches thick, may be filled with a lighter material, such as corrugated cardboard.

— *Solid-core doors*: A solid-core flush door, usually $1\frac{3}{4}$ inches thick, has a dense center of hardwood blocks or particleboard glued together within the internal stile and rail framework that is hidden under the veneer.

— *Interior doors*: Interior doors are manufactured in wood, flat panel, six-panel composite, and French doors. They do not need to be as sturdy as exterior doors. Hollow-core flush interior doors are common. In areas where space is limited, the design may call for you to install a pocket door.

— *Exterior doors*: Exterior doors are manufactured in wood, fiberglass, metal-insulated, sliding-glass, and terrace doors. They provide weather protection and security while allowing people to move from the inside to the outside. While wood doors are still most prevalent, steel and fiberglass doors are gaining popularity.

— *Prehung doors*: Installing prehung doors is highly recommended. Prehung units do not cost much more than slab doors and the components needed to make them operational, but they can be installed in a fraction of the time needed to fabricate a complete door unit.

A prehung door usually comes complete with a split jamb and prefabricated trim. The door can have either lower-cost fingerjoint trim or solid trim. Either trim is fine if it is to be painted, but fingerjoint trim looks out of place when it is stained.

Door installaion

When framing rough openings for door installations, you must allow room for shimming the door. Rough openings should generally be 2 to 2½ inches larger than the width of the door to allow enough room for the jamb. The header is normally framed 3 inches higher than the door height. This height must consider the type and thickness of floor material being used. The door must be hung straight and plumb to operate properly. Interior door frames are made up of two side jambs and a head jamb and include stop moldings upon which the door closes. The most common of these jambs is the one-piece type. The two- and three-piece adjustable jambs are also standard types. Their primary advantage is in being adaptable to a variety of wall thicknesses. Doors are either right-handed or left-handed. Your client can determine the handedness by facing the door as it is swinging toward them. A door that is left-handed has the latch on the left, while a right-handed door has the latch on the right. The swing of the door can be crucial in kitchen projects.

Window installation

Sometimes it is necessary, or at least desirable, to replace existing windows. Adding windows is a job that anyone with basic carpentry experience can usually handle. However, the process can get difficult at times. Ductwork, a plumbing vent, or a chaseway for electrical wires may be located in the same place you want to put a new window. Local code requirements might insist that new windows be added as the use of space is changed. There are a wide variety of window styles from which to choose. Double-hung windows are the most common type; single-hung windows are not used very often. Casement windows, awning windows, bay windows, fixed glass, and bow windows are some additional types.

Cutting in the rough opening for a new window can be a little tricky. However, once the wall is opened up, framing the window opening is pretty simple. Examine the structure of the wall before including major wall changes. Some windows are held in place with a nailing flange. The flange is set against the exterior wall sheathing and screwed in place. The wall studs of balloon-framed houses carry the load of the second floor and roof; cutting into them may be best handled by a subcontractor. Siding is installed over the flange.

Not all windows have nailing flanges. Some windows are made so that they are nailed into place through their sides. Follow the manufacturer's recommendations when installing any window. When preparing to cut in a new window, it is important to remember to start on the inside of the building. If you work from the inside and discover an obstacle that could prevent the window installation, you need to only patch the interior wall, but if you start the work from the outside, you have to repair the siding and sheathing, which is a much larger project. Once the window hole has been cut out on the inside wall, you can see if there are going to be any problems installing the windows in the desired location. If there is no reason to change plans, you can continue with the process. This process entails the alteration of existing framing to accommodate a header, jack studs, and cripple studs. Some of the exterior siding and wall sheathing also must be cut away.

The space for the new window is termed rough opening. Its dimensions are supplied by the manufacturer of the window. These are usually inches larger to provide for thermal expansion and contractions, as well as building settling, shrinkage, or binding, which can distort the new frame. This space is shimmed with tapered slivers of wood shingles to adjust, level, and fasten the window inside the rough opening. The last step, when the rough opening is completed, is installing the window. This step usually goes smoothly. It is the early stages of this job that present you with the most problems. To keep the risk to a minimum, work from the inside out.

Double-hung windows include heavy sash weights concealed behind the frame's side jambs. Connected via a rope-and-pulley system, the weights provide a counterbalance that not only makes the sashes easier to open, but also holds them in any vertical position you choose. A series of stops fitted to the jambs provides channels in which the sashes slide. Check the top view and note that though the outside bind stop is more or less permanently affixed, the parting stop and inside stop can be pried loose if you want to remove the sashes.

Newer double-hung windows replace the weight-and-pulley mechanisms with a pair of spring-lift devices. With both types, the lower sash comes to rest behind a flat stool; its outside counterpart, the sill, slopes so water can run off. Trim-called casing at the sides and top, and an apron below-covers any gaps between the jambs and the wall material. Casement windows open and close door-fashion, usually with the help of a crank-type operator. With some double-glazed casements, though, the grilles snap to the inside of the window to facilitate cleaning or are absent altogether. As with double-hungs, sliding sashes open up only 50 percent of the total window area for ventilation.

Some have one fixed and one sliding sash; with others, both sashes slide along continuous tracks. Sliding windows may have wood or metal construction. Awning sashes tilt outward, under the direction of a scissors- or hinge-type cranking system. Some awnings slide downward as they tilt, so they can be opened to an almost horizontal position for maximum air flow. Jalousie windows also let in lots of air; each turn of the crank pivots a series of glass slats for maximum flow control. The frames here consist of short metal channels at either end of the slats. Those glass-to-glass joints tend to leak air, so jalousies are usually found only in breezeways, porches, and other zones not-normally heated.

Skylight installation

Cutting a skylight into an existing roof is not a big problem. However, the location of a skylight may be restricted by barriers such as electrical lines, heating ducts, or structural framing. Moving the location is less costly than rerouting utility lines or making structural changes. Skylights can be purchased in a size that allows them to fit between existing rafters. A rule of thumb concerning size is to buy a skylight with an area of 10 to 15 percent of the area of the floor in the room. To install them, you simply cut a hole in the roof, set the skylight in place, and seal around it. In vaulted ceilings, the job is not complicated at all.

If there is attic space between the roof and living space, the task takes oil a few twists-alight box must be built. Building a light box is really quite simple. Once you have located a place for the skylight, a plumb bob is used to find an appropriate spot on the ceiling below. A hole is then cut in the roof for the skylight, and the ceiling is also cut out, providing you with a hole in the roof and a corresponding hole in the ceiling below. Lumber is then used to frame the light box. The framing can be attached to the rafters on either side of the holes.

The inside of the light box should be framed so that the skylight can give maximum light. Once the framing is complete, drywall can be hung and finished. Larger skylights may span two or more rafters. To install these, rafters must be cut and new framing installed to maintain the roof's structural integrity.

Skylights are available in many different shapes and sizes. Some are operable-they can be opened-and others are fixed. Operable and fixed skylights look much the same. They both allow the same amount of light to enter a home, but operable skylights also provide ventilation. Improvements in glass permit the use of large areas of glass without mullions, which are the support strips used between the panes of glass. Glazing options in good-quality glass skylights provide insulation, shield rooms from the sun's ultraviolet rays, and create a buffer against outside noise. The choice of flooring style affects several construction factors that must be dealt with early on.

Wood Floors System

Wood floor systems and concrete slab floors are the two most common types of floor systems. Concrete slab floors are used when there is no basement or crawlspace. Wood floor systems are used when a house has a basement or crawlspace. A wood floor system can be thought of as a wood platform on which the house is built. The platform is usually built of structural wood or engineered joists. Both types of joists are covered by subflooring. Subflooring is a panel material, such as plywood.

The structure of a wood floor system generally does not need to be altered unless you are installing a new piece of equipment that would exceed the bearing or weight capacity of the existing wood platform. Before ordering materials or beginning the preliminary work of preparing the subfloor for new flooring, check the basic floor and supporting structure. In older homes, you may find that the wood flooring system has sagged due to settling and shrinkage, creating a dip in the flooring surface. This settling does not necessarily mean that a structural weakness exists. A number of nonstructural changes may be required. Thoroughly inspect the existing flooring for indications of problems.

If the existing floor is being removed as a part of the project, you can examine the subfloor. If the finish flooring is to remain, you need to inspect the subflooring from the underside by going into the crawlspace or basement. From this vantage point, you should be able to examine the floor joists, foundation, and subfloor, and determine the extent of any water damage and estimate how much subflooring needs to be replaced. Especially look for signs of a spongy or deteriorating subfloor, which indicates that there is or has been water leaking on the subfloor. Spongy or deteriorated subfloor may indicate more extensive damage due to leaks in plumbing or walls and roof.

Insects, such as termites and carpenter ants, as well as animal nesting, is unseen from above the floor. Termites build tunnels across masonry to reach the wooden framework. The surface appears solid while they consume the centers of the wood members. Professional exterminators and structural repairs affect time and costs. During this inspection, check the plumbing and electrical runs for condition or modification problems. If you find any indication of structural damage, notify the client of the damage and the anticipated cost to correct the problem.

The masonry foundation should be sound, with no crumbling mortar or loose or missing bricks or stones. Block or poured concrete foundations are more obvious, and cracking in mortar, while common, can worsen due to frost and moisture penetration. Repointing is advisable. Large separations or cracking may indicate a problem in the footer. These conditions may be outside the scope of a cabinetmaker, but they must be brought to the attention of the client. Changing the cabinet work or adding a partition over an uneven floor makes installation more time-consuming. Proper structural repairs may actually be more cost-effective, requiring fewer cosmetic cover-ups.

If the finish flooring is sheet goods, the entire existing finish floor has to be removed and replaced. If the floor is ceramic or vinyl tile, it may be possible to remove only the affected portion and replace it once the subfloor has been repaired. Once the floor surface has been levelled, you can install a new finish floor. If you are installing a new finish floor material, it is generally best to remove the existing flooring materials rather than overlaying the existing flooring with new flooring.

Many installers install new underlayment whether they remove the old flooring or not. Existing imperfections in the old finish flooring usually end up showing through the new flooring material at some point. The advantages of laying new flooring over old are that you bypass the messy job of removing old flooring, and you gain some soundproofing and insulation. Some disadvantages are that you are unable to inspect the subflooring and make corrections, and there may not be enough space left above to install appliances, such as the dishwasher.

Check with the flooring manufacturer for specific instructions and requirements for flooring underlayment. Keep in mind that the failure to follow specific recommendations can void some manufacturers' warranties. An extremely important matter to be aware of is that a variety of old flooring materials were manufactured with asbestos in them. Asbestos is no longer used in flooring materials, but if you are remodelling a house, it may already exist in the flooring. If you have reason to believe that the existing flooring contains asbestos, leave the flooring in place. Do not sand it.

Concrete floor slab: In a house with a concrete floor slab, the problems are somewhat different. Concrete slabs are prone to cracking due to stress on the slab or soil movement beneath the slab. If you are to install a new finish floor on an existing concrete slab, an existing crack might cause a tile floor to crack along the line of the existing crack. If you are installing sheet goods, the crack might telegraph through the new finish flooring. A crack can be masked by using a cleavage membrane material manufactured for this purpose.

Whether or not there are problems with the concrete slab, completely remove the existing finish floor before installing a new floor. Old adhesive from the existing flooring needs to be completely removed so there is a good smooth surface for the new flooring. Because plumbing, piping, and sometimes heating ductwork or piping is installed before pouring the concrete slab, any additional or relocated plumbing rough-in will probably require cutting or breaking out part of the existing floor slab. When the concrete slab is patched, feather the joint between the existing slab and the patch so that the joint does not telegraph through the new finish floor.

Finish flooring must be compatible with the materials beneath it. Not all types are suitable for all kinds of conditions. Almost any kind of flooring material can be used over a wood floor system, including ceramic tile, vinyl, and hardwoods. Wood is affected by moisture, so only laminated products should be considered for rooms below grade. The best finish floor materials over a concrete slab are sheet goods or vinyl, ceramic tile installed with an organic adhesive, and hardwood parquet flooring.

If installing wood strips over a concrete slab, the best approach is to place the floor on sleepers or screeds. Sleepers are treated 2-by-4s laid flat on the slab. The sleepers must be protected from moisture by a vapour barrier. If the slab has no existing vapour barrier beneath it, ground moisture will penetrate to the sleepers. A layer of mastic, covered by 15-pound, asphalt-saturated felt paper, and finally another coat of mastic is needed. A layer of poly sheet between the sleepers and the final flooring is advised. For air circulation, a gap ½ inch between last board and nail works well. Rows of staggered sleepers 12 to 16 inches on center are placed at right angles to the flooring.

Putting the floor on sleepers allows a strip wood flooring system, but the, floor will be at least 2 inches higher than in adjacent rooms. Either use finish floor materials that can be installed directly on the concrete slab or find a transition between adjacent flooring materials. With proper preparation, a concrete subfloor, because it is rigid, can serve as a base for almost any type of flooring. Other subfloors are more flexible and are not suitable for rigid materials, such as masonry and ceramic tile, unless they are built-up with extra underlayment or floor framing. The finished floor is only as good as the material over which it is laid, so it is essential that the subfloor is properly prepared to guarantee a smooth surface. Assuming the substructures are sound and sturdy, the subfloor must be adequately prepared to receive the new flooring. Subflooring is used over the floor joists to form a working platform and base for finish flooring. It usually consists of square-edge or tongue-and-groove boards no wider than 8 inches and not less than ¾ inch thick or plywood that is ½ to ¾ inch thick, depending on species, type of finish floor, and spacing of joists.

Subflooring boards may be applied either diagonally or at right angles to the joists. When subflooring is placed at right angles to the joists, the finish floor should be laid at right angles to the subflooring. Diagonal subflooring permits finish flooring or butt joints to be laid either parallel or at right angles to the joists. End joints of the boards should always be located directly over the center of the joists. Plywood subfloor is nailed to each joist with two 8d nails for widths under 8 inches and three 8d nails for 8-inch widths.

The joist spacing should not exceed 16 inches on center when finish flooring is laid parallel to the joists or where parquet finish flooring is used, nor should it exceed 24 inches on center when finish flooring at least 25/32 inch thick is at right angles to the joists. Where balloon framing is used, blocking should be installed between ends of joists at the wall for nailing the ends of diagonal subfloor boards. Plywood should be installed with the grain direction of the outer plies at right angles to the joists and be staggered so that end joints in adjacent panels break over different joists.

Plywood should be nailed to the joist at each bearing with 8d common or 7d threaded nails for plywood that is ½ to ¾ inch thick. Space nails 6 inches apart along all edges and 10 inches along intermediate members. When plywood serves as both subfloor and underlayment, nails may be spaced 6 to 7 inches apart at all joists and blocking.

Use 8d or 9d common nails or 7d or 8d threaded nails. If necessary, lay an underlayment, of untempered hardboard or plywood directly over the subfloor to raise the surface of new flooring to the same height as the old. Be sure to ensure a level transition between the new floor and adjacent rooms and make it unnecessary to trim door casings, doors, or moldings. In some instances, the addition of new flooring and plywood underlayment may interfere with the replacement of appliances. In these cases, be sure to remove the old flooring.

Underlayment: Correctly installed, underlayment provides a flat, uniform surface, eliminates irregularities in the subfloor, strengthens the floor, and creates a more secure and stable surface for laying finish flooring. It comes in 4-by-8-foot sheets. For underlayment, choose either ¼-inch plywood or hardboard or up to ½-inch particle board. Do not install underlayment in exceedingly moist or humid weather or at times when the atmosphere is unusually dry. Techniques for installing underlayment vary, depending on whether the subfloor consists of plywood sheets or individual boards.

Check the subfloor for uneven areas with a long, straight 2-by-4 laid on edge. Correct the low spots by shimming from below; protruding joints or fasteners will be revealed later on a new glossy surface. Loose joints will later crack through. A new type of underlayment on the market that is gaining popularity is a fiber-reinforced underlayment, which provides an excellent base for a variety of floor coverings. This type of underlayment is smoother, more durable, and more moisture-tolerant than conventional wood-based underlayments. It is made by blending cellulose fiber and gypsum throughout the panel, giving it a uniformly smooth surface. Its high-density surface provides superior indentation resistance compared to traditional plywood underlayment. In addition, it is fire-resistant.

Resilient flooring preparation

Most resilient flooring is so pliable it conforms to irregularities in the subfloor. For this reason, it is essential that care be taken to prepare the subfloor properly to guarantee a smooth surface. If the surface that is to be covered with new flooring is rough, the finished job is not going to look good. When preparing an old floor for new vinyl, always install new underlayment. Hardboard or plywood that is 4 inch or thicker works well. It provides a clean, porous base for the adhesive that secures the vinyl in place. It is best to have the old floor removed before adding the underlayment. It might be necessary, even when new underlayment is installed, to fill cracks that form between the sheets. It is also important to make sure that nails and screw heads are not protruding from the underlayment. Any that stick up are going to show in the new vinyl. Most of today's resilient floorings can be installed on any grade. A few, though, should not be laid on concrete in contact with soil.

Ceramic tile preparation

Unless it is installed over a perfectly sound subfloor, the most carefully laid ceramic tile floor will eventually reveal flaws, and cracks will appear. Inspect the subfloor from above and below for any necessary repairs. Inspect the floor structure and joists, look for loose boards or a random low spot in a subfloor, which indicate defects. If the subfloor and structure are sound, you can lay ceramic tile over subfloors made of plywood panels or individual boards. Use an underlayment suitable to your selected adhesive, such as fiber-reinforced concrete. Traditionally, ceramic tile was installed on floors using the mud-set method-the tile was set in a bed of mortar. The mud-set method allows the ceramic tile to be set level even if there are dips or imperfections in the subfloor when using plywood. Fiberglass-reinforced board is currently recommended. When using these underlayments, a thin-set adhesive method may be recommended by the tile manufacturers. Since you will be raising the level of the floor itself, check the bottoms of the doors for adequate clearance. If necessary, trim the door. A wood base is suitable if the boards or panels are securely fastened to the joists. Baseboard trim, heating elements, and existing cabinetry will also be affected.

Ceramic tile can now be installed much more simply than the mud-set method using a thin layer of adhesive applied with a trowel. It requires a very flat, rigid surface, meaning that board floors or damaged resilient tile must be covered with plywood or underlayment such as the fiber-reinforced concrete before the tile can be laid. Adhesives have been developed that permit installation of ceramic tile in an area with some moisture, making it an appropriate choice to cover a below-grade concrete slab.

Preparing a proper base for any type of wood flooring can be more demanding than putting in the new flooring itself. Wood floors are seldom installed in rooms below grade or in areas subject to dampness. It is important to check an on-grade concrete slab carefully for moisture before installing wood flooring; be certain it will stay dry over the years.

Similarly, the space below a standard floor supported by joists and beams should be properly ventilated and protected from moisture for wood flooring to be laid over it. If there is already an old floor in place, the best approach is to expose the subfloor. Leaving the old floor surface increases the weight of the system and takes away from the headroom. If you want to leave an old floor in place, cover it with asphalt felt, as you would a wood subfloor. Strap flooring is laid lengthwise in a room and normally at right angles to the floor joists. A subfloor of diagonal boards or plywood is normally used under the finish floor. Strip flooring of this type is tongue-and-grooved and end-matched. Strips are random lengths and may vary from 2 to 16 feet or more. The tongue fits tightly into the groove to prevent movement and floor squeaks. All of these details are designed to provide beautiful finished floors that require a minimum of maintenance. Blind-nail boards without damaging the finish. Drive nails into the tongue with a nail set. Use a block and bar to tightly force the board tongue into the groove without damaging it.

Parquet (block) flooring

Parquet (block) flooring is made in a number of patterns. Blocks may vary in size from 4-by-4 inches to 9-by-9 inches and larger. Solid wood tile is often made up of narrow strips of wood splined or keyed, together in a number of ways. Wedges of the thicker tile are tongue-and-grooved, but thinner sections of wood are usually square-edged. Plywood blocks may be 8 inch and thicker and are usually tongue-and-grooved. Many block floors are factory-finished and require only waxing after installation.

Whichever of the three types of wood flooring your client has chosen, preparing a reliable base requires the same steps. Wood floors are typically laid over a concrete slab, over a wood subfloor supported by joists and beams, or, in some cases, over an existing floor, depending on the old floor's composition and condition and on the kind of wood flooring you plan to install. Strips or planks can be fastened to a wood floor or subfloor or to plywood or 2-by-4-inch sleepers installed over a dry, level concrete slab.

If the concrete is uneven, it is best to build a subfloor suspended over the concrete base. Parquet flooring requires a solid, smooth, continuous subfloor, whether of boards or plywood panels, concrete, or even resilient flooring. Laminated wood tiles can be laid directly in mastic on a thoroughly dry concrete slab that has a waterproofing membrane below or above to keep it dry, but blocks of solid wood pieces are best installed over a plywood base built over the slab. Unlike parquet tiles, strip-and-plank flooring can't be cemented directly to concrete. If you don't want to build a subfloor, lay a polyethylene vapour barrier, fasten down 2-by-4-inch sleepers, and then nail the flooring to the sleepers. Be sure the concrete is properly sealed against moisture. If the floor is cold, lay rigid foam insulation between the sleepers. Allow some space above the foam for air circulation. A single layer of polyethylene film laid under new wood flooring is usually considered adequate moisture protection for a dry slab floor.

A wood subfloor, either plywood or boards, should be covered with a plywood underlayment. The combined thickness of subfloor and underlayment should be 1 ¼, inches with underlayment at least ⅝, inch. If the combination is not thick enough, cover it with a layer of ⅝-inch exterior-grade plywood. The laying of wood strip flooring should be completed after the other interior wall and ceiling finish is completed, windows and exterior doors are in place, and most of the interior trim, except base, casing, and jambs, is applied, so that the flooring will not be damaged by construction activity.

Masonry flooring preparation

Masonry flooring can be laid over a ground-level concrete slab or a suspended wood floor. However, putting masonry over a suspended floor in a frame home can be complicated because of the weight. If setting masonry over a wood floor, the floor must be protected by a moisture barrier of asphalt felt. Masonry exerts tremendous weight and should be laid over concrete. A concrete slab provides the best-possible subfloor.

Make sure the slab is clean so that mortar will bond to it. Slate or flagstone may be set in a bed of mortar on a concrete slab or in mastic or adhesive over a wood subfloor. Preparing a base for masonry flooring is simple if the flooring is to be laid over a concrete slab at ground level. If masonry flooring was planned as part of the original building, allowances have been made for the extra weight, and the support system was planned accordingly. But if brick or stone flooring is being laid in an older home as part of a remodelling project, the old floor, in most cases, will need reinforcing.

Always consult a building design professional before putting masonry flooring over any subfloor other than a ground-level concrete slab. Stone is available in rough-hewn pieces or in uniform tiles. You need a thick mortar base over a concrete slab to lay a flooring of rough-hewn stone. The irregularity of the material makes it necessary to provide a cushion of mortar that compensates for the differences in thickness from piece to piece. You can use thin-set mortar for stones that can be cut into pieces of uniform thicknesses, such as slate and marble. Keep in mind that the thickness of these stones, plus the mortar bed, raises the height of the floor considerably. Though most bricks can be used for both walls and floors, pacers are intended specifically for floors. Pavers are available in regular or slightly less than regular thicknesses, or as splits, which are half as thick as regular bricks. Full pavers can be laid on a concrete slab; splits require a concrete slab topped with a mortar bed or spread with thin-set adhesive.

Wooden subfloors require the lighter-weight splits. Because this precut material is a lighter floor, it requires less structural support than rough-hewn stone in a full bed of mortar. The subfloor requirements are the same as those for ceramic tile. If installing a masonry floor, particularly one of natural stone, be sure to check the local building code for subfloor requirements.

6

MECHANICAL SYSTEMS IN KITCHEN

A kitchen builder must be familiar with mechanical systems, such as plumbing; gas; electrical; heating, ventilation, and air-conditioning (HVAC); and cooking ventilation.

PLUMBING SYSTEM OF KITCHEN

The plumbing system of the home provides a means of bringing water to an outlet and a means of taking used water away. Because most of a plumbing system is hidden inside walls and floors, it may seem complex and overwhelming; however, kitchen plumbing needs are fairly simple and straightforward. In today's kitchen, water is needed at many places, no longer just the kitchen sink. Water must be supplied to the dishwasher, food disposer, water purifier, ice maker, and special preparation or service areas, such as a bar or vegetable sink. It is also necessary to provide a means of draining wastewater away from each of these sinks and appliances.

Once installed, the plumbing system is relatively permanent. Changes to existing systems are usually expensive because they require walls to be opened and holes to be cut in floors and ceilings. The effect changes may have on rooms located below or above the kitchen, or both, can also increase costs considerably. The total plumbing system includes all pipes, fixtures, and fittings used to convey water into and out of homes. It can be divided into three basic areas:

— The water-supply system

— The drainage system

— The fixtures and appliances

The object of it all, of course, is to make water available where it is wanted in the home, and to get rid of water, plus wastes, after it has served its purpose.

Water-supply System

In every plumbing system, there must be a source of water and pipes to carry it to the fixtures. This water-supply system must be adequate to ensure the homeowner has pure water for drinking, to supply a sufficient quantity of water at any outlet in the system, and to furnish the homeowner with hot or cold water, as required. The main supply line coming into a house carries cold water. This source is provided by either a municipal water company or a private underground well.

If the water source is a municipal supplier, the water passes through a meter that registers the amount of water used. From this main supply line (through one pipe), a branch splits off and is joined to a hot-water heater. From this point, branches lead to the various fixtures and faucets in the home. The water supply to fixtures and appliances is controlled with faucets and valves. The supply mains should be graded to one low point in the basement so that a drain cock permits complete drainage of the entire supply system. Any portion of the piping that cannot be so drained must be equipped with a separate drain cock. The water-supply system should deliver water to the sink and appliances in the quantity and rate needed.

The size of pipe, number of fittings, the length of pipe from the main, the pressure available, and the number of other fixtures in use at the time determine the rate at which water flows from the faucet. In remodelling projects, if new plumbing fixtures are added, the pipe size of risers and main arteries (or branches) might need to be increased. The service from the main or well should be underground to avoid freezing or mechanical damage. A valve to control the water (the main shutoff) should be located inside the house near the entrance of the water-service pipe. The water meter (if installed) is usually located at this point.

The size of the water piping from the main to the individual fixtures is determined by the number and type of fixtures served by the pipe. These two relationship can be used as a general "rule-of-thumb:" a) For service to three or more fixtures, use ¾ inch (2-cm) pipe. b) For service to two or fewer fixtures, use ½-inch (1.3-cm) pipe.

Each fixture is supplied by a fixture-supply pipe. Table 1 shows the minimum sizes of supply pipes for specific fixtures.

Table 1. Minimum sizes for fixture water-supply lines

Fixture	Supply pipe size (in inches)
Clothes dryer	¾ inch (2 cm)
Clothes washer	¾ inch (2 cm)
Dishwasher	½ inch (13 mm)
Hose bib	½ inch (13 mm)
Hot-water heater	¾ inch (2 cm)
Ice maker	⅛ inch (3 mm)
Kitchen sink	½ inch (13 mm)
Laundry tub	½ inch (13 mm)
Sink risers	¼ inch (6.3 mm)

For most fixtures, a ½-inch (1.3-cm) pipe should be run to the fixture's cutoff valve. Under most codes, the water service to the house might be a ¾,-inch (2-cm) pipe, but a 1-inch (3-cm) water service pipe is a better choice. The lamer water pipe allows for future expansion and provides a higher volume of water to the interior system. Each supply pipe should be equipped with a valve or "stop" so that repairs can be made to an individual fixture without interrupting service to other fixtures in the house.

Water heaters: Hot water is obtained by routing cold water through a water furnace. This heater may be part of the central heating plant or a separate unit. When part of a central system, a separate hot-water storage tank is generally provided to hold the heated water. On the other hand, when a separate heater is used, the water is stored within the unit. A separate heater unit may be electric, oil, or gas-fired, but all are automatically controlled by a preset thermostat.

Each style of heater comes in a wide variety of sizes. All automatic heaters have the necessary internal piping already installed, and the only connections required are the hot- and cold-water and fuel lines. Oil or gas-fired water heaters also require flues to vent the products of combustion. A new hot-water heater might be necessary when new plumbing is added to the present system. Even if the present water heater is functioning properly (not scaled up or rusted out), there may not be sufficient hot water available for the family.

Actually, the size of the hot-water storage tank needed in the house depends on the number of persons in the family, the volume of hot water that may be needed during peak-use periods, and the recovery rate of the heating unit. A good rule to follow when estimating the capacity of the tank required is 10 gallons per hour for each member of the family.

The recovery rate of water heaters varies with the type and capacity of the heating element. Temperature and pressure-relief valves are on all hot-water heaters and hot-water storage tanks. Their function is to relieve pressure in the tank and water pipes should any other piece of control equipment in the system fail and the water temperature reach a point high enough to cause a dangerous pressure that would rupture the tank and pipes. Another important device on the heater is the drain cock or valve. Located at the bottom of the storage tank, the drain cock or valve allows for the draining of the tank. A shutoff is also located on the cold-water intake pipe.

New dishwashers and laundries add to the hot-water draw. Make sure the equipment has the capacity to handle them. In some houses, the distance from the water heater to the point of use may be quite far and may result in long waiting periods for hot water. A circulation line can be installed so that hot water is always available at each fixture. As an alternative to the circulating system, a separate water heater should be considered for the remote area.

Water softeners: In some areas of the country, it is necessary to make hard water soft by piping the domestic water supply through a device called a water softener. Most water softeners have few moving parts and consume little power. The water is treated as it flows through a special chemical that removes the objectionable minerals that make the water hard. Depending on the hardness of the water, the rate of consumption, and the unit's capacity, there comes a time when the chemical must be regenerated or the equipment must be cleaned and renewed. Different types of chemicals and equipment may be required to treat a specific water-hardness problem. For this reason, an analysis of the water should be made. This test may be performed by various local agencies or with a kit that can be obtained from a plumbing supplier.

Drainage System

This system also known as drain-waste-vent system. Drainage is the complete and final disposal of the wastewater and the sewage it contains. A drainage system, therefore, consists of a) The pipes that carry sewage away from the fixtures b) The place where the sewage is deposited.

The concept of plumbing centers on two physical principles-pressure and gravity. When water is delivered to an outlet, some provision must be made to drain away waste or excess water. The drainage system differs from the water supply in one very important respect. In supply lines, water flows under pressure. In the drainage lines, flow is entirely by gravity, and the pipes must be designed and installed carefully to ensure flow at a velocity adequate to keep the pipes clean. Because they are small in diameter and do not depend on gravity, supply lines are easily rerouted.

The drainage system is also more complex than the supply system in that it consists of three parts, all of which are needed in every installation, even if only one fixture is served. The flow of wastewater starts at the fixture trap, the device that stops sewer gases from entering the house. It flows through the fixture branches to the soil stack. It continues through the house drain and the house sewer and finally reaches the city sewer system, or, in a private system, a septic tank. Waste stacks carry only water waste. These parts are as follows:

— Raps are water seals that carry the wastewater to the drain lines and prevent the backflow of air or sewer gas into the house. The liquid seal blocks rising sewer gases from entering the room. Traps should be accessible and as close as possible to each fixture. Sometimes they are part of the fixture. Plumbing codes restrict the distance a sink's trap can be located from its drain/vent line. The trap never empties and retains enough water to maintain the seal.

Trap styles are: S-trap. deep seal P-trap, and running-trap, P-trap, or P-traps using a J-bend fitting which connect the fixture and the drain pipe. When the fixture drains, water flows through the trap and into the drain pipe. Most traps used today are P-traps, which drain into the wall by way of a 90-degree trap arm. On existing installations, you might also find S-traps, which drain into the floor via a 180-degree trap arm.

— Drainage lines are pipes, either vertical, called stacks, or horizontal, called branches, that carry the discharge from the fixtures to the house sewer. They are usually concealed in walls or floors. The pipes receiving the discharge from the water closet are known as soil lines. Those receiving the discharge from other fixtures are known as waste lines. Some plumbing codes require a grease trap in the waste line from the kitchen sink. Others specifically prohibit them. This trap, which is designed to prevent grease and oil from entering the sewer, must be cleaned frequently for efficient operation.

— Vent lines are pipes extending upward through the roof. They allow air to flow into or out of the drainage pipes, thus equalising air pressure in the drainage system and protecting the water seal in the traps. Without a vent pipe, the rush of water down a drain could cause a siphoning action that would pull the water seal out of the trap and let sewer gases enter the home. The vent pipe is generally located right behind the sink.

The relationship between the trap, the drainage line, and the vent line is very important and has a great influence on the location of plumbing fixtures, particularly in remodelling work where the relocation of fixtures is desired. Actually, the required maximum distance from a trap to a vent does not usually present any problems in residences, except when island sinks are used. This problem can usually be solved by using a drainage line large enough for the distance to the nearest vent.

The actual span varies from one locality to another, but generally speaking, a sink cannot be moved more than 3 to 4 feet without either adding or extending branch lines; in some situations, an entirely new run of piping from basement to roof may be needed. Remember that some plumbing code regulations do not permit sinks or other water-using appliances anywhere other than along a wall. All vents must terminate outside the house. The vent terminal must be carried through the roof at full size. It must be at least 3 inches in diameter to prevent clogging by frost. A new fixture could be added below or above an existing fixture as long as the lower fixture is the one with the greater flow.

The drain/waste lines from each fixture or group of fixtures are connected to the building drain. The building drain takes the waste material to the sewer system or septic tank. The building drain must be installed with the proper slope-¼, inch per foot. Steeper slopes provide higher velocities, increasing the carrying capacity of the pipe, and tend to keep the drain pipe clean. A septic tank treats waste right on the property in an enclosed tank. They are watertight receptacles that receive the discharge of the drainage system. The liquids are discharged into the soil outside of the tank in what is referred to as a tile field; the solids in the waste biodegrade in the septic tank. The city sewer system carries waste away from the property. If adding new fixtures to the kitchen, double-check that the capacity of the septic system can handle the additional fixtures. If the residence is hooked up to a city sewer system, be sure the waste line is properly sized to handle the total fixtures.

Fixtures

The fixtures provide the required means for using the water. In this sense, a faucet on the outside of the house is a fixture, as well as a laundry tub in the basement, or a dishwasher, or a toilet. Each has a purpose connected with the homeowner's use of water, and each must have certain features to serve its purpose. Fixtures can be costly plumbing items and should exactly suit the homeowner's needs.

Be aware that most building codes require plumbers to have a special license, so unless you have that license, you need to hire a plumbing contractor. Some areas have exceptions; however, the work must still be approved and checked by the local building inspector. Although most plumbing systems are based on national codes, local building codes may vary from those in an adjoining city or town. When you are installing a kitchen, all plumbing work must be done in accordance with local plumbing codes. The primary purpose of a plumbing code, as well as of a building code, is to protect the health and safety of the homeowner.

Plumbing Materials

Regional preferences and area building codes generally dictate what type of pipe must be used for both new construction and remodelling projects. However, builders should be familiar with the major types of plumbing pipe used. Plastic piping is lightweight and one of the easiest pipings to use. In new construction, it is becoming the water piping of choice. However, it is important to be aware that its use is restricted by some building and plumbing codes. As with all plumbing, be sure to check all codes before using these materials. Some types of plastic piping include polybutylene (PB), chlorinated PVC (CPVC), polyethylene, acrylonitrile-butadiene-styrene

(ABS), and polyvinyl chloride (PVC). PB and CPVC pipe are used in water-supply systems. PB is very flexible and extremely durable. This pipe is available in long rolls, eliminating the need for joints. It is flexible and resistant to damage from back-filling. If comparing costs, ease of installation, and effectiveness, polybutylene pipe is hard to beat. When installed properly, it is one of the best materials for carrying water. CPVC is a rigid pipe that tends to be brittle and is prone to cracking under stress. But once it is installed correctly, CPVC gives reasonably good service, as long as it is not subjected to abuse, and can last a long time. CPVC and PB are suitable for both hot-and cold-water applications. Whenever feasible, it is best to eliminate joints in underground piping, and with CPVC, you cannot eliminate the joints in long runs.

Polyethylene pipe has long been used as a water-service pipe. It also comes in large rolls, eliminating the need for underground joints. The plastic pipe is durable and resistant to backfilling accidents. Polyethylene is probably one of the most frequently used pipe for modern water-service installations. ABS and PVC are both commonly used in drain (DWV) systems. They are very simple materials to work with and can be cut with any fine-toothed handsaw.

The home electrical system could be grounded through metal water pipes. When adding plastic pipes to a metal plumbing system, be certain the electrical ground circuit is not broken. Use ground clamps and jumper wires to bypass the plastic transition and complete the electrical ground circuit. Clamps must be firmly attached to bare metal on both sides of the plastic pipe.

Copper (technically called tubing, not pipe), though somewhat more expensive than others, is lightweight, versatile, highly resistant to corrosion, and gives many years of good service. It is most commonly used for water supply for remodelled kitchens. It is good water-service pipe, unless the water supply contains a high acid content. Be certain to verify that the pipe thickness is sufficient to meet all building codes.

Galvanised steel piping is notorious for its ability to rust out and clog up, and it is heavy. Whether used for drain, vent, or water service, all galvanised steel pipes should be replaced. It is outdated and serves no purpose in modern plumbing installations. It increases the risk of rust, leaking joints, and restricted water flow.

Cast-iron piping has a long life with few problems and is basically satisfactory for continued service. However, it is one of the heaviest and most difficult pipings to work with. It does only drain-waste-vent duty, though no-hub clamps make smaller jobs not overly difficult for an amateur.

Checking plumbing: Inspection of the plumbing system is not easy because much of the piping is concealed and inaccessible. Be sure to look under any cabinets that have plumbing to find out the types of materials used for water pipes, drains, and vents. It might also be possible to inspect some of the plumbing from the basement, cellar, or crawl space. After completing the plumbing evaluation procedure, accurate assessments can be made on the condition of plumbing systems and how the problems can be corrected.

Leading plumbing: Lead has become a serious problem in plumbing, and one that must be addressed by kitchen builders doing remodelling projects. Its presence depends on when the house was built, what kind of plumbing pipes it has, and what types of water mains connect the building to the water supply system. If you discover any lead bends, traps, or pipes, they should always be replaced when remodelling a kitchen. Soft lead deteriorates over time and problems are sure to arise.

HVAC Systems

Heating, ventilation, and air-conditioning (HVAC) systems are designed to maintain comfort in the home. HVAC systems may be affected by your proposed kitchen project. Changes are governed either by the local plumbing regulations or a separate mechanical code. As with plumbing, a special trade license is usually required in this area of work. Therefore, unless you are a skilled HVAC technician, you should plan on hiring a competent subcontractor to work with these systems. It is always important to make your client aware of two important factors when installing a heating and air-conditioning system: a) The cost of the purchase and installation b) The cost of actually operating the various systems

Kitchen builders must check the type of heat and make sure the designer or architect took the existing system and ducts or radiators into consideration in the design and layout of the room. Probably the most difficult task in providing heating and cooling for a kitchen is finding a suitable location for the terminal device of the heating/cooling system. Generally, the out-side walls of the kitchen are lined with cabinets, making it almost impossible to locate air registers, hydronic baseboards, or electric resistance baseboards on the wall. The various heating systems used in a home are not discussed fully here. However, suggestions as to how they can be employed and installed in a kitchen-new or remodelled-are given here.

Both air-conditioning and heating ducts are fairly easy to reroute, as long as you can gain access from a basement, crawl space, garage wall, or unfinished attic. Radiant heat pipes or other slab-embedded systems may pose problems.

Home heating systems can be classified by the fuel they use or by heating medium. The medium can be warm air, hot water, or steam. Fuels are natural gas, fuel oil, or electricity. Water and steam heat the house with radiators piped from a boiler. Warm air is generated by a furnace and is widely favoured because it is easy to add a central air-conditioning unit and a central humidifier. Electric resistance heaters are easy to install, but electric rates make them expensive. Warm-air systems deliver heat to a room through wall, floor, baseboard, or ceiling registers or diffusers. Air returns to the furnace through return grilles. If the kitchen being remodelled does not have a register, one can be added in a kick space with a duct elbow to route heat into the room through a toekick grille.

Warm-air systems: Registers for warm-air systems and small electric resistance blower-operated units can be located in the toe space beneath lower cabinets. These units are acceptable for heating, but registers in the toe space present problems of proper air distribution for cooling applications. If they are used, they should be considered for heating use only, and provision should be made so that they may be blocked or turned off in summer when the cooling system is in operation. In new construction, provisions can be made for using toe-space registers for heating and auxiliary registers located on the side walls for cooling, if the installed system is one that provides both heating and cooling.

For remodelling work, the relocation of ductwork can sometimes present serious difficulties, particularly if the house is built on a slab or if there is a finished ceiling in the basement below the kitchen. If the "new" kitchen is located in an addition to the house, it is possible to extend the ductwork to provide for heating and cooling the addition. Before this is done, the existing furnace should be checked to see that it has sufficient heating and/or cooling capacity for the addition. The blower unit must also be checked to see that it is capable of delivering the additional air needed in the new room. It may be necessary to replace the blower assembly or the blower motor to increase the air-handling capability of the system, even though the furnace burner has sufficient heating capacity. It is also possible to increase the air-handling capacity of the system by speeding up the blower.

In general, this is not a good practice, since the increased blower speed normally increases the noise level from the furnace. Be aware that when remodelling for a kitchen or room adjacent to a heating unit, moving walls or surfaces too close to the heater or ductwork is hazardous. Each heating unit has minimum safe clearances that are included with the manufacturer's installation information or, in some instances, shown on a sticker on the unit. If in question, consult the subcontractor or manufacturer before planning to move a partition.

A heater must have adequate air for combustion. It must not be enclosed in such a way that cuts off its air supply or impedes its flue or exhaust. Most forced warm-air systems can support another register or two if the furnace is centrally located. A zoned heating system designed to heat the addition may be the best answer. Quite often, the HVAC plan you receive with design plans may be very schematic, and the dedicated areas for running ductwork may not be indicated or planned for in the design.

HVAC systems require a substantial amount of space, and cramping the ductwork areas only leads to awkward installations that can cause the HVAC system to be inefficient or noisy. If the addition of any bump-outs or chases for the ductwork will affect the cabinet layout, this information should be determined and reported to the dealer or designer so that modifications can be made before cabinets are ordered. When remodelling around a hot-air system, registers can be added or relocated. When planning the kitchen, consult the manufacturer or a subcontractor before finalising a design.

Hydronic (hot-water) systems: In a forced hot-water system, a boiler heats water that circulates through pipes. The pipes lead to fan coil units, convectors, or radiators. These units radiate heat to the room air. Convectors consist of a core of fins that are heated by hot water. The air passing over these fins is warmed. Fan coil units work on the same principle, but have small fans that push the warm air out into the room. Earlier hot-water systems operated by gravity and did not have a circulating pump.

A circulating pump can be added on this type of hot-water system. In small kitchens or in corridor or U-shaped kitchens, the walls are lined with cabinets, making it difficult to locate baseboard units. A valance unit can be used, or the radiation necessary to offset the heat loss of the kitchen can be located in an adjoining breakfast area or other space immediately adjacent to and open to the kitchen. The HVAC subcontractor can tell you if the system can be modified or if convector or fan coil units can be relocated.

The pipes often run through walls, so you need to trail the path to determine if pipes inside a wall need to be removed or modified. When adding to a hydronic system, be sure the new radiator units are made of the same metal as the old, or it is a sure invitation to corrosion. In extreme cases where the equipment cannot be located in an adjacent space, part of the wall space must be left free for the installation of a convector with or without an integral fan unit to help distribute the warmed air.

Hydronic systems can be modified to suit if a kitchen is part of a new addition. The addition may be heated using the existing furnace; consult the subcontractor. Two methods to add on to an existing system are zone valves or an additional circulating pump and piping. Zone valves are electronically controlled units that are actuated when heat is required in the room. Heated water is pumped by a circulator through the zone valve to baseboard convectors. A circulating pump may be added to the existing system if that unit is not adequate to move the needed hot water. New piping, baseboard convectors, and a pump are installed with little disturbance to the existing heating system.

Electric Heat

If electric ceiling cables or panels are used in a kitchen, there is no particular problem except interference from the soffit work over the upper cabinets. Other electric resistance-type heaters are available, including panels of glass or metal that are mounted on the wall; units that have a small fan that circulates the heated air; and hot-water baseboards in which the water is heated by electrically heated elements similar to those used in a water heater. Also available are resistance units that may be inserted in the branch supply ducts of a central-air duct system. For kitchen installations, a small unit or units that resemble warm-air system registers may be installed in the toe space of the base cabinets. These units are equipped with small blowers to provide air circulation over the resistance elements. If wall space is not available for baseboard units and a toe-space installation is also not practical, electric cable can be applied to the ceiling. It is also possible to install electric-resistance panels on the ceiling to furnish radiant electric heat. They are used with plastered or plasterboard ceilings. The wires are fastened to the ceiling before installing the finished wall surfacing. These panels are rectangular in shape and resemble acoustical tile. With electric-resistance heating, a separate cooling system must be installed.

Subfloor Radiant-Heating Systems

Many manufacturers have introduced electric cable floor warmers that act like heating coils, permanently placed beneath wood, tiles, and even carpet. They are supplementary heating sources of warmth that evenly radiate heat upward, where it does the most good. Most of the new types on the market are mounted on top of the subfloor, have certified insulated cables, and are powered by their own 120-volt box with its own thermostat. In addition, rather than having to design around radiators or typical baseboard heat units, these heating systems are built in under the floor, giving designers more options.

The homeowner has more even heating and more space. These systems rely on electricity to provide heat (from 8 to 15 watts per square foot, depending on the floor material) and are designed as a secondary heat source, not the main heat source for the home. Major benefits to these systems is that, unlike forced hot-air systems, these radiant systems cannot spread dust, pollen, or germs throughout the house and, once installed, are maintenance-free.. These subfloor heating systems can be placed under most any flooring materials-hardwood, ceramic tile, carpet-however, they are not recommended for under linoleum.

Radiators: While radiators provide a good form of heating and are often found in older homes, they are a real problem when one sits right where new, cabinets are desired. There are three basic solutions to the problem of a radiator in the kitchen:

— *Cover it.* Build a cover that matches or complements the rest of the new kitchen design. Make sure this cover allows proper circulation to heat the kitchen adequately.

— *Move it.* Is there another location in the kitchen for the radiator? Perhaps moving it to another wall might improve the kitchen design and the heating, although this option can be costly. If a radiator is moved, it probably will still have to be covered.

— *Replace it.* The old-style radiator can often be replaced with a new base-board unit that gives more versatility in decorating the walls. These old radiators are generally cast iron and are of column, large-tube, or small-tube design.

  Columns and large-tube radiators are no longer manufactured, but small-tube radiators are still available. When radiators are replaced by modern equipment such as convectors, finned tubes, or baseboard radiators, the replacement must be sized to supply a similar amount of heating. It is always best to consult the literature published by the manufacturer of the equipment for the exact amount of heat output of the unit.

It is possible to combine heating and cooling in a central system. This is usually a good choice. It is also possible to have a separate central cooling system. In addition, window air-conditioning units or through-the-wall units may be used to cool the kitchen. This option eliminates the need for ductwork, but it is not as attractive, and it might not be as efficient. With individual units, occupants can control their own comfort. It a central unit is used, some people can be chilly while others are warm. Independent units are easy to install, unlike central units, which require extensive ductwork and considerable time to install.

Window units fit into the opening of a double-hung window, and special units are available for installation in casement windows. The units vary in cooling capacity from as small as 5000 Btuh to 35,000 Btuh. Room air is circulated through the unit, where it is cooled, dehumidified, and filtered. A condensate drain is not necessary since the moisture condensed from the air is evaporated into the outdoor air. The units are electrically operated, and many of the small ones can be plugged into existing electrical outlets. The larger units require 220 or

240 volts and use up to 200 amperes of electricity. They require a separate circuit installed specifically for the air-conditioning unit.

Through-the-wall units are simply window units that have been provided with a metal sleeve built into the wall, which makes the installation more permanent. The chief advantage of the through-the-wall unit is that the window is not obstructed by the air conditioning unit, and the unit may be placed high on the wall so that the distribution of the cooled air is more efficient. The chief disadvantage of the through-the-wall unit is that when the unit must be replaced after some years of service, it may be difficult to find another unit that fits the sleeve. Some manufacturers have standardised the size of the sleeves, but there are still many nonstandard units.

Heat pumps: Heat pumps have become one of the most popular forms of home heating and cooling because of their excellent energy efficiency. They provide both heating and cooling in one system, and they can be installed almost anywhere. While the heat pump's source of energy is electricity, it does not produce heat directly from the electric current. Heat pumps use electricity to move heat from one place to another. In the heating mode, the heat pump extracts heat from outside of the house and delivers it inside. In the cooling mode, it extracts heat from the house and takes it outside.

Sometimes the chimney flue seems to run right through the kitchen. If you're lucky, it is already in the wall. If not, there is a problem. A chimney flue cannot be readily moved and enclosed in the wall like a heating duct. A chimney flue, however, can be boxed in the same manner as pipes. Another solution is to accept the limitations of the flue location and design around it. It can be boxed with drywall and hidden, or it can be dramatised and highlighted.

Electrical Considerations

Another aspect of the kitchen of equal importance to its dual role as a work and living area is adequate electrical provision. Because of all that can be done with electricity in a kitchen, the biggest part of a house's electrical load-up to 80 percent of the total house wattage-is drawn by kitchen appliances and lighting. Because electricity offers such convenient power, more and more power will be used to make the storage, preparation, and cooking of foods and cleanup after meals more convenient and time saving for the homeowner.

A new kitchen usually means more wiring for new appliances and relocated circuits. A trade license is usually required to handle electricity, so in most instances, you need to hire a subcontractor. However, as the builder, you must become knowledgeable about electrical requirements and codes and be confident that you understand their impact on each project. It is important to have a general understanding of electricity so you can inspect the existing electrical service, if applicable, to recognise what may need to be modified, and intelligently discuss the project with an electrical contractor.

Power from the utility comes in through a service entrance to a meter that keeps track of the consumption. The power then continues on to a service panel; which breaks it down into a series of circuits. These circuits deliver current through-out the house. At the service panel, fuses or circuit breakers control individual circuits and protect against fire, which could develop if a circuit draws more current than it is designed to handle. In most newer installations, the safety devices are called circuit breakers. In an older home in which the original wiring is intact, the service panel may contain fuses rather than breakers.

A single circuit breaker controls a 120V circuit. Any 240V circuit is controlled by two circuit breakers that might be connected with a plastic cap. Any 240V circuit serves only one outlet, such as a dryer or electric range. A 120V circuit might serve as many as a dozen outlets, as long as the total amperage of the lights and appliances does not exceed the amperage rating of the circuit breaker or fuse. If a circuit is overloaded or shorted, the breaker automatically breaks the flow of current. Ground circuits are an important part of the wiring. Electrical current flows, under pressure, through the wiring in the house.

The amount of current going through a wire' at a given time is based on the number of electrons passing a certain point each second. The pressure that forces these electrons along their route is known as voltage. Electrical current goes to the service panel on what is called "three-wire" service. Each of the two hot wires supplies electricity at approximately 120 volts. The third, or neutral, wire is maintained at 0 volts. These wires provide both 120-volt and 240-volt circuits in the house. Some small appliances may operate on low-voltage current, usually around 10 or 12 volts, but possibly ranging from 6 to 24 volts. Their voltage is cut down by a small transformer wired in anywhere between the appliance anti the service panel.

Portable appliances and devices are readily connected to an electrical supply circuit by means of an outlet called a receptacle. A duplex outlet is one that has two receptacles. A receptacle with two slots is a 2-wire receptacle. Newer houses have 3-wire receptacles, which have two slots and a round hole. The third wire on the three-wire receptacle is used to provide a ground lead to the equipment that receives power from the receptacle. The three-wire receptacle takes the regular two-prong plugs still found on some appliances.

However, it is wise to ground a receptacle and is required by electrical codes. Another feature of modern receptacles is polarisation, in which one slot is larger than the other to accept modern polarised plugs. The larger slot connects to the white neutral wire, the small slot to the hot wire, ensuring that the switch always interrupts the flow of current so no current can flow in when the switch is off. If polarity is reversed, an exposed socket can give a shock even when the switch is off and the light or appliance isn't running. Wherever there is an outlet or any other place where wires are joined, it must be done in a junction box. These metal or plastic boxes come in many sizes and shapes, with knock-out holes so wiring can be brought in from any direction. They usually are nailed to studs, joists, or floor plates.

Electric Service Expanding

If you open the door of the service panel, you see all of the circuit breakers or fuses. If you see blank slots with no breakers, they are places where new breakers can be installed to expand the house electrical system with more circuits. In remodelling a kitchen, you almost surely want to add circuits. You might be able to combine some circuits that have light loads to create an open slot or two for expansion. Older houses often were rated at only 60 amps for the entire house.

Today, houses are likely to need 150 or 200 amps. The main breaker on the service panel should show the house rating. It is usually a double breaker in line with all the others that is larger and a different colour. This rating might be the number "60" or "100" molded or pressed into the tops of the two breakers. In any kitchen remodelling, consider upgrading to 150 or 200 amps to provide circuitry for future needs. The service ampere rating is obtained by adding together the current required for general lighting, major appliances, motors, appliance circuits, and other special circuits. Circuit breakers should be placed in an easy-to-reach location in or near the kitchen, so the homemaker does not have to hunt for it in a dark basement or garage.

Most residential wiring today is done using nonmetallic sheathed cable (NM cable). NM cable contains three or more individual wires, each with their own colour-coded insulation. The number of the conductors grouped together in the cable is dependent on the type of circuit you are running. The size of wire used in the conductors determines the available amperes in the circuit. The sizes are designated by gauge number. As the numbers increase in numerical value, the amperes decrease. Be sure to check the incoming wire size.

Kitchen Wiring

Modern kitchens require an adequate supply of electricity. Of course, adequate wiring in a kitchen includes general-purpose circuits for lighting, branch circuits for small appliances, and individual major-appliance branch circuits. The recommendations may vary from city to city, depending on standards and codes. There are several basic wiring requirements common to all kitchen layouts. Depending on its size and layout, your client's kitchen will probably contain all or most of these, perhaps more. Using the cabinet layouts and floor plan, be sure to plot out an electrical plan to ensure that your clients receive all the wiring needed in their kitchen while helping to eliminate waste.

Running future-use wires when walls are open is a lot easier than working with them after everything is sealed up. If a designer is drawing up the plans, he or she should also provide an electrical plan, as well as a lighting plan for the electrician to work from; these plans include a table of electrical symbols. It is important to remember that no matter who provides the plan, it is best to have it verified by a local electrical inspector.

Wiring colour coding: To ensure universal wiring and safety, all electrical wiring today is colour-coded. The individual wires in the cable each have a coloured jacket to simplify the proper installation. The neutral wire is always white. The ground wire is either bare or colour-coded green. Hot wires are coloured black, red, or any colour other than green, white, or bare.

Grounding and ground-fault circuit interrupters (GFCIs): All new wiring in a home is required to be grounded (a safety measure built into every home electrical system), whether the existing wiring is grounded or not. In some instances, officials will make you upgrade the existing wiring if it is ungrounded and appears unsafe. Grounding is accomplished through the use of a third wire in the circuit and provides an alternate route for any leaking current, protecting the circuit and family members from shock.

The main grounding wire connects all the metal parts within the electrical system to the service panel and from there to a ground source, usually a metal cold-water pipe, or a grounding rod buried in the earth or in the building's foundation. Older homes may have the metal plumbing used as a ground. Code compliance is vital when remodelling this type of home. Previously installed plastic pipe that may have been inserted between sections of metal plumbing may have destroyed the grounding to sections of the house not within your contracted area. Be aware that although your project does not involve major rewiring, you may still want to consult a professional electrician during the estimating phase.

When connecting appliances, fixtures, receptacles, or any other metal electrical component, always look for the green grounding screw and be certain the ground wire in the NM cable is connected to it. A remodelled kitchen almost certainly requires more circuits than that and a lot more outlets. These circuits should be divided so that approximately half the kitchen is on each circuit and can also extend into areas immediately adjacent to the kitchen.

These two circuits should be for receptacles only and should not include any lighting. While two 20-ampere circuits are generally sufficient, some thought should be given to providing one or even two additional 20-ampere appliance circuits.

When adding one light or moving an existing light, simply adding wiring from an existing switch may be easily accomplished when an additional receptacle is desired and the circuit you plan to put it on will not be overloaded. Each stationary appliance, such as a cooktop or an oven, requires a separate, dedicated circuit. The circuit size must be sufficient to serve the appliance's amperage rating as listed on the appliance nameplate. To wire a kitchen for convenience, each of the major work centers, as well as the various supplementary ones, makes its own electrical demand.

Smoke detectors and Noise abatement: Under current code regulations, a smoke detector is required in a kitchen. Requirements can mandate that the smoke detector be hard-wired and connected so that if one detector goes off, they all sound an alarm. Battery-powered detectors may be sufficient; however, check the requirements of local authorities.

Noise can be a problem in both a new and a remodelled kitchen. During the meal-preparation hours, it is not unusual for several appliances to be used at the same time. With all of this activity, the noise level in the kitchen can reach a point where it causes great discomfort, as well as disturbs other areas throughout the house. Noise can be kept at a reasonable level if the following antinoise steps are taken.

— One of the first things to consider is the installation of sound-insulating walls. Application of an extra layer of material on a wall helps, but a staggered stud wall that allows weaving of insulation material through the studs gives a great deal of sound protection.

— Level the refrigerator and freezer to eliminate annoying vibrations. Either appliance is properly balanced if the door closes automatically from a half-open position.

— Dishwashers are very noisy because of the tremendous water activity. Choose a dishwasher that has more insulation and other sound-deadening features built into it or wrap the sides with insulating material to prevent transmission of sound to cabinets and countertops.

— Mount the dishwasher, food waste disposer, compactor, and other similar appliances on springs or pads to prevent vibrations from being transmitted through the floor, walls, and countertops.

— Use rubber isolation gaskets at the mount of food waste disposers to prevent the sink bowl from amplifying the grinding noise.

— Heavy-gauge stainless-steel sinks vibrate less than thinner ones; porcelain on cast iron is still quieter. Wooden cabinets reflect less noise than metal ones.

— Place rubber bushings behind cabinet doors to stop banging. Check the drawer slides, and if they are noisy, replace them with quiet ones.

— The hum of a fluorescent light often annoys people. Use rubber mounts combined with ballast to eliminate hum.

— Make sure room air conditioners and vent fans are properly mounted to avoid excess vibration. Ductwork should be designed without reduction in size and with a minimum of turns.

— Install air chambers or pneumatic antihammer devices in the water lines to stop any hammering noises.

— Long runs of hot-water supply creak or snap as they expand or contract. Differences up to 100 degrees F can exist in piping and can cause expansion of up to ⅛ inch in 10 feet. Noise occurs when expanding pipe is forced against its hangers or surrounding structural members. Allow space for growth at the end of long runs where pipes change directions.

— Holes cut through common walls for plumbing or heating may leak noise. Seal all holes with a resilient material to isolate noise and seal against air leaks, either vertical or horizontal.

— Remember that acoustical ceiling panels or tile, carpeting, and fabrics used for curtains and tablecloths absorb most of the sound that reaches them.

— Move the vent fan from the range in the kitchen to an outside wall in the attic, utility room, or basement.

— Noise transmits to other rooms through lighting fixtures, electrical outlets, and heating ducts. Seal these with insulating material. Use insulating panels over the ceiling wallboard and under floor underlayment.

— Avoid placing any switches or outlets back-to-back. Position junction boxes on opposite sides of the same wall so there is 36 inches (91 cm) of lateral distance between them.

— Attach ceiling fixtures so that fasteners are set into furring strips attached to the ceiling joists with spring clips. The clips will absorb any noise that may develop in the fixture.

7

Stoves and Ovens

Kitchen Stoves

A stove is a heat-producing device. Typically the word is used to refer to a kitchen appliance used for either generating warmth or for cooking. In British English, however, the term cooker is normally used for the cooking appliance, and stove for a wood or coal-burning room heating appliance. There are many types of stoves. A kitchen stove is used to cook food, and refers to a device which has both burners on the top (also known as a cooktop or range or hob) and an oven.

Stoves may generate heat by:

- burning of:
  - natural gas
  - heating oil
  - wood, coal, or synthetic heating pellet
- electrical resistance (by way of a heating element)

The basic free-standing stove is the most common type. It is self-contained, finished on both sides, sits on the floor, and is usually placed between two base cabinets or at the end of a line of cabinets. Some free-standing stoves have a second, smaller oven mounted above the cooking surface.

Figure 1. A glass-ceramic cooktop

A variation of the free-standing style is the slide-in stove, which is self-contained and rests on the floor. The sides are usually unfinished, but end panels are available when either side is visible.

A drop-in stove is permanently installed flush with the base cabinets and is supported on a low cabinet base. A drop-in stove is a good choice for an island design because it is flush with the surrounding counter and is built-in.

Porcelain enamel is the material most frequently used for stoves because it is resistant to heat, acids, stains, and scratches and because its colour will not fade or yellow with use. Baked or synthetic enamel is a paint material applied at high temperatures. This finish resists knocks and blows better than porcelain enamel but cannot withstand abrasion.

Enamel is usually less expensive and is considered less durable than porcelain enamel. Stainless Steel is available in matte and glossy finishes. It is very durable, corrosion and stain-resistant, easy to clean; and does not dent easily, but it may discolour if overheated. Chrome-plated surfaces will not chip, scratch, or dent easily. However, heat may cause chrome to discolour, turning it blue-brown over time. Vitro-ceramic is a new material imported from West Germany. It is noted for ease of cleaning. This is not the same glass material that was previously used on ceramic cooking surfaces. The colour does not yellow with time and it is easy to clean and maintain. Vitroceramic is used in the construction of several smooth-glass cooking surfaces.

Electronic controls are now found on stoves as well as cooktops and ovens. Electronic controls may increase the initial cost of an appliance, but they are a good investment because they offer more precision and reliability than mechanical controls. Available on stoves are a variety of cooking timers that keep time from 5 minutes to 4 hours. They have reminder options, automatic shut-offs, buzzers or chimes, or warning lights to indicate completed cooking times. Timers help save energy because they prevent overcooking.

Many new stoves have built-in venting. A high-low stove may have venting from the top oven, where air is vented through a wall. Other stoves may have down-draft systems that must be vented through floors or walls. A down-draft ventilation system is a good choice for an island or peninsula kitchen design because it eliminates the need for an overhead exhaust system.

History of Stoves

In Europe, the history of the kitchen stove begins in earnest in the 18th century. Before, people cooked over open fires fuelled by wood, which first were on the floor or on low masonry constructions. In the Middle Ages, waist-high brick-and-mortar hearths and the first chimneys appeared, so that one didn't have to kneel or sit anymore to cook. The fire was lit on top of that construction; the space underneath was used to store and dry wood. Cooking was done mainly in cauldrons hung above the fire or placed on trivets. The heat was regulated by placing the cauldron higher or lower above the fire.

Open fire has three major disadvantages that prompted already 16th century inventors to look for improvements: it is dangerous, produces a lot of smoke, and the heat efficiency is poor. Attempts were made to enclose the fire to make better use of the heat it generated and thus reduce the wood consumption. A first step was the fire chamber: the fire was enclosed on three sides by brick-and-mortar walls, covered by an iron plate. This technique also caused a change in the kitchenware used for cooking, for it required flat-bottomed pots instead of cauldrons.

Only in 1735 the first design that enclosed the fire completely appeared: the Castrol stove of the French architect François Cuvillies was a masonry construction with several fireholes covered by iron plates with holes. It is also known as a stew stove. Towards the end of the 18th century, the design was refined by hanging the pots in holes through the top iron plate, thus improving heat efficiency even more.

Figure 2. Raised kamados

Chinese and Japanese civilisations had discovered the principle of the closed stove much earlier. Already from the Chinese Qin Dynasty (221 BC - 206/207 BC), clay stoves that enclosed the fire completely are known, and a similar design known as *kamado* appeared in the Kofun period (3rd - 6th century) in Japan. These stoves were fired by wood or charcoal through a hole in the front. In both designs, pots were placed over or hung into holes at the top of the knee-high construction. Raised *kamados* were developed in Japan during the Edo period.

Iron Stoves

In the 18th century the first iron stoves appeared. An early example is the Franklin stove, a wood burning stove said to have been invented by Benjamin Franklin in 1742. It had a labyrinthine path for hot exhaust gases to escape, thus allowing heat to enter the room instead of going up the chimney. The Franklin stove, however, was designed for heating, not for cooking. Benjamin Thompson at the turn to the 19th century was among the first to present a working iron kitchen stove. His Rumford stove used one fire to heat several pots that were also hung into holes so that they could be heated from the sides, too. It was even possible to regulate the heat individually for each hole. His stove was designed for large canteen or castle kitchens, though. It would take another 30 years until the technology had been refined and the size of the iron stove been reduced enough for domestic use.

Stewart's Oberlin stove was a much more compact iron stove, patented in the U.S. in 1834. It became a huge commercial success with some 90000 units sold in the next 30 years. In Europe, similar designs also appeared in the 1830s. In the following years, these iron stoves evolved into veritable cooking machines with flue pipes connected to the chimney, oven holes, and installations for heating water. The originally open holes into which the pots were hung were now covered with concentric iron rings on which the pots were placed. Depending on the size of the pot or the heat needed, one could remove the inner rings.

Gas and Electric Stoves

All these stoves were fired by wood, charcoal, or coal. The first gas stoves were developed already in the 1820s, but these remained isolated experiments. At the world fair in London in 1851, a gas stove was shown, but only in the 1880s did this technology start to become a commercial success. The main factor for this delay was the slow growth of the gas pipe network. The first gas stoves were rather unwieldy, but soon the oven was integrated into the base and the size reduced to fit in better with the rest of the kitchen furniture.

In the 1910s, producers started to enamel their gas stoves for easier cleaning. A high-end gas stove called the AGA cooker was invented in 1922 by Swedish Nobel prize winner Gustaf Dalen. It is considered to be the most efficient design and is a much sought after kitchen must have in certain circles-despite the hefty price tag. The AGA, and similar products such as the Rayburn Range are examples of always-on stoves which continue to burn fuel even when cooking is not being performed. Stoves such as these are often used instead of boilers or furnaces to supply hot water and central heating to the rest of the house.

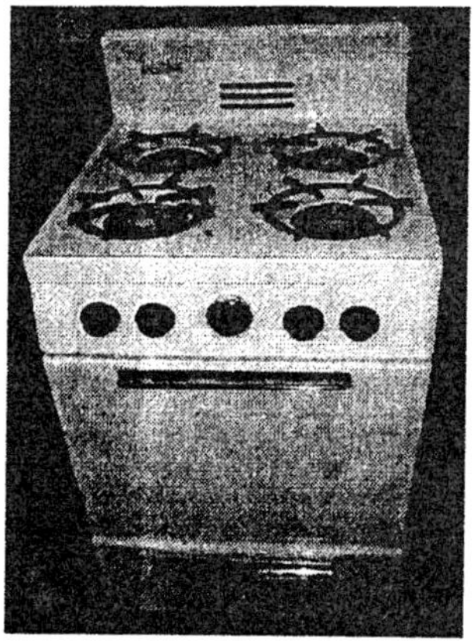

Figure 3. Gas stove

First attempts at building electrical stoves were made in the 1880s, but its real debut was at the Chicago World's Fair in 1893, where an electrified model kitchen was shown. But like the gas stove, the electrical stove had a slow start, partly due to the unstable technology, and partly because first cities and town needed to be electrified.

By the 1930s, the technology had matured and the electrical stove started to slowly replace the gas stove, especially in domestic kitchens. Gas and electric stoves are the most common today in western countries. Both are equally mature and safe, and the choice between the two is largely a matter of personal preference and preexisting utility outlets: if a house has no gas supply, adding one just to be able to run a gas stove is an expensive endeavour. In particular, professional chefs often prefer gas cooktops, for they allow them to control the heat more finely and more quickly. On the other hand, chefs often prefer electric ovens because they tend to heat food more evenly. Today's major brands offer both gas and electric stoves, and many also offer dual-fuel stoves combining gas cooktops and electric ovens.

Ovens and stoves, throughout history, have one thing in common, they will burn the person who comes in contact with their hot metal surfaces, for instance, the oven rack's front edge. Devices to protect the hands, such as oven gloves, have been developed, but need to be used consistently, to be effective; so people still get burned.

Modern stoves are typically considered a basic appliance in homes in developed nations. Along with the refrigerator, a stove is typically located in the kitchen room. Many modern stoves typically have from three to six burners or hotplates of various sizes and power levels, an oven, and knobs for controlling heat on burners, which may be located on the backsplash, on the cooktop, or on the front of the stove closest to one's hips. Middle to high-end models also may feature locking mechanisms for the oven door, convection cooking, automatic cleaning mechanisms that raise the oven temperature to over 260 degrees Celsius and reduce accumulated food spills to ash, one or more timers, a digital display, and may even be programmable such that they start and stop heating at preset times.

Modern Cooking Systems

Halogen Cooking System

The halogen cooking system is one of the newest cooking units available. Its tungsten halogen lamps appear to produce virtually instantaneous heat and light. The halogen unit surface is made of vitro-ceramic. This new, smooth surface is also used for some of the induction cooking systems.

Figure 4. Halogen cooking system

Induction Cooking System

The induction cooking system is quite new to many consumers. It is fast, safe, and energy efficient. Target temperatures can be instantly achieved and very low temperatures can be easily maintained to eliminate burning. The cooking surface stays cool, so less heat escapes into the kitchen. Only the cookware, which must be magnetic, and the food get hot-not the entire cooking surface.

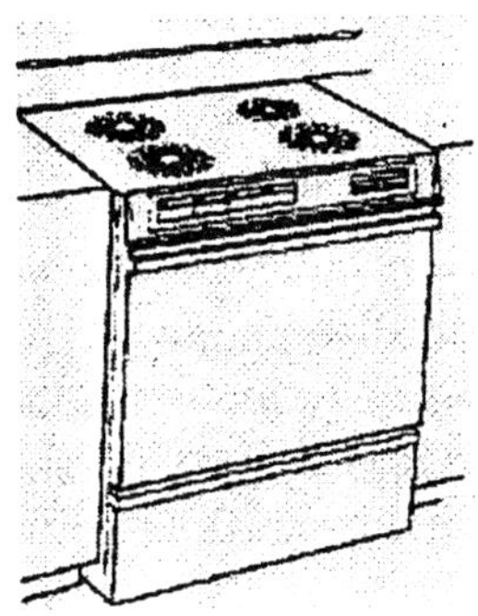

Figure 5. Induction cooking system

Solid-disk Cooking System

The solid-disk cooking system is somewhat new and currently very popular. European design, ease of cleaning, and evenness of cooking are some of the reasons for its popularity. The disk requires

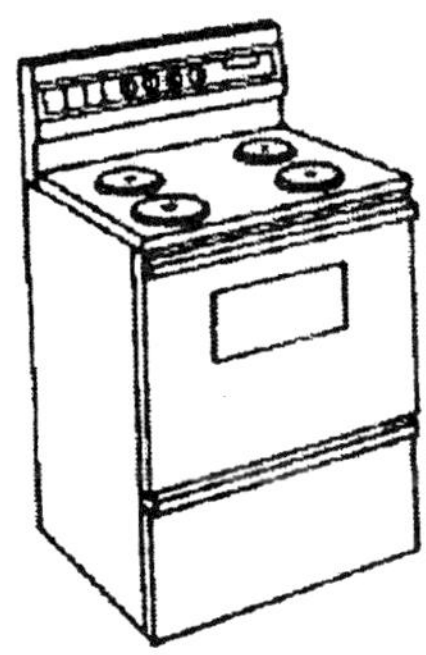

Figure 6. Solid-disk cooking system

frequent application of a special cleaning treatment to keep it looking new. Since the solid disk is made of cast iron, it is slow to heat-up, cooks evenly, and retains heat well. Energy can be saved by turning the element off and using the retained heat to complete cooking.

Convertible Cooking System

The convertible cooking system stoves can be custom designed simply by unplugging a module and plugging in a different one. There are modules for induction, halogen, solid-disk, conven-tional-coil, and glass ceramic cooking. Extra modules are also available for deep-fat frying, griddling, grilling, barbecuing, and wok cooking. Convertible cooking surfaces work well in open kitchen areas because an overhead exhaust unit is not needed due to the presence of down-draft ventilation systems.

Figure 7.
Convertible cooking system

Pilotless Gas Cooking System

Pilotless gas stoves are relatively new. Elimination of the continually burning pilot light results in big energy savings. It also keeps the kitchen cooler. The new gas stoves are easier to clean. On many of the new gas stoves, the top lifts up or off so burners can be easily removed and cleaned. In addition, the knobs, burner bowls, and cookware supports can be easily removed for cleaning.

Figure 8.
Gas cooking system

Beverage Can Stoves

Figure 9. Pepsi can stove:

A beverage can stove is a homemade, ultra-light backpacking stove. The simple design is made entirely from cans and burns denatured alcohol. Countless variations on the basic design exist. Pepsi cans are often used because they have a bottom shape that lends itself to securing the stove's inner wall, and because of this the stoves are sometimes called Pepsi can stoves.

The Pepsi can stove weighs 0.4 oz (10 g) and will boil two cups of water in five minutes with two tablespoons of fuel. Total weight, including a windscreen/ stand can be less than one ounce (30 g). Due to the low weight compared to commercial stoves and their fuel canisters, backpackers can save about one pound (450 g) of pack weight with this stove. This advantage may be lost on long hiking trips however, because the stove is less efficient and requires more fuel, especially when cooking for more than one person.

The stove is made from two aluminum can bottoms. An inner wall is cut and rolled from can material. A ring of holes is pierced into the top with a pin. Parts are glued with high temperature epoxy, or sealed with thermal foil tape. Total height is less than two inches (50 mm), though dimensions can be increased to hold more fuel or decreased to take up even less space.

The choice of aluminum has several advantages; light weight, low cost, and good thermal conductivity to aid vaporisation of fuel. Alternative construction materials have been used, including stoves made of tin cans such as cat food tins, tuna cans, and juice cans - the basic design is very similar. Windscreens/stands can be fabricated from tin cans, cut to size and with ventilation holes added.

The stove is designed for one or two people. When used to cook larger meals, it is less efficient than a more powerful stove that delivers more heat to a pot. This is because a longer cooking time is required, during which more heat is lost to the surroundings. To use the stove, a small amount of fuel is poured into the stove and ignited. The pot is then placed above the stove, on a windscreen or stand. The flame is small at first, only burning from the inner chamber. Once the fuel has warmed up, requiring about one minute, its vapour will pass through the perforations and form a ring of flame. Enough heat from the flame is passed to the fuel to maintain full combustion until fuel runs out.

Portable Stoves

A portable stove is a stove specially designed to be portable and lightweight, such as for camping. There are several main types based on the type of fuel used:

— Simple single-burner stoves, often without any controls at all, using solid or liquid fuel which is placed in the burner before ignition.

— Single-burner stoves using volatile liquid fuel in a pressurised burner-tank combination.

— Single or multi burner bottled gas stoves, providing controls for the heat setting similar to a kitchen cooktop.

— Gravity-fed spirit stoves, with priming pans.

Simple Single-burner Designs

The simplest stove is a burner that contains the fuel, and which once lit burns until either it is snuffed or the fuel is exhausted. The rise in the popularity of extreme lightweight equipment for extended backpacking, and the increasing restrictions on the use of campfires in most wilderness areas, have made these small stoves extremely popular.

The two most popular of these are the solid fuel stove, using Hexamine tablets, and the liquid fuelled stove using methylated spirits. Both types are available commercially. There are also many designs published for similar home-built stoves, like the Pepsi can stove. While solid-fuelled stoves may be refuelled while burning with care, with a liquid-fuelled stove it would be reckless to attempt this. Both solid alcohol fuel and stoves for using it are produced by Esbit, and fuel is produced by several other makers. While most brands of firelighters can be used in such stoves, some types will produce a troublesome residue that may be impossible to remove from cookware, and will taint any food exposed to the flame or fumes. One popular make of simple liquid-fuelled stove is the Trangia, available in many different models from a single bare burner to an integrated expedition cooking system. Some of these come with a sealing cover, allowing the burner to be packed while containing fuel.

Pressurised Burner Stoves

There is some controversy over the invention of the pressurised burner. Most have given the credit to F.W. Linqvist, who was granted a patent for a kerosene-fuelled burner in the late 1880s and went on to develop the Primus brand name of stove into a market leader. However, some have suggested that he bought the design.

The Primus stoves and their imitators were a significant advance over previous designs that had used a wick to supply liquid fuel to the burner by capillary action. Instead the Primus burner vaporised the fuel in a loop of pipe, and used this to both supply the fuel to the burner as a gas and to maintain pressure in the fuel tank. Initial pressure was provided by a small hand-operated pump. It was also necessary to pre-heat the burner with methylated spirits. This burner design was also successfully adapted to portable lamps, lighthouse lamps and blowtorches.

Pressurised burner stoves are now available to burn almost any volatile, inflammable liquid, including alcohol, diesel or other motor fuels, kerosene, jet propellant, and many others. Work is proceeding on vegetable-oil burners. Some can burn multiple fuels or even mixtures. Some require special low-residue stove fuel, others are either designed to resist clogging or to be easily and regularly cleaned of the residue. Most provide some control over the amount of heat produced. Some fuels permit preheating with the fuel, others require use of a more volatile fuel, such as methylated spirit or alcohol priming paste, for preheating the burner. Most provide an integrated pump for initial pressurisation, others require the use of a separate pump, while a few need no pump but pressurise themselves when the burner is preheated.

Although heavier than the simpler designs and more complex to maintain and operate, these stoves can heat food more quickly, and as standard issue to many units in the second world war they enjoyed a large base of competent users in the years immediately following. Another advantage is that hydrocarbon fuels have a higher heat content weight for weight than alcohol fuels, so for extended expeditions the weight advantage of alcohol-fuelled stoves is reduced or even reversed.

Gas-Cartridge Stoves and Refillable Gas-bottle Stoves

The greatest variety in designs is in this category. They include gas-cartridge stoves and refillable gas-bottle stoves.

In most of these the gas is stored as a liquid under pressure, but vaporises immediately it leaves the storage bottle and so arrives at the burner as a gas.

Smaller, lighter designs tend to use non-refillable gas cartridges containing butane, propane or a mixture of hydrocarbons. There is little compatibility between different makers and systems, and cartridges for older stoves are often unobtainable. In addition, the single-use cartridges are considered objectionable by some on environmental grounds.

Refillable gas bottles are heavier and tend to be used on larger stoves intended for car-camping or expedition base camps. However a great variety of gas-fired stoves is available, some integrating the gas cylinder, some connecting it by a hose.

Gravity-fed Spirit Stoves

The traditional "spirit stove" still found in many pleasure boats is a unique design, largely replaced by gas stoves but still with a following. It consists of a tank that supplies methylated spirit under gravity to the burner or burners, where it is vaporised and burned. Around each burner is a priming pan used to preheat the burner. To light the stove, the burner is first turned on to allow a small amount of fuel to pass through the burner and collect as a liquid in the priming pan. The burner is then turned off, and the fuel ignited to preheat the burner. When the fuel in the pan is almost all gone, the burner is turned on again, and fuel passes into the burner where it is vaporised and passes through the jets. These stoves look and even sound a bit like pressurised-burner stoves, but the fuel tank is under no pressure. They remain popular for small boats owing to the minimal fire risk they pose in a confined space.

Liquid-fuel and Gas-fuel Stoves

Most stoves can use either liquid or gas fuel, but not both (One exception is Primus Omni/Multi-Fuel). Gas-fuel stoves are simpler to operate than liquid fuelled stoves. The gas, being already pressurised, flows from the fuel canister into the burner, where it ignites, in the same manner as a domestic kitchen stove.

Liquid-fuel stoves are more complex because the liquid fuel must be vaporised prior to burning. To accomplish this, the stove design brings the fuel line containing the liquid fuel near the flame of the burner. The heat from the flames converts the liquid fuel to a gas before it reaches the burner, where it mixes with air and is ignited.

Stoves operating with liquid fuels must be heated or primed before the burner is turned on. Many stoves require the operator to open the fuel valve briefly without igniting the fuel, so that it flows into a small pan. This small quantity of fuel is then lit and allowed to burn down. When the fuel valve is opened again, the fuel vaporises from the heat of the pan. Some stoves do not have this apparatus, and must be preheated by the application of an external heat source such as a solid fuel block.

In many stoves, the priming pressure is generated by a small hand pump that forces air into the fuel container. As the fuel is consumed, the pressure decreases according to Boyle's Law, so the pump must be operated occasionally during use to maintain steady stove operation. Liquid fuel stoves are the most popular for backpacking in United States. They generally operate well in cold weather. Liquid fuel costs less than gas fuel generally. Some forms of fuel, such as kerosene or fuel oil, are readily available worldwide.

Disadvantages to liquid fuelled stoves include they require priming, hence some skill is needed to operate them properly. Using liquid fuel stove in a tent is difficult or even dangerous. The fuel does not burn as cleanly as gas fuelled stoves. Soot builds up on cooking vessels eventually. Spilt liquid fuel poses a fire hazard, and can soil equipment. The odour of the fuel may also attract dangerous wild animals.

Gaseous fuels have many advantages; the fuel burns cleanly. They are quite simple to use, just adjust the fuel flow with a valve and light the burner. Since the gasious fuel quickly dissipates, the fire hazard associated with leaking fuel is reduced. Safety is also increased because there is no priming. Gas fuel bottles of a particular make may be widely available in some countries but not in others, so international travellers have to be particularly careful.

Some disadvantages of gas fuel are the difficulty of transferring fuel from one container to another and the difficulty of accurately gauging how much fuel remains in a container. Gas fuel is somewhat less efficient than liquid fuel, meaning more fuel volume is required for the same heat output. Gas fuelled stoves usually do not operate well in colder temperatures. Butane in particular, does not vaporise well at low temperatures which makes stoves fuelled with butane unsuitable for cold weather camping. Boiling point of butane under normal pressure is -1°C and under this temperature butane cannot be used as a fuel for gas stove. The temperature where use of butane becomes impractical is even higher (around 5°C). Propane-butane-isobutane mixtures used in most containers are suitable to temperatures of -10°C. Pure propane boils at -42°C which is the actual limit of usability of propane stoves. Gas fuel canisters tend to be heavier than liquid-fuel bottles, because it must be stored under greater pressure. When a canister runs out, it may have to be treated as hazardous waste. Canisters tend to deteriorate and leak if stored for several years.

Solid-fuel Stoves

A quantity of liquid fuel sufficient to cook a meal, if simply placed in a container and ignited, would burn violently and consume itself in a matter of seconds, and a similar quantity of gas fuel would simply explode. The primary design principle of stoves that use these fuels is to provide a steady flame and prevent the fuel's escape. Solid fuel, however, is more manageable.

A solid-fuel stove may consist of no more than a metal plate to hold the fuel, a set of legs to keep it out of contact with the ground, and some supports for the cooking vessel. This design is highly scalable, and may be used for anything from tiny backpacking stoves to large portable woodstoves.

While admirably simple, solid fuel has many disadvantages. First of all, its burn rate may be controlled only by varying the amount of fuel placed on the fire, while fluid fuels may be controlled precisely with valves. Second, no solid fuel burns completely. It produces considerable amounts of ash and soot, which soil both the stove and the cooking vessels. Some of the chemical energy of the fuel remains locked up in the ash and soot, so solid fuel releases less heat, gram for gram.

Firewood may often be used in solid-fuel stoves, but manufactured fuels are also available. One type is sold in the form of small blocks, on the order of a centimeter in size. Sterno is a viscous fluid that is also used in solid-fuel stoves. Simple stoves are sometimes used in ice houses and large tents, both to provide warmth and for cooking. They burn wood, and have a small flue used to exhaust the smoke. When used in tents, they are used in a larger tent made of fabric that does not burn readily, and are most often used in base camps that move infrequently.

The widespread use of backpacking stoves began with increased awareness of the environmental impact that backpackers had on the areas where they travelled, beginning in the 1950s in parts of Europe and the 1960s in the United States. Prior to their use, the usual practice when backpacking was to build an open fire for cooking from available materials such as fallen branches. The fire scar left on the ground would remain for two or three years before the vegetation recovered. The accumulation of fire scars in heavily travelled areas detracted from the pristine appearance that backpackers expected, leading to more widespread use of stoves.

Ovens

An oven is an enclosed compartment for heating, baking or drying. It is most commonly used in cooking and pottery. Two common kinds of ovens are gas ovens and electric ovens. Ovens used in pottery are also known as kilns. In cooking, the conventional kerr oven is a common kitchen appliance and is used for baking, broiling, roasting and heating food. Food normally cooked in this manner includes meat, casseroles and baked goods such as bread, cake and other desserts.

Culinary historians credit the Greeks for developing bread baking into an art. Proper front-loaded bread ovens originated in Ancient Greece. The Greeks created a wide variety of doughs, loaf shapes and styles of serving bread with other foods. Baking developed as a trade and profession as bread increasingly was prepared outside of the family home by specially trained workers to be sold to the public.

The Greeks also pioneered sweetbreads, fritters, puddings, cheesecakes, pastries, and even wedding cakes. Often prepared in symbolic shapes, these products were originally served during special occasions and ceremonies. By 300 AD, the Greeks had developed over seventy different kinds of bread.

An oven window and light make it easy to check the progress of baking items without opening the door. Opening the door wastes energy and can effect baking results. Some oven windows have three panes of heat-resistant glass with air trapped between each pane which minimizes heat loss through the window.

However, a window is a convenience only if the consumer can see through it clearly.Factors affecting visibility are the colour of the glass, the brightness of the oven light, and the coarseness of the screening that is often used to reinforce the glass.A proper seal is vital to keeping heat inside the oven for efficient operation and excellent baking results. A silicone rubber seal can withstand very high temperatures, thus has a long life. Strong springs are important to hold the oven door tight against the seal.

One of the newest features found in ovens is convection cooking. It is available in portable, full-size, free-standing, and built-in wall ovens. In convection ovens, a fan blows the heated air over and around food, increasing the rate of moisture evaporation and thus decreasing cooking time.

The oven temperature can be reduced 25 to 50 degrees when cooking with convection because of the air circulation and more even cooking. Shorter cooking times and lower temperatures add up to important energy and dollar savings. Because convection ovens use forced-air for cooking, noise level is a consideration. It should be low enough to not be irritating.

Some manufacturers are making combination ovens as an option to conventional gas or electric ovens. These combination ovens allow microwave-convection, microwaveconventional, or convection-conventional cooking in a single large oven. The consumer can cook with either method or combine them for faster cooking. Some combination ovens can reduce cooking time by one-third.

Microwave Oven

Microwaving is a method of cooking where food is bombarded by microwaves (usually with a microwave oven) which excite the water, fat and sugar molecules in food. Microwave energy is a natural phenomenon that occurs when electric current flows through a conductor. Microwaves are a form of electromagnetic radiation that is very similar to sunlight and radio waves. The microwaves do not heat glass, ceramic, and plastic containers. One advantage of microwaving is that small amounts of food can be heated very quickly, making it useful for reheating leftovers.

A disadvantage of microwaving is that food which is microwaved does not undergo some of the chemical reactions, such as browning, that make the food both visually attractive and give it a different flavour. Primitive microwave ovens often do not cook the food evenly, leading to a concern that bacteria easily killed by more traditional cooking methods may survive the quick cooking time in "cold spots", though the food item as a whole is cooked to a safe average temperature. This can be overcome by leaving the food to stand for a few minutes when cooking is completed. Some high-end microwave ovens are combined with a convection oven; they cook the food using microwaves and hot air simultaneously to achieve both the fast cooking time and the browning effect.

Using a microwave for cooking a large food mass is difficult due to limited penetration of microwaves. However, microwave ovens are used in some fast food chains, and special microwave bags are available for cooking fowl or large joints of meat.

Professional chefs generally recommend using microwaves for a limited set of tasks, including melting fats (such as butter) and chocolate, cooking grains like oatmeal and grits, cooking rice, thawing frozen meats and vegetables before cooking by other methods, and quickly reheating already-cooked foods. A common myth is that a microwave oven cooks from the centre of the food outward. However, most foods only have their outermost inch heated by the microwaves, and the rest of the food is heated via conduction. Similarly, foods with both air and water content allow the microwaves to penetrate fully, heating the entire item with the microwave radiation.

Using a microwave to boil liquids is potentially dangerous, due to the possibility of superheating. In a microwave, liquids can be raised quickly to a temperature above the boiling point before major bubbles form, especially if the liquid is purified and in a very clean glass vessel. When a liquid in a superheated state is disturbed, it can suddenly and unexpectedly boil violently, leading to a risk of scalding. This effect is rare, even for scientists who try to deliberately recreate it, and any seed whatsoever for boiling is likely to prevent the problem. Boiling water with, for instance, a teabag already in it will prevent any dangers by providing a seed, as will using a mug that is not perfectly clean.

The risk greatly increases when the liquid has already been boiled once in the same container. This situation can occur if the user of the oven boiled the liquid once, forgot about it, then came back later to boil it again. The first time the liquid boils, the seed bubbles are used up and largely eliminated from the liquid as it cools down. When the liquid is heated again, the lack of seed bubbles allows superheating, and creates the risk of a steam explosion when the liquid's surface is disturbed.

Placing something in the liquid before heating can mostly alleviate this risk. If you are planning to mix something with the liquid you are heating, such as tea or hot chocolate, adding it before heating will ensure that the liquid boils properly. Otherwise, placing a wood object, for instance a chopstick, in the water before heating will also work. All that is necessary to prevent superheating is the presence of seed bubbles, so any liquid that has been allowed to sit undisturbed for a period of time is more prone to superheating.

Care should be taken when removing heated liquids from a microwave. Make sure that the hands are protected from possible liquid boil-over, place the container on a level, heat-proof surface, and stir liquid with a warm spoon. Also, never add powdered substances to the container taken from the microwave, due to the addition of a large amount of seed bubbles and the potential for violent, spontaneous boiling. It is advised that the liquid be poured slowly into another container that already contains the powder.

Metal objects, such as metal utensils, in a microwave oven can lead to dangerous situations. Metals do not absorb microwaves effectively. Instead, metals reflect microwaves, thereby preventing the latter from reaching the food. If the microwaves are not absorbed inside the oven, the oven can be damaged by electrical arcs and overheating of the microwave source. Thin metal layers, such as metal foil and mugs with metal trim, can melt or burn due to the strong electrical currents that are generated in metal objects. However, small solid metal objects, such as spoons, in combination with a large amount of absorbing food or liquid, normally do not lead to problems.

With wireless computer networks gaining in popularity, microwaves can disrupt wireless network transmissions because the microwave creates radio waves at about 2.4 GHz. This is about the same frequency that 802.11 wireless networks use, so microwaves in use may interfere with network signals, as the specific frequency varies slightly.

Characteristic features of microwave oven

A microwave oven is a kitchen appliance employing microwave radiation primarily to cook or heat food.

A microwave oven consists of:

— a magnetron,

— a magnetron control circuit,

— a waveguide, and

— a cooking chamber

Figure 10. Microwave oven

A microwave oven works by passing microwave radiation, usually at a frequency of 2450 MHz (a wavelength of 12.24 cm), through the food. Water, fat, and sugar molecules in the food absorb energy from the microwave beam in a process called dielectric heating. Most molecules are electric dipoles, meaning that they have a positive charge at one end and a negative charge at the other, and are therefore twisted to and fro as they try to align themselves with the alternating electric field induced by the microwave beam. This molecular movement creates heat. Microwave heating is most efficient on liquid water, and much less so on fats, sugars, and frozen water. Microwave heating is sometimes incorrectly explained as resonance of water molecules, but this occurs only at much higher frequencies, in the tens of gigahertz.

The cooking chamber itself is a Faraday cage enclosure to prevent the microwaves escaping into the surroundings. The oven door is usually a glass panel for easy viewing, but has a layer of conductive mesh to maintain the shielding. Since the mesh width is much less than the wavelength of 12 cm, the microwave radiation can not pass through the door, while visible light can. Professional chefs generally find microwave ovens to be of limited usefulness.

With wireless computer networks gaining in popularity, microwave interference has become a concern among those with wireless networks. Microwave ovens are capable of disrupting wireless network transmissions due to the fact that the microwave creates radio waves at about 2450 MHz. This is about the same frequency that wireless networks use, so microwave ovens in use can interfere with network signals and cause connection issues.

A microwave oven does not convert all electrical energy into microwaves. A typical consumer microwave oven could consume 1100 W, and deliver 700 W of microwave power. The remaining 400 W are dissipated as heat by components of the oven. The main source of energy loss is the magnetron tube which is much less than 100% efficient at generating microwave output from the power source. Lesser amounts of power are consumed by the oven lamp, AC power transformer losses, magnetron cooling fan, food turntable motor and control circuits. This waste heat does not end up in the food but is mostly expelled from the cooling vents on the oven and heats the air in the kitchen. Most of the actual microwave power will end up heating the food inside the oven, unless the microwave oven is loaded with a very small amount of absorbing food. In that case, the magnetron element will reabsorb the microwaves, which can lead to overheating and a fire risk.

Solar Oven

A solar oven or solar cooker is a way of harnessing the sun's power to cook food. A metal box forms the simplest solar oven. A set of large mirrors or a large Fresnel lens to focus sunlight to a single point may also be added. On a sunny day a black baking tray or cooking pot can convert thousands of watts of light into heat, in addition to any infra-red. Temperatures in a typical oven can reach 400 degrees F (200°C). Apart from the obvious need for sunlight and the need to aim the solar oven before use, using a solar oven is not substantially different from a regular oven. However since they use no fuel they are free to run. Humanitarian organizations are promoting their use worldwide to help slow deforestation and desertification caused by the need for firewood with which to cook. The first known western solar oven was built by Horace de Saussure in 1767.

Diffusion of innovations theory, discussed in the book of the same name by Everett Rogers, discusses adoption of solar ovens in Lesotho. Although solar ovens were safer and cheaper to use than oil burning ovens, Lesotho women resisted using them. Agencies such as the Peace Corps have tried to use "change agents" to influence the women. But these change agents have differed from the women in class and norms and were not effective in spurring change. Researchers have found that the diffusion process works better if the change agent trains a local aide who belongs to local social networks and can better influence locals.

Types of Solar Ovens

The available designs of solar ovens fall into three main categories: the box, parabolic, and panel designs. The feature common to each oven design is the shiny reflective surface that directs the sun's rays onto a dark cooking vessel. Each category has advantages when compared on their heating ability, ease of construction, ease and safety of use.

Box cookers

Box cookers are the most common type made for personal use. Despite the name "box" cooker, they are made in both circular and rectangular shapes. Box cooker consist of an enclosed inner box covered with clear glass or plastic, a reflector, and insulation. There is a wide variety of patterns and plans that can be adapted to work with available materials. While they do not heat quickly, they provide slow, even cooking. Box cookers are very easy and safe to use, and fairly easy to construct.

Parabolic cookers

Parabolic cookers reach higher temperatures and cook more quickly than solar box cookers, but are harder to make and use. Most commercial ovens are a form of parabolic cooker. Parabolic cookers require more precision to focus the sunlight on the cooking vessel. If the sunlight is not focused exactly on the cooking vessel, the food will not cook. When the parabolic oven is used, the temperature must be watched so the vessel does not overheat, burning the food. The risk of burns and eye injury is greater with homemade parabolic designs. While they provide excellent results when used correctly, they are not easy to build at home and require great care to use.

Panel cookers

Panel cookers are flat reflective panels which focus the sunlight on a cooking vessel without inner box common in box cookers. Panel cookers are the easiest and least costly to make, requiring just four reflective panels and a cooking vessel, but they are unstable in high winds and do not retain as much heat when the sun is hidden behind clouds.

Convection Oven

Convection ovens use heated air that is forced into the oven by fans located in the back of the oven, generally for cooking food. By moving heated air past the food, convection ovens operate at a lower temperature than a standard conventional oven and they can cook food more quickly. They are mostly used in industrial and commercial applications, but can be purchased for the home as well. With a convection oven there will be about a 25 to 30% decrease in cooking temperature and a 20% decrease in cooking time as compared to a conventional oven.

Figure 11. Convection ovens

Convection ovens are highly versatile units. They're ideal for cooking, warming, roasting, re-thermalizing and baking. Whether you're roasting a turkey or baking croissants, convection ovens cook evenly and thoroughly.

Convection ovens are available in gas or electric and in various configurations, including full-size, half-size, stackable, and as part of a traditional bake oven.

Convection ovens are highly versatile and ideal for cooking, warming, roasting, re-thermalizing and baking. Convection ovens work by forcing heated air, via fans located in the back of the oven wall, over and around the food racks. By moving heated air around the food product, convection ovens do the same job as a rotary oven in a lot less time and using a lot less space.

Convection ovens operate at lower temperatures than standard conventional ovens and they cook faster, saving an operator both time and energy. In a convection oven, product that is placed with little space between pans will still cook evenly. Convection ovens offer the operator more flexibility to cook, bake, or steam inject. With a convection oven, you'll generally see about a 25 to 30% decrease in cooking temperature and a 20% decrease in cooking time when compared to a conventional oven.

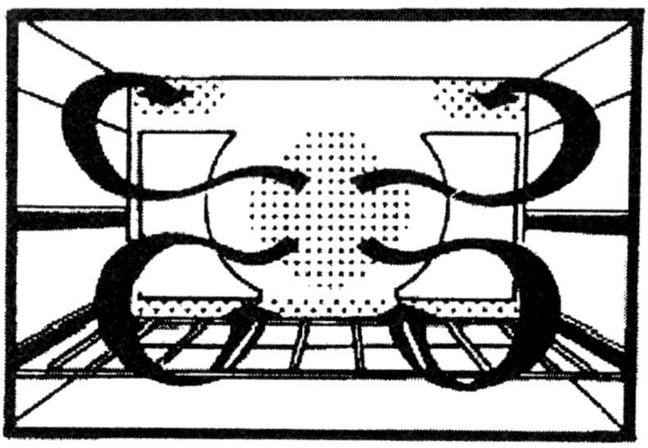

Figure 12. Convection oven air movement

Convection cooking reduces product shrinkage and, in some cases, can result in an extra serving. You can use a convection oven to bake and roast anything from meats to pizza, pastries, and crusty breads. One can bake delicate pies and pastries in a convection oven. When these ovens first came on the market, the moving air would create uneven meringues and custards. Today, with the "gentle bake" and diffused air circulation, uneven cooking is no longer a concern. Although both of these ovens use convection to carry heat, only one of them has the word "convection" in its name. The difference between them is that while a standard oven waits for natural convection to move heat slowly from the heat source to the food, a convection oven uses a fan to drive heat rapidly from source to food. While natural may sound appealing, a convection oven is simply better than a standard oven.

In natural convection, hot air's buoyancy carries it upward through cooler air. Hot air is less dense than cool air and it floats upward the same way a bubble floats upward in water. With the heat source at the bottom of the standard oven, warmed air floats upward to touch and heat the food above it. But the airflow pattern in a standard oven is erratic, unpredictable, and easily upset by the very food that it's trying to cook. If you overfill the oven, the food won't cook properly. And even when the oven is almost empty, heat is transferred more efficiently to the bottom of the food than to its top so it's easy to burn the bottom. But in a convection oven, hot air is stirred rapidly throughout the oven. Heat flows evenly into the food from all sides, leading to speedy and balanced cooking. The tops of foods brown and crisp nicely and the bottoms rarely burn. If it weren't for the added expense of the fan and the modest space the fan takes up inside the oven, convection ovens would *be* the new standard ovens.

Dutch Oven

A Dutch oven is a thick-walled metal cooking pot with a tight-fitting lid. A camping, cowboy or chuck wagon Dutch oven has three legs and a flat, rimmed lid, so that coals from the cooking fire can be placed on top as well as below. This provides more uniform internal heat and lets the inside act as an oven. They are ordinarily made of cast iron, although some are aluminum.

Figure 13. Dutch Oven

Modern dutch ovens consist of a covered, shallow cooking pan set on legs and heated from below with a built-in electrical heating element.

The dutch oven is also a slang name for a practical joke played on bedmates by restraining them under the covers after you have passed gas. Also refers to slang term used to describe the smoking of cannabis or marijuana in a sealed enviroment such as a small room or car for the purpose of inhaling the residual smoke long after the smoking implement has been emptied, thus providing a further high. This is also known as hot-boxing, clam-baking, or fish-bowling.

Cooking techniques such as roasting, baking simmering, stewing, frying, boiling, steaming, and many others are easily done on the campfire with only a single utensil, the dutch oven. Think of the possibilities, delicious fresh baked bread that will rise up and lift the lid, cobblers made from berries picked fresh at the campsite, incredible deep-dish pizzas, stews, quiches that melt in your mouth, cornish game hens roasted to perfection, and imagine a chocolate cake a foot in diameter. These and many, many more are very possible and sometimes easier than they are at home.

All recipes use one of two dutch oven techniques, cooking with your dutch oven or cooking in it. The first is when the food is placed directly in the bottom of the dutch oven. In the second method, food is placed in a second dish and this dish is then placed onto a trivet in the bottom of the dutch oven. The reason for the trivet is to elevate the dish above the bottom of the oven to prevent burning.

In shopping for an oven, you should look for one that is obviously well made. Look at the bail handle, it should be of heavy gauge wire and securely attached to molded tangs on the side of the oven. Ovens that have riveted tabs should be avoided. Most oven handles will lay down against the side of the oven in both directions, but if you look hard enough, you will find some that allow the handle to stand up at a 45 degree angle on one side. This allows you easier access to it when positioning or removing the oven from the fire. Another area that bears close examination is the handle on the lid. It should be a loop attached to the lid on both ends and hollow in the centre allowing it to be easily hooked. Stay away from the ones that have a molded solid tab on the lid for a handle. These are very difficult to grasp and manage with a load of coals. The loop style offers much better control. While examining the lid, check that it has a lip or ridge around the outer edge. The lip keeps the coals from sliding off of the lid.

Another feature to look at is the legs. The most common variety is one with three legs, although flatbottomed ones and four legged ones can also be had. For outdoor cooking, legs are a necessity, they maintain the height of the oven above ground allowing air for the coals underneath. The flat bottomed ones can be set up on rocks or up on steel tent pegs.

The last option to look at is a second handle attached to the lid or upper rim on the oven base. Some ovens are offered with a skillet type handle attached to the lid. This, in theory, is a good idea, but in reality they seem to be more in the way than of assistance. The handle does assist in using the lid upside down as a skillet or griddle but when using it as a lid, they get in the way of the bail handle and also misbalance the lid when lifting by the centre hoop. They also tend to be in the way during storage and packing situations.

Fixed handles on the oven base, with one exception, should be absolutely avoided. The theory behind these handles was to make the oven easier to position in a deep fire pit. If you insist on considering the handle, take a couple of red bricks with you to the store and place them in the oven. Then give her a lift by the handle and you will see the uselessness in the handle. A loaded 12" oven can weigh 20 to 25 pounds, a real wrist breaker. The one exception is a small tab sometimes offered which is about 1 to 1-1/2" deep and 2-3" wide on the upper lip of the oven. This tab makes pouring liquids from the oven very easy and its small size never cause storage or packing problems. When someone mentions "Dutch Oven" most people immediately think "Cast Iron", but dutch ovens are supplied in aluminum also. An aluminum oven weighs only 6-1/2 to 7 pounds opposed to around 18 pounds for the cast iron oven. There are advantages and disadvantages to each.

The most obvious aluminum advantage is weight, 11 pounds lighter. Additionally, because aluminum doesn't rust, care is restricted to simple washing with soap and water. Aluminum tends to heat faster requiring less preheating time but they don't retain the heat very long after the coals are removed. Also because aluminum reflects more heat than cast iron, more coals will be required to reach and maintain a set temperature. Also on windy days, you will see a greater variation in temperature than one of cast iron. Where weight is very critical, most of the disadvantages can be overcome. For canoeing, backpacking or trips where weight is a problem, aluminum ovens are the answer.

Dutch ovens owned by cooks who understand their subtleties are kept in places of honour, sanctuaries reserved specifically for them. On the other hand, ovens owned by cooks who can't seem to keep the potatoes from burning to the bottom or who can never get the chicken to look anything but a pasty white, are quickly relegated to some obscure location where they will be "out of the way." For the unsuccessful current user, the interested but uninitiated, or anyone who just wants to cook better, the seven secrets outlined below will provide a firm foundation for the creation and consumption of mouth-watering Dutch oven meals fit for even the most discriminating palates.

Automatic Oven Cleaning

Self-cleaning (pyrolytic) is the true self-cleaning system. It uses high heat during a special one to three-hour cycle to decompose food soil and grease. During the cycle, which is clock controlled, the oven door is latched and locked. The door cannot be opened until the oven cools. When self-cleaning ovens were first introduced, consumers were concerned about how much energy they might use in the cleaning cycle. The new self-cleaning ovens, gas and electric, are sealed tighter and have more insulation than conventional and continuous-cleaning ovens. They actually save enough energy during normal baking to clean the oven six times a year, which is more than most consumers clean. It actually costs less to operate and clean a selfcleaning oven than to operate and buy cleaning solutions for a regular oven.

Figure 14. Ovens

Continuous cleaning (catalytic) uses a porous coating on the oven walls that partially absorbs and disperses the food soil and grease. This cleaning process takes place during normal baking and keeps the oven presentably clean, but the racks and door parts must be cleaned by hand. This special oven coating cannot be cleaned with soap, detergent, or commercial oven cleaners without causing permanent damage. In addition, the continuous cleaning oven does not look as clean as the self-cleaning oven.

For aluminum ovens, the cleaning is the same as for ordinary pots and pans. Use soap, water and scrub as usual for your other pans. More often than not, cleaning cast iron ovens is much easier than scrubbing pots and pans. For cast iron ovens, the clean process is in two steps. First, food is removed and second, maintenance of the coating. To remove stuck on food, place some warm clean water into the oven and heat until almost boiling. Using a plastic mesh scrubber or coarse sponge and no soap, gently break loose the food and wipe away. After all traces have been removed, rinse with clean warm water. Soap is not recommended because its flavour will get into the pores of the metal and will taint the flavour of your next meal.

After cleaning and rinsing, allow it to air dry. Heat over the fire just until it hot to the touch. Apply a thin coating of oil to the inside of the oven and the underside of the lid. Allow the oven to cool completely. The outside will need little attention other than a good wipe down unless you see signs of rust forming. As a suggestion, it is a good idea to keep a scrubber for cast iron and never use it with soap.

8

Cookware and Bakeware

Cookware and bakeware are types of food preparation containers commonly found in the kitchen. Cookware comprises cooking vessels, such as saucepans and fry pans, intended for use on a stove or range cooktop. Bakeware comprises cooking vessels intended for use inside an oven. The terms cookware and bakeware are not exclusive, and it is possible for a single utensil to be used as both cookware and bakeware.

Knowledge of cooking vessels before the development of pottery is minimal due to the limited archaeological evidence. It has been possible to extrapolate likely developments based on methods used by latter peoples. Among the first of the techniques believed to be used by stone age civilizations were improvements to basic roasting.

In addition to exposing food to direct heat from either an open fire or hot embers it is possible to cover the food with mud or large leaves before roasting to preserve moisture in the cooked result. Examples of similar techniques are still in use in many modern cuisines. Of greater difficulty was finding a method to boil water. For people without access to natural heated water sources, such as hot springs, it was possible to prepare a small pit lined with stones and filled with water.

Heated stones could then be placed in the water to raise its temperature. In many locations the shells of turtles or large molluscs provided a source for waterproof cooking vessels. Bamboo tubes sealed at the end with clay would have provided a usable container in Asia, while the inhabitants of the Tehuacan Valley began carving large stone bowls that were permanently set into a hearth as early as 7000 BC. A final cooking vessel available to early civilizations were the stomachs from animals killed by hunters.

The development of earthenware pottery allowed for the creation of fireproof cooking vessels in a variety of shapes and sizes. Coating the earthenware with some type of plant gum, and latter pottery glazes, converted the porous container into a waterproof vessel. The earthenware cookware could then be suspended over a fire through use of a tripod or other apparatus, or even designed to be placed directly into a fire or coal bed. The development of bronze and iron metalworking skills allowed for cookware made from metal to be manufactured although adoption of the new cookware was slow due to the much higher cost.

After the development of metal cookware there was little new development in cookware, with the standard Medieval kitchen utilizing a cauldron and a shallow earthenware pan for most cooking tasks with a spit employed for roasting. By the 17th Century, it was common for a western kitchen to contain a number of skillets, baking pans, a kettle, and several pots along with a variety of pot hooks, and trivets. In the American colonies, these items would commonly be produced by a local blacksmith from iron while brass or copper vessels were common in Europe and Asia.

Improvements in metallurgy during the 19th and 20th centuries allowed for pots and pans from metals such as steel, stainless steel and aluminum to be economically produced.

DIFFERENT TYPES OF COOKWARE

Cookware consists of different types of pots and pans that are used for specific purposes. Some of the pieces of cookware can be substituted for a type you may not have and still accomplish the type of cooking you need to perform. Pots and pans are available in different sizes and made of different types of material. Some materials are better than others when used for specific cooking methods. When selecting the cookware for your kitchen, you should take the following points into consideration:

— *Budget*: How much can you afford to spend on the pots and pans you purchase? You should purchase the best quality that you can afford. It will be well worth it in the long run. Otherwise, you will find yourself replacing them in a short time.

— *Cooking Habits*: How much will you be cooking? Do you eat out a lot and buy convenience food or do you like to prepare meals from scratch? Will you be entertaining a lot?

— *Cuisine*: Will you be making a lot of pasta, soups, or stir-fries? There are special pots and pans that assist in preparing these types of food.

— *Quantity*: Will you be cooking for 1, 2 or several? Having the right size cookware will be important when preparing your food.

Cookware Materials

Cookware is made from many different materials. Understanding the differences will assist you in making the best choice for your needs.

Lined copper

Copper is one of the more expensive materials used to make pots and pans. It conducts heat evenly and is very responsive to heat. It heats up quickly and will also cool down quickly when removed from the heat, preventing sautés and delicate foods from burning and becoming overdone. Because copper distributes heat so evenly and efficiently, it is the best choice for frying and sautéing, but it is also a good choice for many other cooking methods. One problem with copper is that it interacts with everything it comes in contact with.

Moisture in the air causes it to form a film on it that is poisonous and salty food causes a chemical reaction that can make food have a metallic taste. To make the copper pots and pans safe to use, they are lined with tin, silver or stainless steel to protect any surface that would come in contact with any food. Another drawback with copper is that because of how it reacts to everything it touches, it needs to be polished regularly to keep its bright copper shine. To care for copper cookware, hand wash with hot soapy water and avoid using abrasive materials to clean. Use copper polish to keep copper from tarnishing and free from white spots. The interior should be re-tinned every couple of years, depending on usage.

Stainless steel

Stainless steel cookware is moderately priced. It is the most versatile material to use because it keeps its bright shine and has good tensile strength, preventing it from denting easily. Stainless steel is a good material for any type of pan because it does not corrode and does not react with alkaline or acidic materials. The one problem with stainless steel is that it does not conduct heat well. To combat this problem, pots and pans made from stainless steel have should have a thick aluminum or copper core in the bottom of the pan to help conduct heat more evenly and make the pan more responsive to heat.

In the better quality pans, the aluminum or copper core also runs up the sides. You may find a stainless steel pan with an aluminum or copper plate on the bottom but if the plate is not thick enough, it will not do an efficient job of conducting heat evenly. To care for stainless steel cookware, wash with hot soapy water. A nylon scouring pad or nylon scraper can be used to remove stuck on food. There are stainless steel cleaners that can also be used to remove stains and bring a shine back to the cookware.

Aluminum

Aluminum cookware is fairly inexpensive in comparison to cookware made from other materials. Aluminum is lightweight but fairly strong. It is a good conductor of heat and does not easily distort when exposed to high temperatures. Aluminum works well for sautéing and frying foods because if its heat responsiveness. The drawback of aluminum is that it reacts to acidic and alkaline foods, causing it to corrode and affect the taste of the food being cook. Aluminum is generally used as a core heat conductor, or coated with stainless steel or an anodized coating to protect the food. To care for aluminum cookware, wash the pans with hot soapy water. Avoid washing the cookware in hard water because it tends to darken the aluminum. To remove stains, use a cream of tarter and water paste.

Anodized aluminum

This is aluminum that has been given a special finish to protect it from corrosion. It is a good conductor of heat and the special finish makes it stick-resistant. It is a good choice of material to look for in pots and pans for most any type of cooking. Pots and pans made from anodized aluminum are not dishwasher safe and can be dark in colour, making it hard to see slight colour changes in the food being cooked. To care for anodized aluminum pans, do not cook foods that are highly acidic or alkaline in them because they have a tendency to cause pitting in the coating. They should be washed by hand in hot soapy water rather than in a dishwasher where the strong detergent would damage the surface of the cookware. To avoid scratching the finish, do not use abrasive materials on the surface of anodized aluminum cookware.

Cast iron

Cast iron cookware is inexpensive to moderately priced. It is fairly heavy and conducts heat evenly. It heats slowly but once it is hot it holds the heat well. This makes it good for deep frying and slow-cooking. It can be used on top of the stove and in the oven. Drawbacks to cast iron are that it rusts, stains and becomes pitted when exposed to air, moisture and certain foods. To care for cast iron cookware, do not wash in soapy water but try wiping clean with a paper towel. Run hot water over stuck on food to help loosen and remove. After your cast iron pot has been washed it should be dried thoroughly. To prevent the pan from rusting, rid it of any excess moisture by setting it on the stove over high heat until all moisture has evaporated and coat with oil before storing.

Non-stick

These pots and pans have had a coating applied to them that prevents food from sticking and makes clean up easier. The non-stick surface is really an advantage when cooking some foods, such as omelettes, and when reheating sticky foods, such as rice. It also reduces the amount of fat that is normally required when cooking. The non-stick surface is less efficient when using certain cooking methods, such as sautéing, because the coating interferes with the transfer of heat from the underlying pan. To care for non-stick cookware, use hot soapy water and avoid using abrasive pads or powders.

If food does stick to the pan, soak in hot water to loosen stuck on food. A nylon scouring pad, nylon scraper, or nonabrasive cleaner can also be used to help remove stuck on food. Do not wash in a dishwasher. Also protect the non-stick surface by only using wooden, plastic, or coated utensils when cooking.

Porcelain enamel

Porcelain enamel is applied as a coating only on pots and pans made of other material, such as cast iron or aluminum. It prevents them from corroding or reacting with the food being cooked in them. A pan coated with porcelain cannot be used for sautéing or frying but will work as a saucepan or roaster. To care for porcelain enamel cookware, wash with hot soapy water. For stuck on food, soak in hot water to loosen. A nylon scouring pad, nylon scraper, or nonabrasive cleaner can also be used to help remove stuck on food. Porcelain enamel can be cleaned occasionally in the dishwasher unless it has a non-stick interior surface. Limit the use of a dishwasher to avoid the strong detergent dulling the enamel surface.

Tempered glass

Available as flameproof and ovenproof glassware. Both types of glassware hold heat well but are not heat responsive. The flameproof glassware, which is fairly expensive, can be used in the microwave, on the stovetop and in the oven. It heats unevenly, resulting in hot spots that cause food to stick. Ovenproof glassware can be used in the microwave and in the oven, but if used on the stovetop, it must be used with a diffuser. To care for tempered glass, wash in hot soapy water and soak to loosen stuck on food. Do not use metal scrapers or abrasive powders to remove stuck on food.

Pots and Pans

There are many types of pots and pans available for different cooking methods. Many of the types can be used for more than one method. Shown below are some of the different types and a brief description of each.

Braiser pan

A round or oval-shaped pan with two stay-cool handles and heavy domed cover. This is a heavyweight pan made of anodized aluminum or stainless steel. Both types of material contain an aluminum or copper core layer in the middle that runs all across the bottom and up the sides, which spreads heat evenly through the pan.

Figure 1. Braising pans

Braising pans can be used on the stovetop and in the oven. It is important that the cooking vessel has a tight fitting lid so that the liquid does not evaporate. They are available in depths ranging from 2 to 3 inches and in various sizes ranging from 10 to 13 inches in diameter or 2 ½ quarts to 6 quarts. This pan could also be used as a casserole pan.

Casserole

A round or oval pan with steep sides, which ranges in size from 2 quarts to 12 quarts. The casserole pan can be found made from many different materials. It is available made from the same high quality materials as a saucepan or you may find it made from glass, ceramic or earthenware. It may have a cover but many times the cover is not used when cooking the food in a casserole.

Figure 2. Casserole pan

Depending on the material it is made from, it may be used on the stove top but is generally used in the oven. It is used for cooking one-dish meals and the meal is served at the table in the casserole pan.

Chef's pan

A medium depth pan that generally has flared or rounded sides but is sometimes found with straight sides. It has a flat bottom and wide mouth, which accelerates the evaporation of liquids. A chef's pan most often will have a long handle and a tight fitting cover. It is made of a metal with a thick ground base that allows temperature changes to occur rapidly as the level of the heat applied to it changes, either increasing or decreasing for the best heat conduction.

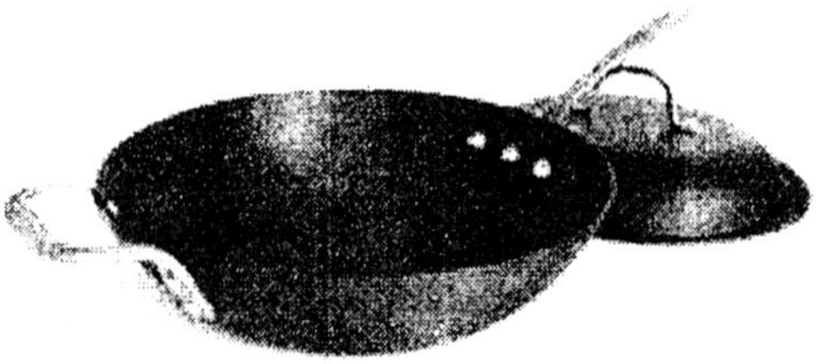

Figure 3. Chef's pan

Chef's pans are available in a variety of sizes such as 2, 3, 4, 5, or 6 quart. The height of the sides make it easier for sautéing, frying or steaming greater amounts of foods, allowing sufficient space for turning and stirring of the contents. Chef's pans are very similar to saucier pans and either pan can be used interchangeably.

Double boiler

A double boiler consists of two pans where one sits inside of the other. The bottom pan is slightly larger so the top pan can fit inside. The bottom pan contains hot water and the top pan holds the ingredients that are being cooked. This type of pan is used when making delicate sauces that have a tendency to separate if cooked on direct heat.

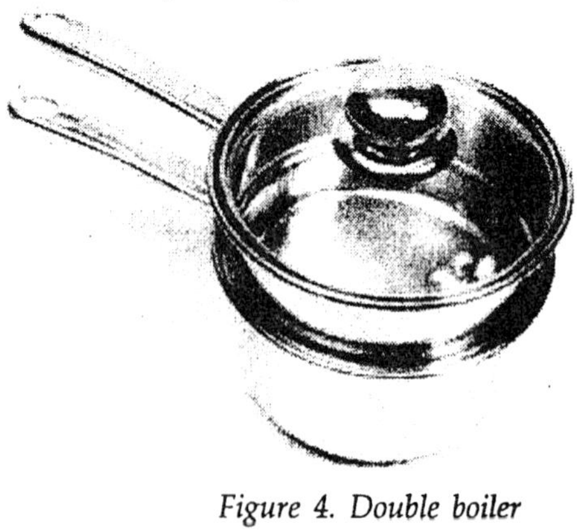

Figure 4. Double boiler

Double boiler are often made from stainless steel but can also be found made from other materials, such as enamelled steel, aluminum, and glass.

Dutch oven

A round or oval, heavyweight pot with a domed cover. A Dutch oven has steep sides that range in depth from 2 to 4 3/4 inches and range in size from 2 quarts to 6 quarts. You will find them made from stainless steel, anodized aluminum and cast iron. They are used for pot-roasting, stewing, braising, boiling pasta and making soup. They can be used on the stovetop and in the oven. Dutch ovens are a popular cookware item used when camping. Some cast iron models have legs, making it easy to set the pot over coals or a campfire.

Figure 5. Dutch oven

Frying pan/Skillet

A frying pan has a flat bottom with short sides that are flared or sloped, which makes it easier to toss and turn food with a spatula. The pan should be made of heavyweight material that is responsive to heat, such as lined copper, stainless steel with a copper or aluminum core, anodized aluminum or cast iron.

Figure 6. Frying pan

There are also frying pans available with non-stick surfaces. It is used for frying foods but can also be used for sautéing. Frying pans are available in several sizes, such as 6 ½", 7", 8", 9" 10", 11", 12", and 14". They are available in depths of 1 ½" to 3" and generally come with a cover.

Grill pan

A heavy metal pan that consists of ridges spaced evenly across the bottom that closely simulate the grilling process when cooking various meats and foods. They are available with shallow sides and with deeper sides similiar to a frying pan.

Figure 7. Flat Iron Grill Pan

The ridges raise the food off thc bottom surface of the pan, which helps prevent the food from steaming as it cooks. The ridges also serve as a method for allowing the fat contained in some foods to drain away from the food and collect in the spaces between the raised ridges. Many grill pans are made from cast iron.

Figure 8. Skillet Grill Pan

Cast iron needs to be seasoned but there are manufacturers who produce enamel surfaced and factory seasoned cast iron grill pans. Cast iron pans are also heavy and the handles get extremely hot, making them hard to handle. Even though cast iron is bulky, it is still the best material for a grill pan because of its ability to retain heat and to heat evenly. They are available in round, square, and rectangular shapes and range in size from 9 to 12 inches. There are also double burner sizes available.

Omelette pan

An omelette pan is basically the same as a frying pan. It is available made from the same type of material as frying pans and is generally shaped the same.

Figure 9. Omelette pan

An omelette pan with a non-stick surface is beneficial when making omelettes because it allows the eggs to release from the pan, making them easier to turn or flip. The omelette pan is also available in an oval shaped pan that is generally 10 to 12 inches long. The oval pan works well for cooking foods such as omelettes, fish filets, and shell steaks. The most common sizes for round pans are 8, 10, and 12 inches.

Roasting pan

A rectangular shaped pan with low sides, which allows the heat from the oven to expose the entire surface of the meat to create a browned exterior. The pan is generally used with a rack to prevent the meat from sitting in its own juices and stewing instead of browning. See Roasting Racks. There are several sizes available. Select a size that allows approximately 2 inches between the side of the pan and the meat. Also, be sure that there is at least 2 inches of space between the outside of the pan and the sides of the oven so that there will be proper air circulation.

Figure 10. Roasting pan

The roasting pans are available made from several different materials, such as stainless steel, stainless steel with an aluminum or copper core, aluminum with non-stick surfaces, anodized aluminum, lined copper and granite.

Roasting pans with high cover

An oval shaped pan with deep sides and a large domed cover. It generally has a flat rack included on the bottom of the pan. They are available in several sizes and material, such as granite, anodized aluminum, and stainless steel.

Figure 11. Roasting pans

The meat is cooked with the cover on, which acts as an oven in an oven, resulting in the meat cooking more quickly and in a moister environment. This results in moist, tender meat. The deep-sided roasting pan, generally without the cover, is also used for casseroles.

Saucepan

A round pot with high straight sides and a flat bottom that is used for several purposes, such as cooking vegetables, heating soup, and making sauces. The standard saucepan has straight sides but there are other styles available that are used for special purposes.

Figure 12. Saucepan

A saucepan known as a Windsor has sides that flare out and another known as a saucier has sides that are rounded. They are used to provide more exposed surface to speed up reducing a sauce by allowing more evaporation and they make it easier to stir and whisk food out of the corners.

Saucepans are made of a sturdy material that is heat responsive, such as lined copper or stainless steel with an aluminum or copper core or bottom plate. They are available in several sizes. A small saucepan holds 1 to 1 ½ quarts, a medium holds 2 quarts, and a large saucepan holds at 3 or more quarts. Most saucepans come with a snug fitting cover.

Sauteing pan

A pan very similar to the frying pan, only it has short, straight sides. It has a heavy gauge bottom and is made from a material that is heat responsive, such as lined copper, stainless steel with a copper or aluminum core, or anodized aluminum. It is used for sautéing foods but can also be used for frying foods. The pan should have a long handle and it generally comes with a cover. Some of the larger models have a loop handle opposite the long handle that is used to assist in lifting the pan.

Figure 13. Saute pan

The saute pan is available in various sizes, ranging from 6″ to 16″ in diameter, and 2 ½″ to 3 ½″ in depth.

Sauteuse pan

An round, lidded pan with small handles that is often used to sauté or braise a variety of foods. With short to medium height outward sloping sides, a sauteuse pan is a utensil for cooking casseroles, stews, and pasta dishes as well as meat and poultry dishes. Common in European households, this pan has a small curved handle on each side instead of a single straight handle and is typically available in sizes ranging from 2.5 quarts to 7 quarts.

Figure 14. Sauteuse pan

Stir-Fry pan

A round, deep pan that may have straight sides with a slightly rounded base or more commonly a round base that slopes out and upward. Stir fry pans are available with several different sized handle lengths that can be selected to match the cooking process. The pan allows heat to be well distributed across the base while the sloping sides make it easier to stir and turn ingredients as they cook. The Asian pan referred to as a "wok" is one traditional type of stir-fry pan while other versions are often available with bases and sides that are thicker in substance, not as curved, nor as deep as the wok pan.

Figure 15. Stir fry pans

Stir fry pans are often used to prepare and quickly sear multiple ingredients that go well together including various meats and vegetables mixed with sauces. The stir fry pan is good for cooking food in a small quantity of oil and for retaining the colours and textures of the various ingredients.

Stockpot

A deep, straight-sided pot that is taller than it is wide. It has two, securely attached, loop handles that are big enough to easily allow the use of potholders or oven mitts. It is used for simmering large amount of liquid, such as stock, soup and stews, but also works well for thick soups, chilli and for boiling pasta.

Figure 16. Stockpot

The pot does not need to be made of anodized aluminum or copper to promote responsive heat reaction but should have a heavy bottom to protect against burning and scorching. Stockpots are available in sizes ranging from 6 quarts to 20 quarts and generally include a cover. 10, 12 and 14 quarts are standard sizes that will satisfy many uses. You will find stockpots made of several different materials, such as stainless steel, aluminum, anodized aluminum, copper, and non-stick materials.

Pasta Insert: A perforated insert that fits inside a stockpot. The insert acts as a colander for draining pasta and is generally made of stainless steel.

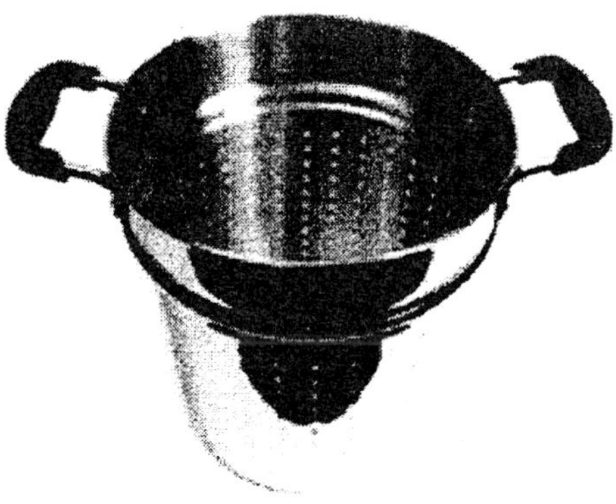

Figure 17. Pasta Insert

Wok

A bowl shaped pan that is used to quickly cook food over high heat. It is available with a rounded or flat bottom. The traditional type wok has a rounded bottom and is used over a flamed heat source, such as a gas burner. The flat bottom wok was designed to use on an electric burner or a ceramic stovetop but can also be used on a gas stove. The rounded woks come with a ring that should be placed over the flames to hold the woks steady. Woks are available made from various materials, such as carbon steel, cast iron, stainless steal with aluminum inner layers, and metal with a non-stick coating applied.

Figure 18. Wok

Cast steel and cast iron woks must be seasoned before they are used for the first time. Some varieties of woks have one long handle, some have two short handles and others have a long handle on one side and a short one on the opposite side. The wok is approximately 4 inches deep and can be 12 to 16 inches in diameter. The wok is most often used for stir-frying but can also be used for sautéing, steaming, deep-frying,

Roasting racks

There are various types of racks available and they are

generally made from stainless steel or a non-stick coated metal, which makes clean up a lot easier. You may want to have a couple of the different types because some racks work better for different uses. Be sure it is big enough and sturdy enough to hold the piece of meat you will be cooking and that it fits into your roasting pan. When placed in the oven, there should be at least a 2″ space between the meat and the top of the oven. A brief description of the most common type of racks is shown below.

Flat Racks: A simple rack that lays flat in the bottom of the roasting pan. It is available in a rectangular or oval shape and is made of thin wires running parallel to each other the length of the rack. It will have a couple of wires running at a right angle to help support the parallel wires. It does not work well for poultry because the legs and wings have a tendency to fall through the wires.

Nonadjustable V-racks: Made of v-shaped pieces of metal that are attached to a frame that has handles on it. This rack works well to cradle the roast or bird and hold it in place, but because the metal bars are generally so far apart, the wings and legs of a bird fall through. This makes it difficult to turn the bird if necessary or to remove it from the rack without tearing the wings and legs.

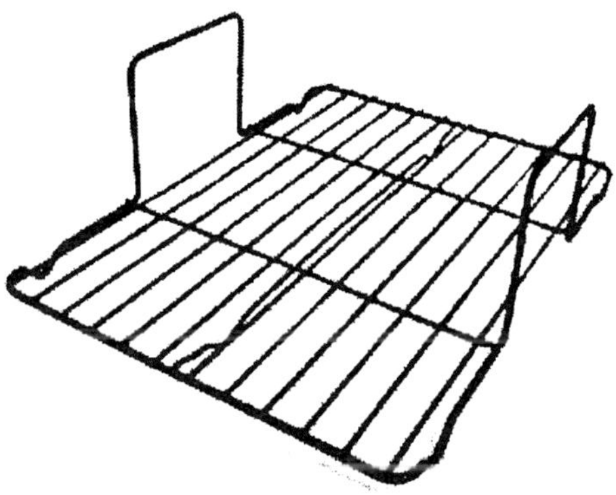

Figure 19. Flat Racks

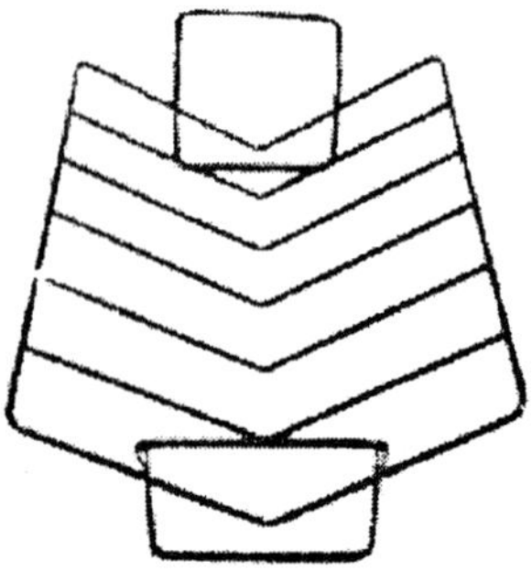

Figure 20. Nonadjustable V-racks

Adjustable V-rack: This V-rack has two sides made of thin wires attached to a base. The sides can be adjusted to change the width of the V that they form. This allows you to better fit the rack to the meat you are placing on it. A problem may occur if you have to turn the roast or bird on the rack because the rack has a tendency to collapse.

Vertical Racks: This type of rack has vertical prongs that are attached to a round base. The prongs are inserted in the cavity of the bird and it is cooked looking as if it is standing up. The wire prongs inserted into the bird help to speed up the cooking time by conducting heat into the bird. Roasting the bird in this manner also provides a crispier skin but it also makes more of a mess in the oven because you have fat splattering in all directions.

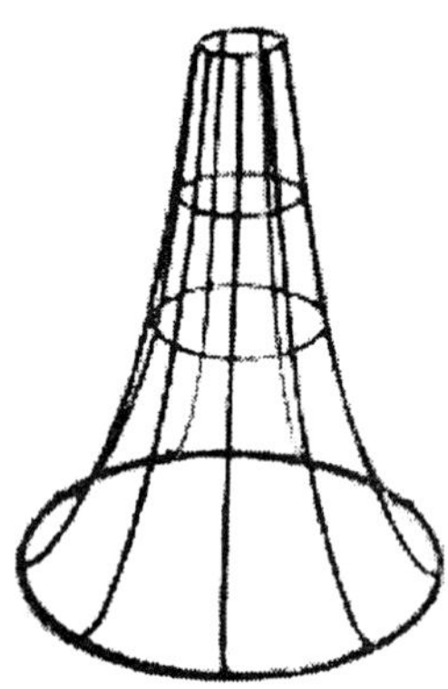

Figure 21. Vertical racks

The other problem with this rack is that it can only be used on chickens or other birds of that size.

Basket Rack: A U-shaped piece of perforated metal that has a handle on each end. The rack resembles a basket. The U-shaped rack cradles the meat and when used for a chicken, it holds the wings and legs next to the body. It produces the crispiest skin on a chicken due to its ability to conduct heat. It is sometimes referred to as a cradle roasting rack. This rack only works for small birds and roasts that are 5 pounds or smaller.

Microwave cookware

Cookware for the microwave is different than other cookware. Most cookware that is used on the stovetop or in the oven cannot be used in a microwave oven. Microwave cookware is generally made from glass, ceramic or plastic and not all glass, ceramic and plastic containers are microwave safe. If a container is not microwave save it can heat up in the microwave and become a safety hazard.

Most plastics work well in the microwave oven but not all. If their label indicates that they are able to withstand boiling water and if it states that they are dishwasher safe, they should be able to withstand the heat from the microwave. Glassware for the microwave should be heat-resistant. Non-heat-resistant glass cannot withstand the high and uneven heat from the microwave. Ceramic cookware should be unglazed.

Glazed ceramic absorbs the microwave energy too quickly, which can cause it to break or become heated to a high temperature. The best style of microwave cookware to use is a dish that has shallow sides and is round or oval in shape. There are microwave cookware sets available that contain different size and shape containers that are suitable for the microwave.

To test a dish or container to see if it is microwave safe, fill a 1-cup glass measuring cup with water and place it next to the dish or container in the microwave. Start the microwave on high power and run for 1 minute. After a minute, check the water and the container you are testing. The water should be hot but if the container is also hot, it is not microwave safe.

Cookware Sets: You can purchase prepackage sets of cookware where the different pieces have been selected for you. You can generally gain some cost savings when buying the pieces in a set over buying them separately but be careful that all the pieces are pots and pans that you will use. It should include a saucepan and lid, a frying pan, and a stockpot. A roasting pan would be another worthwhile piece in the set. Sets are available in different size groupings. If purchasing a set, select the best one possible for the amount you have allocated by paying close attention to the quality of the pieces and to what pieces you are getting in the set.

If the set has several pieces that you will hardly ever use, it may make more sense to purchase one of higher quality that has fewer pieces that are all commonly used. You will also want to select a set that is made from a material that is versatile enough to use for different cooking methods. Stainless steel with a copper or aluminum core or bottom plate would be good choice. Anodized aluminum cookware would also be a versatile choice. If a cookware set will not give you the essential pieces for most of your cooking needs, consider buying separate pieces of basic pans you need to start.

There are four basic pans shown below that will satisfy the majority of your cooking needs.

— *Saucepan*: Purchase a 2 qt. saucepan, which can be used for making sauces, reheating soups, pasta, and rice. A stainless steel pan with an aluminum base, which would be moderately priced, is a good choice for this pan.

— *Frying Pan/Skillet*: A 12 inch pan would be a good size to be used for several purposes, such as frying meats, potatoes, pancakes and eggs, and can also be used for stir-frying, sautéing and making one dish meals on the stovetop. It should be purchased with a cover and be made out of stainless steel with a copper or aluminum core, or a non-stick aluminum pan with a non-stick coating would provide a pan with easier clean up and one that required the use of less fat.

— *Roasting Pan*: A roasting pan, which should be purchased with a rack, can be used for roasting meat and poultry. It can also be used to make one-dish meals that bake in the oven, such as lasagna. An aluminum pan with a non-stick coating would provide a pan that is lightweight, heats evenly, and is easy to clean up.

— *Stockpot*: An 8 to 12 quart size pot would be a good standard range of size to provide a pot that can be used for many purposes, such as making stock or soup, boiling long strands of pasta, cooking sweet corn, and boiling seafood. For a moderately priced pot, select a stainless steel pot with an aluminum base, which will provide you with a pot that will conduct heat evenly.

Bakeware

Bakeware Pan Sizes

When you are preparing to create a recipe that requires the use of bakeware, you should first determine whether you have the proper size pan. There are many different types of bakeware, such as, round pans, square pans, rectangle pans, tube pans, bundt pans, jelly roll pans, loaf pans, springform pans, roasting pans, and casseroles. Your recipe will suggest that you use a certain size and type of pan. If you do not have the pan requested, you can generally substitute a similar size pan without any problem. The information below will help you make the appropriate substitution

Select a pan that is as close to the same size as the pan the recipe indicated to use. The pan should have approximately the same volume capacity and when filled, the ingredients should be close to the same depth as they would be in the original size pan. To find the surface of a pan use the equations below:

Square or Rectangular Pans:		Width x Length *9″ x 13″*	 =	Total Square Inches *117 Square Inches*
Round Pans:	Step 1.	Diameter ÷ 2 9″ ÷ 2	 =	Radius 4.5″
	Step 2.	Radius x Radius x (3.14) *4.5″ x 4.5″ x 3.14*	 =	Total Square Inches *64 Square Inches*

— If the pan is close in size and volume to the original, the cooking temperatures and times should not have to be adjusted.

— When measuring a pan, measure from inside edge to inside edge so that you are not including the thickness of the sides in your measurement. Measure the depth by placing the ruler inside the pan and measuring from the bottom up to within ¼ inch of the top edge. If the pan has slanted sides, be sure to keep the ruler straight and do not slant when measuring.

— Measure volume by filling the pan with water and then pouring the water into a measuring cup to measure how much water is in the pan, or you can also measure the water as you pour it into the pan.

— Be careful substituting a pan when the recipe indicates that a tube pan should be used, such as an angel food cake pan or a bundt pan. Generally the recipe requires this type of pan so the heat is distributed properly. This is necessary for the food to get to its proper doneness.

— If you select a glass bakeware dish or a dark, non-stick pan, reduce the oven temperature by 25°F.

— If selecting a pan that results in the depth of the ingredients to be thinner, reduce the cooking time by 10 to 15 minutes. If the depth of the ingredients is thicker, increase the cooking time by 10 to 15 minutes. Be sure to use the visual indicators to test for the proper doneness.

— If a casserole dish has to be substituted for a different size when making a savoury dish, use the same guidelines as for baked goods. Use a dish that holds close to the same volume and if you substitute one that will affect the depth of the ingredients, adjust the cooking times to use less time for thinner depths and more time for thicker depths.

The table below shows the sizes and volume of some of the common bakeware pans. The table will help to assist you in selecting a successful substitution.

Table 1. Bakeware Pan Sizes and Volume

Bakeware Pan Size	Approximate Volume	Bakeware Pan Size	Approximate Volume
Round		Loaf	
6″ x 2″	4 cups	8″ x 4″ x 2 1/2″	4 cups
8″ x 1 1/2″	4 cups	8 1/2″ x 4 1/2″ x 2 1/2″	6 cups
8″ x 2″	6 cups	9″ x 5″ x 3″	8 cups
9″ x 1 1/2″	6 cups	Bundt	
9″ x 2″	8 cups	7 1/2″ x 3″	6 cups
9″ x 3″	12 cups	9″ x 3″	9 cups
10″ x 2″	11 cups	10″ x 3 1/2″	12 cups

Pie	
8″ x 1 1/2″	4 cups
9″ x 1 1/2″	5 cups
9″ x 2″	8 cups
10″ x 1 1/2″	6 cups
Square	
8″ x 8″ x 1 1/2″	6 cups
8″ x 8″ x 2″	8 cups
9″ x 9″ x 1 1/2″	8 cups
9″ x 9″ x 2″	10 cups
10″ x 10″ x 2″	12 cups
Rectangular	
11″ x 7″ x 2″	6 cups
13″ x 9″ x 2″	14 cups
Jelly Roll	
10 1/2″x 151/2″ x 1″	10 cups
12 1/2″ x 17″ x 1″	12 cups
Springform	
8″ x 3″	11 cups
9″ x 2 1/2″	10 cups
9″ x 3″	12 cups
10″ x 2 1/2″	12 cups

Tube	
8″ x 3″	9 cups
9″ x 3″	12 cups
9 1/2″ x 4″	16 cups
10″ x 4″	16 cups
Tart	
11″ x 1″	4 cups
Muffin Cup	
1 3/4″ x 3/4″	1/8 cups
2 3/4″ x 1 1/8″	1/4 cups
2 3/4″ x 1 1/2″	1/2 cups
3″ x 1 1/4″	5/8 cups
Casserole	
1 quart	4 cups
1 1/2 quart	6 cups
2 quarts	8 cups
2 1/2 quarts	10 cups
3 quarts	12 cups
4 quarts	16 cups

When selecting a substitution according to the pan's volume , that you need to allow room for expansion of certain foods as they cook. Certain types of food need more room for expansion than others. Fill the pan as directed by the instructions on the recipe. If you select a pan that has a comparable volume to the original size suggested by the recipe, it should allow the necessary room for expansion.

9

KITCHEN KNIVES

A knife consists of a blade, a tang and a handle. A knife is a sharp-edged hand tool used for cutting. The tang is an extension of the blade into the handle. Some knives have a handguard, so that fingers cannot slip onto the edge and be cut. A fuller, sometimes called a blood gutter or blood groove, is a groove on the side, along a blade.

According to a popular myth, it lets bleeding occur from an artery without removing the knife. In reality, its only function is to make knives and swords lighter while sacrificing little strength; on most knives it has more decorative worth. Some knives also have a shoulder in which the blade thickens as it meets the handle. In piercing, this helps keep the knife from jamming, for example in bone.

In kitchen knives, it keeps chopped items from moving back toward the hand. The handle of a knife should be made of a non-slip material. For a large knife, it is desirable that the handle is thick enough that one's fingers just meet one's palm when the knife is gripped tightly. A hole in the end of the handles allows the knife to be hung or placed on a lanyard. A knife usually consists of a blade, usually less than 12 inches (30cm) in length, attached to a handle.

The blade of a knife is usually pointed and may have one or two cutting edges. Knives have been used as tools and weapons since the Stone Age. The first knives were flint or other rock, chipped or ground to an edge, sometimes with a handle. Later on with advances in smelting and metallurgy the blades were made of bronze, iron, then steel. While the materials have changed over time, the basic design remains the same.

Together with the fork and spoon, the knife has been a common eating utensil in the West since the Middle Ages. In the West, multi-purpose pocket knives are probably the most common knives carried today, and the importance of the knife as a weapon is declining.

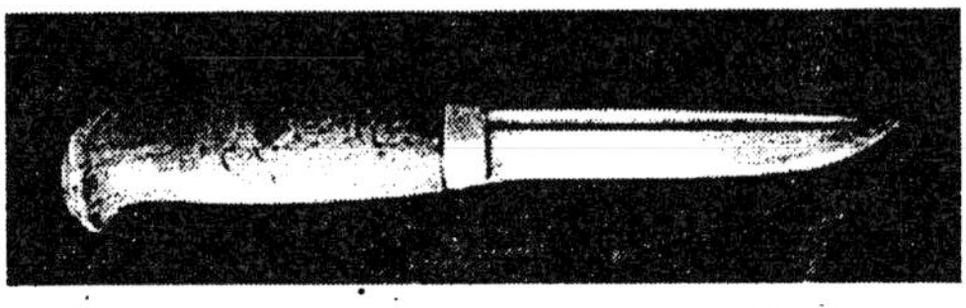

Figure 1. Traditional Finnish puukko knife

Materials of Making-Knife

Blades are usually made of steel(s); though there are a few knives using materials like high tech ceramic and titanium, these are very uncommon. Stainless steels have gained popularity in the latter half of the twentieth century because they are highly resistant to corrosion (though they can rust under extreme conditions).

Steels having high carbon but low chromium content are prone to rust and pitting if not kept dry. As of 2004 there are a variety of exotic steels and other materials used to form blades. Knife manufacturers such as Spyderco and Benchmade typically use 154CM, VG-10, S30V, and CPM440V (aka S60V), as well as high-speed high-hardness tool steels like D2 and M2.

Other manufacturers sometimes use titanium, cobalt, and cobalt containing alloys. All three are more ductile than typical stainless steels, but have quite a vocal support group despite concerns about health effects of cobalt content. The craft of Damascus steel may be lost, but marketers today misuse its name to apply to pattern welding, which creates layered and admired patterns. The cost of the process restricts it to high-end knives. There is typically more demand for exotic alloys in the utility, outdoor, and tactical or combat knife categories than there is in the kitchen knife category.

Forschner/Victorinox make decent, inexpensive kitchen knives; high-end manufacturers include Wüsthof, Global, Henckels and Böker (Tree Brand). Some manufacturers, particularly of kitchen knives, make ceramic blades; these are harder and stay sharp longer, but because of their brittleness, chip and break more readily.

All knife steel is martensitic, which means that small crystal grains and lattice irregularities, that make it hard, are formed as it cools from austenitic structure while hot to ferritic structure while cold. Knife steel has fairly low nickel content, because nickel tends to keep steel in the austenitic structure, even when cold. Stainless knife steels are high in carbon, but "carbon steel" means there is not also a lot of chromium.

Stainless steel is steel with very high (12-18%) chromium content. It is corrosion resistant (though knife steel is less so than higher nickel stainless steel) because, except in acid, one of the metals or one of the oxides is always stable. Stainless steel usually has particles of chromium (or other alloy metal) carbides. These explain its reputation for long wear (the carbides are harder than the metal) and for being harder to sharpen and not taking as good an edge as rustable, low alloy ("carbon") steel (the ceramic particles themselves cannot be sharpened easily.)

The bulk hardness and toughness of stainless steel tend to be lower than those of low alloy steel. Vanadium and molybdenum are important alloy metals because they make the gain size smaller, which improves hardness and toughness. Vanadium, and perhaps molybdenum, also increase corrosion resistance. Properties of kinife making materials are:

Stainless Steel: Unlike carbon steel, stainless steel blades do not discolor or rust, however, they are not hard enough to maintain the best edge.

High Carbon Stainless Steel: A combination of the best attributes of carbon steel and stainless steel blades. They have the toughness and ability to hold an edge and do not discolor.

Titanium: Titanium blades are made from a mold of titanium and carbides. When compared to steel, titanium is lighter, more wear resistant, and holds its edge longer. The titanium blade is more flexible than steel, they work best for tasks such as boning and filleting.

Ceramic: Ceramic blades are made of zirconium oxide and aluminum oxide. Although they are much more delicate than steel knives, they tend to hold their edge up to 10 times longer. Once the blades have dulled, they must be sharpened by a professional.

Plastic: Plastic blades are used with the primary goal of preventing vegetables and such from becoming discolored from the blade of a knife. Plastic blades are not very sharp and require some force when cutting.

Hollow Ground: A knife blade with concave beveled edges created by starting midway, or lower, from the top of the blade and grinding or tapering each side of the blade thinner toward the bottom, or cutting edge, of the blade. This type of cutting edge results in a very thin and exceptionally sharp edge that can be easily sharpened.

It is a type of blade that is excellent for slicing but not for chopping activities since the higher impact of the chopping action dulls or may chip the blade. Although these blades often have very sharp edges, the blade lacks the balance and longevity of a taper ground blade.

Taper Ground: A knife blade that is manufactured with a single sheet of metal and has been ground so that it tapers smoothly from the spine to the cutting edge. This type of blade desired on knives that are used frequently.

Knife Construction

Tang: The tang is the part of the knife blade that extends into the handle. The length of the tang is thought to be significant in the ability to balance and control a knife. Various manufacturers believe that producing a knife with a tang that extends throughout the full length of the knife is most desirable. Other manufacturers argue that each piece of a knife benefits from using a different metal. Investing in a solid, heavy, well balanced knife that you feel comfortable with is the overall objective.

Metal Rivets: Metal rivets are used to secure the tang to the handle of the knife. To prevent irritation to the hand, the rivets should be completely smooth and lie flush with the surface of the handle. In addition, this will help prevent debris and microorganisms from collecting in the spaces between the handle and the rivets.

Bolster: A bolster is a thick piece of metal (collar or shank) that is placed between the handle and the blade. The purpose of a bolster is to provide safety from the blade and add balance to the knife.

Knife Handles

Wood. Wood handles provide an excellent grip, but requires more maintenance than a plastic or stainless steel handle. Critics argue that wood handled knives absorb microorganisms.

Wood Handles Infused with Plastic: A combination of the best attributes of wood handles and molded plastic handles. They have an excellent grip but do not require the maintenance all wood handles require. They are also not as porous as wood handled knives, preventing the absorption of microorganisms.

Molded Plastic or Composition: Molded plastic handles are much easier to care for than wooden handles. They will not absorb debris and microorganisms and are easily cleaned. Critics argue that handles made with molded plastics become brittle over time and can become slippery in the hand.

Stainless Steel: Metal handled knives last longer and add weight to the knife. Critics argue that they become slippery in the hand.

Shapes

There are a variety of knife blade shapes; some of the most common are listed below.

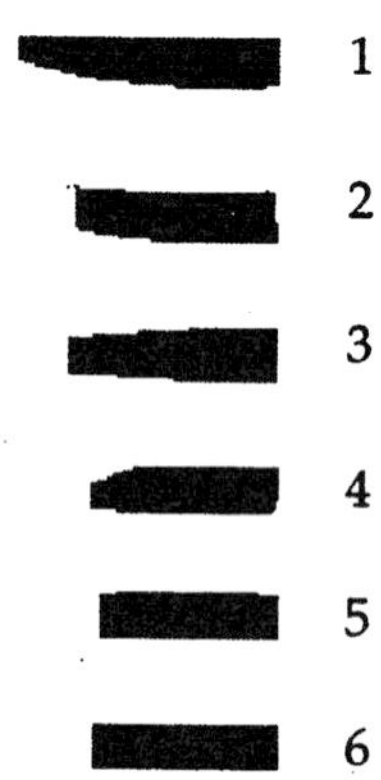

Figure 2. Variety of knife blade shapes

— A normal blade has a curving edge, and flat back. A dull back lets the wielder use fingers to concentrate force; it also makes the knife heavier and stronger for its size. The curve concentrates force on a small point, making cutting easier. Therefore, the knife can chop as well as pick and slice.

— A curved, trailing-point knife has a back edge that curves upward. This lets a lightweight knife have a larger curve on its edge. Such a knife is better for slicing than a normal knife.

— A Double edged or spey blade has two edges. The idea is to make a blade that cuts in either direction, with a strong sharp point. This shape is primarily used for fighting knives because it can cut in both directions and point in line with the handle.

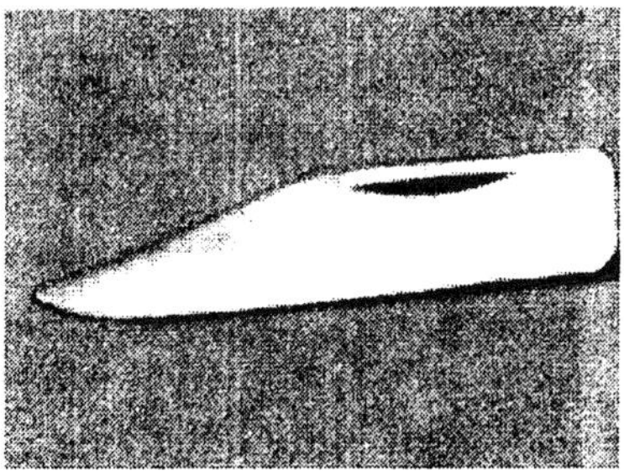

Figure 3. Clip Point blade

— A clip point blade is like a normal blade with the tip "clipped" to make the tip thinner and sharper. The back edge of the clip can have a false edge that can be sharpened to make a second edge. The sharp tip makes the blade exceptional as a pick, or for cutting in tight places. If the false edge is sharpened it increases the knife's effectiveness in piercing. The Bowie has a clipped blade.

— A sheepsfoot knife has a straight edge, and a curved dull back. It gives the most control, because the dull back edge is made to be held by fingers. Sheepsfoot knives are good for whittling, including sheep's hooves.

— An Americanised tanto style knife is thick towards the point. It is superficially similar to the points on most Japanese long and short swords (katana and wakizashi). The traditional Japanese tanto knife uses the blade geometry of (1). The edge is straight. The point is actually a second edge on the end of the blade, with a total edge angle of 60-80 degrees.

An ulu knife is a sharpened half-circle. This sort of blade is all edge, with no point, and a handle in the middle. It's good for scraping, and sometimes chopping. It is the strongest knife-shape. An example is a head knife, used in leatherworking both to scrape down leather (reducing thickness), and to make precise, rolling cuts to form shapes.

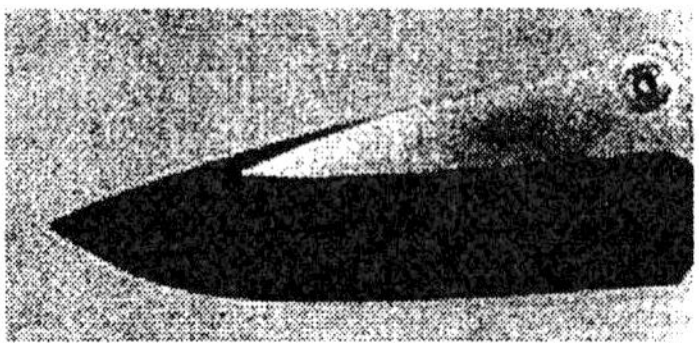

Figure 4. Drop-Point blade

A drop-point blade is very similar to a clip point, but it features the back convexed down, rather than having a clip taken out of it. It handles much like the clip-point.

Form of Knives

Knives exist in several styles:

Fixed Blade Knives

A fixed blade is a knife in which the blade does not fold and extends most of the way into the handle. This type of knife is typically stronger and larger than a folding knife. Activities that require a strong blade, such as hunting or fighting, typically rely on a fixed blade. Some famous fixed blade designs include the Ka-bar and Bowie knives.

Folding Knives

A folding knife is one that has a pivot between handle and blade, allowing the blade to fold into the handle. Most folding knives are small working blades, pocket knives are usually folding knives. Some folding knives have a locking mechanism:

— The most traditional and commonplace lock is the slip-joint. This isn't really a lock at all, and is found most commonly on traditional pocket knives. It consists of a backspring that wedges itself into a notch on the tang on the back of the blade.

— The lockback is the simplest true locking knife. It is found on most traditional locking knives. It is like a slip-joint, but the lock consists of a latch rather than a backspring. To disengage, one presses the latch on the spine of the knife down, releasing the tang.

— The linerlock is the most common today on knives, especially so-called "tactical" folders. Its main advantage is that it allows one to disengage the lock with one hand. It consists of a liner bent so that when the blade opens, the liner presses against the rear of the tang, preventing it from swinging back. To disengage, you press the liner to the side of the knife from where it is attached to the inside of the scales.

— The framelock is a variant of the linerlock, however, instead of using the liner, the frame functions as an actual spring. It is usually much more secure than a liner lock.

— There are many other modern locks with various degrees of effectiveness. Most of these are particular to single brands, most notably Benchmade's AXIS™ lock and SpyderCo's Compression™ lock.

Many folding knives (particularly locking models) have a small knob, or thumb-screw that allows the user to open the knife quickly with one hand. In the middle ages, a dorsal meant a knife with a back, or a one-sided knife. An ansall was a two-sided knife, with a blade on both sides. These terms have since fallen out of use.

Types of Kitchen Knives

The following descriptions and images of knife types are general examples only. Although the basics of each knife style is the same, manufacturers have many variations of how each type of knife looks.

Chef's Knife

Also called a cook's knife. An all purpose kitchen knife that is used for most types of chopping, dicing, mincing, and slicing. Chef's knives come various lengths of 6, 8, 10, and 12 inches. The length of the knife you purchase is significant. The longer the knife, the heavier and more difficult it will be to handle. Small handed cooks should choose shorter blades while large handed cooks will prefer longer blades.

Figure 5. Chef's Knife

Carving Knife

A knife with an 8 to 15 inch blade used for carving large

roasts, poultry, and filleting large fish. The blade edge of a carving knife is either smooth or beveled. The blade should be large enough to carve across the cut of meat, poultry, or fish in one sweep. The blades vary in flexibility.

A carving knife with a rigid blade is used for slicing roasted meats; more flexible blades for poultry; and the most flexible blades are for slicing smoked pork and fish. Carving knives are often sold in sets with a carving fork. A carving fork is designed to hold the meat steady while slicing and keep the hand safe while cutting. These forks typically have two long, curved prongs.Some manufacturers refer to carving knives over 9" as slicers.

Figure 6. Carving Knife

Paring Knife

A small knife with a sharp blade that is generally three to four inches long. It is easy to handle and works well for peeling and coring foods. The blade is typically thin and narrow and tapers to a point at the tip.

Figure 7.Paring Knife

Serrated Knife

A knife with a sharp edge and saw-like notches or teeth. The blade of a serrated knife is 5 to 10 inches long. Serrated knives are difficult to sharpen; therefore many chefs spend less on a serrated knife and buy new more often.

A serrated knife with a long blade is used to slice through food that is hard on the outside and soft on the inside, such as slicing through the hard crusts of bread. A serrated knife with a short, thin blade is intended for slicing fruits and vegetables.

Figure 8.Serrated Knife

Utility Knife

A small lightweight knife, which has a blade that is generally 4 to 7 inches long and is used for miscellaneous light cutting such as fruits and vegetables.

Figure 9. Utility Knife

Boning Knife

A knife with a thin short blade, typically 5 or 6 inches long, used to remove the main bone within a cut of meat, such as a ham or a beef roast. A boning knife will typically have a long narrow blade for ease of manipulation around bones, that is rigid and proportioned to the size of the bones being removed. Bigger cuts of meat require a larger more rigid blade that will not be too flexible and cause injury if it bends too easily, while smaller meat cuts can be trimmed and boned using a smaller less rigid blade.

Figure 10. Boning Knife

Filet Knife

A knife consisting of a thin flexible blade, typically 6 to 11 inches long, used for filleting fish. The narrow blade enables the knife to cleanly move along the backbones of the fish, in and around areas adjacent to bones, and to evenly slice along the skin, removing it easily from the flesh.

Figure 11. Filet Knife

Cleaver

A knife with a wide rigid blade approximately 6 inches in length, which tapers to a sharp cutting edge. This tool is used to chop, shred, pound, or crush food ingredients and materials. The blade of the cleaver is thick, somewhat heavy and well balanced with a beveled cutting edge, which allows for ease of chopping through vegetables or materials as hard a bones with the beveled blade.

The flat blunt side of the blade can be used to pulverize meat. If the handle is flat on the end it may be used to crush seeds, garlic or other similar ingredients. A hole is typically provided on the top end of the blade to allow for ease of hanging this tool.

Figure 12. Cleaver

Santoku Knife

A type of knife commonly used to prepare ingredients for Asian food dishes. This knife is very similar to a chef's knife with a wide blade that has a long straight edge curving up slightly at the end. The main difference is that the santoku knife has a wider blade that is thinner in thickness, shorter in length, and curves up very gradually at the end providing a straighter cutting edge.

Constructed of stainless steel, this knife will typically be expensive to purchase, since it is precision made to be well balanced and well formed for ease of handling and greater control. With a thinner blade than a chef's knife, the santoku can cut smoothly and more precisely through dense vegetables, which may have a tendency to provide more resistance when using thicker width blades.

Versions of this knife are manufactured with either a standard-edged blade or a hollow ground edge, also known as a granton edge. The purpose of the granton style blade is to assist with keeping particles from sticking to the knife edge as it chops small bits of food as well as a friction reducer to provide less drag when chopping, which enables easier and faster motion.

Santoku knives are used for chopping, dicing, and slicing foods into narrow or fine pieces so they can be added as ingredients to enhance the look or flavors of the various foods being prepared. This knife also works well for butterflying boneless chicken breasts, providing a manageability and ease of handling for the cutting required to butterfly poultry.

Figure 13. Santoku Knife

Steak Knife

A knife used for cutting main courses such as steak and chicken. The knife usually has a blade that is 4 to 6 inches long and varies in thickness. Depending on the manufacturer, the blade may or may not be serrated.

Figure 14. Steak Knife

Mincing Knife

A knife that can be used to mince or cut foods into smaller bits for seasoning sauces, soups, salads, and other dishes. Mincing knives can be either single or double bladed to cut a variety of foods into very small pieces. A mincing knife is also referred to as a Mezzaluna, Mezzaluna chopper or Mezzaluna knife.

Another version of a mincing tool is the rolling mincer or rotary mincer. This utensil consists of numerous circular blades, close together mounted on a handle, enabling the user to roll the tool back and forth over the herb as the blades do the mincing.

Figure 15.Single Bladed Mincing Knife

Figure 16. Double Bladed Mincing Knife

Oyster Knife

A kitchen utensil that is used to pry open the hard shell of an oyster or clam in order to remove the meat. Typically, the knife will have a sharp, beveled blade that can be inserted into the tightly closed shell to pry the shell apart. The blade is then used to cut through the muscle and oyster membrane. A round shield is built into the handle in order to keep the knife and hand from going into or through the sharp edged shell.

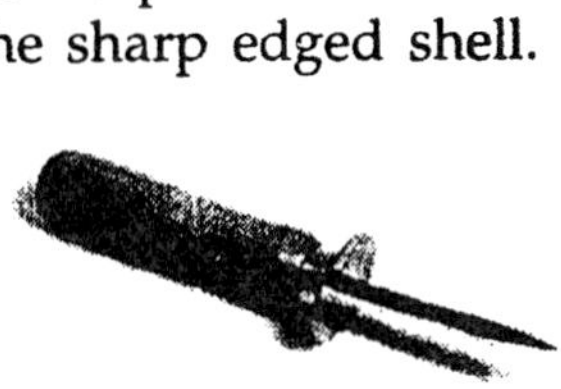

Figure 17. Oyster Knife

Devein Knife

A kitchen utensil that is used to remove the large vein

that runs down the length of a shrimp. A fork can be inserted in the back of the shrimp to pull out the vein or a deveining knife can be used to cut a slit down the length of the shrimp. This tool is inserted at one end of the shrimp and then pushed up through the entire body to remove the vein and the shell at the same time.

Figure 18. Devein Knife

Clam Knife

A kitchen utensil that is used to pry open the hard shell of a clam or an oyster in order to remove the meat. Typically, the knife will have a beveled edged blade that can be inserted into the tightly closed shell, twisting the blade to pry the shell apart. A round shield is built into the handle in order to keep the knife and hand from going into or through the sharp edged shell.

Figure 19. Clam Knife

Grapefruit Knife

Kitchen utensil that is made for ease of cutting the meat of the fruit away from the grapefruit skin when preparing a half grapefruit for serving. There are several varieties of this tool available, either single or double bladed, each containing at least one serrated blade. The dual bladed knives have serrated blades on each end of a handle placed in the center. The curved blade on one end is used for cutting the meat away from the outer skin.

Figure 20. Grapefruit Knife

The second blade may consist of two closely aligned parallel blades or one blade with a slit in the center, each used to cut between the lining that separates the inner meat into sections. The grapefruit knife effectively serves a good purpose of separating the meat sections of grapefruits better than the average kitchen knife.

Cheese Knife

A kitchen utensil that is thinly shaped to cut easily through soft or hard textured cheese. This knife may have a forked tip that is used as a lifter for pieces of cheese as they are cut. This knife may also be referred to as a forked-tip utility knife, which is used as a bar knife for cutting through citrus fruits or spearing garnishes for drinks as may be required for pickles, onions or maraschino cherries.

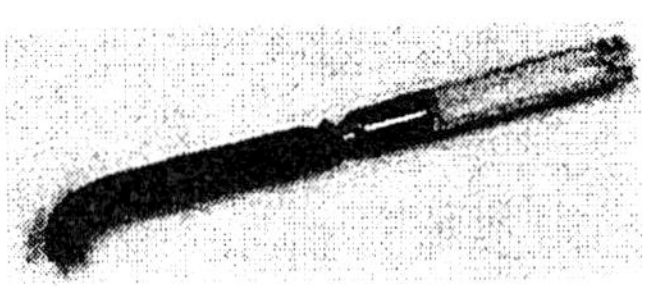

Figure 21. Cheese Knife

Chestnut Knife

A kitchen utensil that is used to score the chestnut prior to roasting. By carving a line, a cross or an "X" into the shell of the unroasted nut, it allows it to breathe during roasting and to resist exploding as the steam builds up. The chestnut knife is short shafted in order to keep the cut confined to the shell without going too deeply to pierce the inner skin.

When preparing, place the nuts in a shallow pan and roast at 425 degrees for .30 minutes or slightly less. Following roasting, the knife can then be used to open the shell to remove the meat. To remove the nut, make a single score/cut fully around the middle of the shell. The nut may stick to the skin, but should be adequately separated to remove the nut easily.

Figure 22. Chestnut Knife

Peeling Knife

Also known as Bird's Beak Knife. Considered to be a type of utility knife that is used for many of the same tasks as the traditional paring knife. The bird's beak knife, which is also known as a "tournée" knife, has a shorter 2 to 3 inch blade than a paring knife and is designed to curve upward on both the cutting edge and the top edge.

Figure 23. Peeling Knife or Bird's Beak Knife

It is a knife that is commonly used to make a type of cut referred to as the tournee cut in vegetables such as carrots, potatoes or squash that is accomplished for purposes of food presentation. This cut is also known as a tourne or tourné cut. Bird's beak knives may also be used to slice soft fruits such as nectarines, plums or peaches and for peeling skins or blemishes from a variety of fruits and vegetables. It is a knife that is also used for cutting decorative garnishes such as rosettes in radishes or fluted mushrooms.

Ceramic Knife

A knife with a blade made from zirconium oxide, also referred to as ceramic zirconia, a very durable and hard substance that is only slightly softer than the hardness of diamonds. With a blade harder than steel, knives made from industrial ceramic do not easily dull and will maintain an exceptionally sharp edge before being required to be sharpened.

Figure 24. Ceramic Knife

Industrial ceramic, which is made by heating the base materials to exceptionally high temperatures, results in a substance that has a high degree of purity, removing most of the impurities that make ceramic materials brittle. Ceramic knives are excellent for slicing through a variety of foods, making thin slices an easy task.

However, use on harder materials, such as bones and hard textured foods may result in chipped or broken blades, due to the hard and rigid blade materials that are not as flexible as more common metals. Also, if the blade hits or is dropped accidently on a hard tile floor, it may chip part of the blade but will not shatter it.

Factory repair of the blade is an option if the blade becomes damaged. Ceramic knives will not need sharpening as often as other metal knives, but will require that the person doing the sharpening be qualified to sharpen ceramic materials.

Slicer

A knife used to slice cooked meat. The blade is long, typically 8-12 inches, with a round or pointed tip. Depending on the manufacturer, the blade may be flexible or rigid. Some manufacturers refer to slicers under 9″ as carvers.

— To extend the lifetime of your knives, wash them by hand. Knives that are washed in the dishwasher are exposed to harsh detergents and scalding temperatures. Damage is likely to occur to the sharp edge of a knife if allowed to be thrashed around in a dishwasher.

— Wipe knives clean immediately after use to prevent the discoloration of the blade. This practice will also help to prevent foods from hardening onto the blade, allowing for ease of cleaning.

— If available, store knives in a wooden or polyethylene knife block. If one is not available, store knives in a sheath or, at a minimum, store the knives away from other utensils to prevent damage to the sharp edges.

— Use a wood or polyethylene cutting board. Wood and polyethylene cutting boards create less resistance to the knife edge than ceramic, metal, or plastic cutting boards.

10

FOOD PROCESSORS

Food processing is the methods and techniques used to transform raw ingredients into food for consumption by humans. Food processing takes clean, havested or slaughtered and butchered components and uses these to produce attractive and marketable food products. Similar process are used to produce animal feed.

A food processor is a kitchen appliance used to facilitate various repetitive tasks in the process of preparation of food. It helps to chop, slice, shred, grind, and puree almost any food quickly and easily. Some models can also assist the home cook in making citrus and vegetable juice, beating cake batter, kneading bread dough, beating egg whites, and grinding meats and vegetables. Today, the term almost always refers to an electric-motor-driven appliance, although there are some manual devices also referred to as "food processors".

Food processors are similar to blenders in many ways. The primary difference is that food processors use swappable blades and disks (attachments) instead of a fixed blade. Also, their bowls are wider and shorter, a more appropriate shape for the solid or semi-solid foods usually worked in a food processor.

Its functions normally consist of:

— Slicing/chopping vegetables
— Grinding items such as nuts, meat, or dried fruit
— Shredding or Grating cheese or vegetables
— Pureeing
— Mixing and kneading doughs

The food processor was introduced to the North American market in 1973 by engineer Carl Sontheimer, who had spent a year adapting a French industrial blender for the home cook. It took a few years for consumers to realise how useful the new appliance could be, but once they did, the food processor became a bestseller. Sontheimer's invention revolutionised food preparation in home kitchens around the world.

Figure 1. An electric food processor

Design and Operation

The base of the unit houses a motor which turns a vertical shaft. A bowl, usually made of transparent plastic, fits around the shaft. Cutting blades can be attached to the shaft; these fit so as to operate near the bottom of the bowl. Shredding or slicing disks can be attached instead; these spin near the top of the bowl. A lid with a "feed tube" is then fitted onto the bowl.

The feed tube allows ingredients to be added while chopping, grinding or pureeing. It also serves as a chute through which items are introduced to shredding or slicing disks. A "pusher" is provided, sized to slide through the feed tube, protecting fingers.

Almost all modern food processors have safety devices which prevent the motor from operating if the bowl isn't properly affixed to the base or if the lid isn't properly affixed to the bowl.

Basic Components of Food Processors

Modern food processors come in three basic sizes: full, compact, and mini. No matter what size they are, however, the basic components are the same: a motor, a bowl with a lid and feed tube, and a set of attachments.

The motor is housed in the base of the appliance, and it is the heaviest part of the device. Full-size machines generally have larger, more powerful motors, and can weigh more than 20 lbs (9 kg). This weight has a utilitarian value: The heaviness of the base gives the appliance stability and ensures that it doesn't move around while the motor is running. Though the first food processor bases were clad only in white, hard plastic, today they are available in a range of stylish colours and with metal and plastic finishes, ensuring that your appliance will fit in with your kitchen decor.

From the motor, a shaft extends upward to power the attachments. The bowl, which is usually made of durable, transparent plastic, fits onto this shaft and locks into position. The lid, usually made of the same material, locks onto the top of the bowl; in many older models, engaging the locking mechanism turns on the motor, but newer models generally have an on/off switch or button.

Figure 2. Parts of an electronic food processor

The lid has a feed tube fitted with a plunger. You can insert food into the device through this feed tube, pushing it down with the plunger. Some models have wider and narrower feed tubes for use with larger and smaller food items. The size of the bowl varies according to the size of the machine:

— Full-size bowls generally have a capacity of 9 to 13 cups.

— Compact-size bowls can accommodate 5 to 7 cups.

— Mini-size bowls can fit 2 to 5 cups.

Some models come with large and small bowls for use with the same base.

The attachments fit over the shaft inside the bowl. Standard attachments for a food processor are an S-shaped blade — also known as a sabatier blade — and shredding and slicing discs.

The sabatier blade sits at the bottom of the bowl. It consists of two small, curved blades arranged on opposite sides of a central plastic pillar that fits onto the shaft inside the bowl. The blades of the sabatier are usually made of metal, but are sometimes made of hard plastic. You may find that metal blades are preferable because they retain their sharpness longer.

The shredding and slicing discs are made of metal and sit at the top of the bowl, over the shaft. You push food down the feed tube and it contacts the disc, at which point it is grated or sliced into the bowl. The holes on the shredding and slicing discs may yield fine, medium, or coarse bits of food. You can purchase these different versions of the discs separately if they are not included with your food processor.

In addition to the standard attachments that came with your food processor, you can supplement your equipment and make your appliance more versatile by buying additional attachments.

Other common attachments include:

— *A dough blade* - This blade is made of plastic or metal and has straighter (less curved) paddles than the sabatier blade. You use this to make dough for bread and pizza.

— *An egg whip* - This attachment has two straight arms with large open paddles at the ends. You use this to beat egg whites and whipping cream, incorporating sufficient air to ensure a fluffy end product.

— *A julienne disc* - This piece has a row of protruding, short, sharp teeth. You use this to cut food into long, thin matchsticks.

— *A French fry disc* - This is similar to the julienne disc but yields larger, fatter pieces.

— *A citrus juicer* - This is a dome-shaped attachment that fits on top of the shaft and turns to squeeze the juice from oranges, grapefruits, lemons, limes, etc.

— *A non-citrus juicer* - This purees fruits and vegetables introduced into the feed tube, collecting the pulp in the middle and straining the juice into the bottom of the bowl.

You can also find a special container to hold all of the attachments in one place, and extra work bowls, which can be handy if you are making several things in the food processor and don't want to wash out the bowl between tasks. Also, some models have different-sized feed tubes and bowls that can be used with the same base. These can help you perform a range of tasks without having to buy two different appliances.

How to Choose a Food Processor

If you entertain often, a food processor can be a lifesaver. Even if you're just cooking for your family, it can save time and let you combine several functions in one appliance.

Steps

1. Analyse your need for a food processor. If you prepare food for large amounts of people and would regularly use the slicing, shredding, chopping and other functions of a food processor, you may be a candidate for buying one.
2. Consider the capacity you need. A 2- or 7-c. bowl is likely to be big enough unless you usually make large quantities of food.

3. Decide whether you need any extra slicing or shredding discs. Most food processors are sufficient without extras, but you may want to add discs now or later.
4. Check special features such as mini bowls, feed chutes, number of speeds, pulsing function and whether blades are reversible.
5. Look for a juicing function if you're interested in making fruit or vegetable juices.
6. Check that the parts are dishwasher-safe. This saves cleanup time.
7. Read warranties carefully, and check on service options and replaceable parts.

Tips

— Be realistic. If you aren't likely to drag out an appliance to grate cheese or shred carrots because it's easier to do it yourself manually, you probably don't need a food processor.

— The heavier the base of your food processor, the less likely it is to move around when it's being used.

— The larger the bowl of the food processor, the more it's likely to cost.

— Make sure you have storage space for a food processor. It can be bulky, especially if it comes with extra discs and bowls.

— The base of a food processor should never be put in a dishwasher or underwater.

How to Use Your Food Processor

The shredding disc quickly and efficiently grates common ingredients like cheese and carrots, and the slicing disc yields perfectly even slices of potatoes and apples in no time at all. You just push the food through the feed tube using the plunger.

Chopping, grinding and pureeing involve a little more technique. Let's illustrate this by learning how to make fresh salsa using your processor.

You know that fresh salsa contains vegetables such as tomatoes and hot chillies; it can also incorporate ingredients like scallions, garlic, and fresh coriander. You might be tempted to just throw all your ingredients into the food processor and turn it on, but you'll end up with something more like gazpacho soup than salsa.

It's better to work in stages, because the different ingredients in your salsa will have different textures: You want the chillies and garlic pureed so that their flavour is distributed evenly throughout; you want the scallions and coriander finely chopped but not pureed, so that small green pieces are visible; and you want your tomatoes in bite-sized chunks. To achieve this variation in size and texture, you're going to have to introduce the ingredients one or two at a time, processing them in turn.

Since the garlic and chilli need the most processing, let's start with them. Peel a clove of garlic, remove the stem from a hot chilli, and throw them in the bottom of your food processor bowl. Then turn it on. You'll see that the garlic and chilli quickly get chopped up, but if your bowl is large, you might find that they get thrown against the side, away from the blades. You will have to turn off the motor and scrape down the bowl, putting the food pieces nearer to the blades again.

You will also find that adding a bit of liquid (a tablespoon of fresh lime juice, water or olive oil would be perfect for your salsa) will help ensure that food thrown against the side of the bowl drips back down to the bottom rather quickly. You'll also find that using a pulse action -

- turning on the motor for one second, turning it off for one second, then turning it on again for one second -- gives the food time to drip down near the blades. Pulsing is one of the most important food-processor techniques; it allows you to keep an eye on the texture of your food to ensure that you don't over-process it.

After 10 to 15 one-second pulses, and several scrape-downs, your garlic and chilli should be pureed. Now let's add the scallion and coriander. Be sure that you wash all the vegetables well, and trim off the roots and ragged bits. Take the plunger out of the feed tube, throw in a scallion and a small handful of coriander, replace the plunger, and use five one-second pulses to chop up the greens, scraping down the sides of the bowl halfway through.

Now, the tomatoes. First, cut them in half lengthwise, then into quarters, and cut off the stem tip. Now feed the tomato chunks into the bowl through the feed tube (with the motor off), and process them with three or four one-second pulses. Voila! Easy salsa, beautifully prepared. Pour your masterpiece into a bowl, season with salt to taste, and grab some corn-chips!

Mixers

A mixer is a kitchen appliance intended for mixing, folding, beating, and whipping food ingredients. Mixers come in two major variations, hand mixers and stand mixers.

A hand mixer, as the name implies, is a hand-held device. It typically consists of a handle mounted over a large enclosure containing the motor, which drives two beaters. The beaters are immersed in the food to be mixed. Hand mixers are often battery-powered.

A stand mixer is essentially the same as a hand mixer, but is mounted on a stand which bears the weight of the device. Stand mixers are larger and have more powerful motors than their hand-held counterparts. They generally have a special bowl that is locked in place while the mixer is operating. Heavy duty commercial models can have bowl capacities in excess of 100 quarts (95 L), but more typical home and commercial models are equipped with bowls of around 4 quarts (4 L). A typical home stand mixer will include a wire whip for whipping creams and egg whites; a flat beater for mixing batters; and a dough hook for kneading. Mixers should not be confused with blenders. Blenders contain sharp blades and typically operate at higher speeds that chop, liquify, or otherwise break down larger food items. A mixer is a much slower device without blades.

Blenders

A blender is a kitchen appliance used to blend ingredients or puree food. The term typically refers to a stationary, upright electrical device, which is to be distinguished from a hand-powered or electric mixer that may be used for similar purposes.

Figure 3. An electric blender

A typical blender is built around a vessel for the ingredients to be blended. At the top of the vessel is a cap to prevent ingredients from escaping when the blender is switched on. At the bottom is a blade assembly, typically removable for cleaning purposes. The bottom seal is most likely watertight. The vessel rests upon a base containing a motor (for turning the blade assembly) with controls on its surface. Most modern blenders offer a number of possible speeds.

In 1922, Stephen Poplawski invented the blender. Stephen Poplawski was the first to put a spinning blade at the bottom of a container. He used his appliance to make soda fountain drinks. In 1935, Fred Osius improved on Poplawski's idea and invented the famous Waring Blender.

Espresso Machines

Espresso consumption has grown tremendously in the last decade or two. There are drive-through espresso shops in parking lots. Sometimes an espresso cart will just park on the sidewalk, like the hot-dog vendors in cities. People have been buying espresso machines for their homes, too. These machines are smaller than the commercial machines found in cafes, but they work on the same principles.

If you go to a cafe or espresso bar and ask for an espresso, what you will get is a shot-sized glass holding a small amount of very strong coffee. There are many different types of espresso drinks, including cappuccino, cafe latte and cafe mocha. All are made with one or more shots of espresso.

A shot of espresso is made by forcing about 1.5 ounces of hot water through tightly packed, finely ground espresso coffee. If everything goes well, what comes out is a dark brown, slightly thick liquid with a small amount of crema (a foam, sort of like the head on a beer) on top.

Figure 4. Espresso machines

There are many variables in the process of making a shot of espresso. The temperature of the water, the pressure of the water, the fineness of the ground coffee and how tightly the coffee is packed are just a few. The skilled espresso maker, or barista, controls all of these variables to produce a quality shot of espresso. Let's start with one of the most crucial variables: the coffee. Espresso coffee is a blend of several different types of coffee beans from different countries. The beans are roasted until they are dark and oily-looking.

A Simple Machine

To force the water through the coffee, the simplest espresso machines use pressure that comes from heating water inside a sealed vessel. These types of machines can be bought for around $50, and there's even one that is made especially to take on a camping trip. They all work on the same principle, so we'll take a look at one of the camping-style machines.

In this type of machine, the coffee is packed into a funnel-shaped piece of metal that has a tube extending to the bottom of the reservoir. A few ounces of water are put into the reservoir and the top is screwed on.

When the water is heated over a fire, pressure builds inside the vessel, and the only way for it to escape is up the tube, through the coffee and out of the tube in the top. Since the end of the tube is under water, the pressure forces the hot water up through the tube.

There are some disadvantages to a machine like this. The pressure in the system depends on the temperature of the water. The temperature required to build up enough pressure to force the water through the coffee might exceed the ideal brewing temperature.

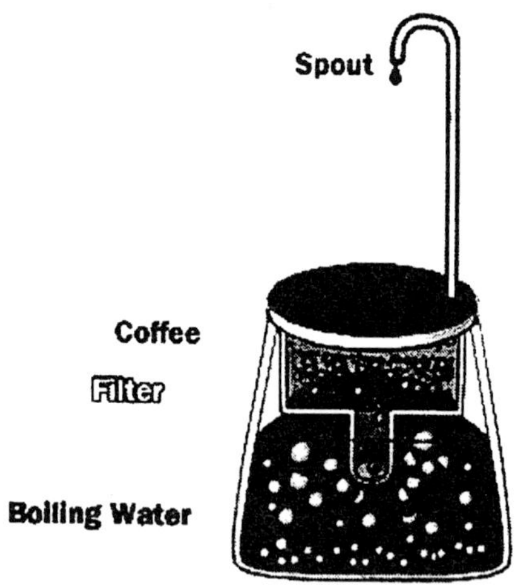

Figure 5. A Simple Espresso Machine

How Espresso Machine Works

Assuming that the machine already has water in it, you start by turning the machine on and waiting for the heater light to indicate that the heating vessel has heated the water to the ideal temperature.

Next, you put the ground espresso coffee into the basket and tamp it down.

You install the porta-filter by twisting it into the machine, and you place one small cup beneath each spout. You then turn the valve to the espresso position. This engages the micro-switch that starts the pump, which pressurises the heating chamber and hot water to about 15 atmospheres (220 psi) of pressure. This forces the hot water through the ground coffee and out of the spouts. Ideally, it should take about 25 seconds for about 1.5 ounces of espresso to come out.

When the espresso has filled the cups, you put the switch back into the middle position. Most likely, you'll want to steam and froth some milk next.

To steam some milk for, say, a cafe latte, you place a container with some cold milk under the steam wand so that the wand is submerged. Then, you turn the valve to the steam position. This energises the resistive heater, which quickly boils the water in the heating vessel and opens the valve, starting the flow of steam out of the nozzle. The pump runs intermittently to keep the heating vessel supplied with water. The steam quickly heats up the milk, and, if you hold the steam nozzle near the surface of the milk, can be used to make froth.

Coffee Makers

Most people who are dependent on caffeine have breakfast with an old friend — the coffee maker! Every morning you scoop in the coffee, add the water and turn it on, but have you ever wondered what is happening inside? How does the water get from the little compartment where you pour it in to the top of the coffee maker, and what is that gurgling sound?

A modern drip coffee maker is a surprisingly simple device. Manufacturers have had 25 years to hone their designs, so these coffee makers are pretty straightforward once you open them up.

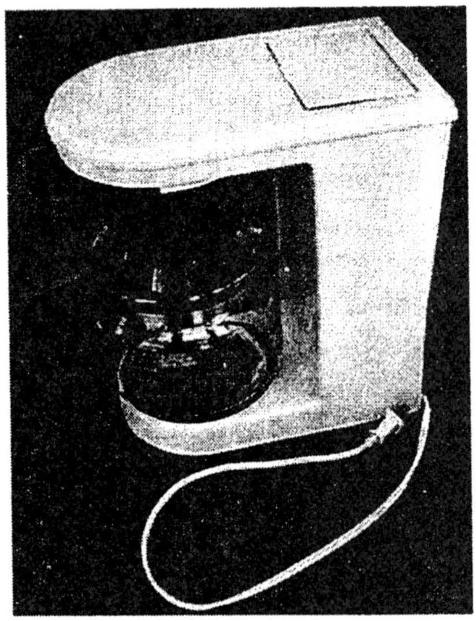

Figure 6. Coffee Maker

If you take off the top of the coffee maker, you find three things:

— There is a little bucket that holds the water when you pour it into the pot at the start of the coffee-making cycle (on the right in the picture above). There is a hole in the bottom of the bucket, and its role will become obvious in a moment.

— There is a black tube that carries the hot water to the drip area.

— There is the drip area (on the left-hand side of this picture). Water arrives here from the black hot-water tube and simply falls through the holes into the coffee grounds.

The heating element is an aluminum extrusion with two parts: a resistive heating element and a tube for water to flow through.

The resistive heating element is simply a coiled wire, very similar to the filament of a light bulb or the element in an electric toaster, that gets hot when you run electricity through it. In a resistive element like this, the coil is embedded in a plaster to make it more rugged. The heating element has two jobs:

— When you first put the water in the coffee maker, the heating element boils it.

— Once the coffee is made, the heating element keeps the coffee warm.

The heating element presses directly against the underside of the warming plate, and a white, heat-conductive grease makes sure that the heat transfers efficiently to the plate. This grease, by the way, is extremely messy. You find this grease in all sorts of devices, including stereo amplifiers, power supplies — pretty much anything that has to dissipate heat.

The coffee maker's switch turns power to the heating element on and off. To keep the heating element from overheating, there are three solid-state temperature sensors.

The device attached directly to the coil is the primary temperature sensor. When it detects the coil getting too hot, it cuts off the current. Then, when it cools down, it turns the coil back on. By cycling on and off like this, it keeps the coil at an even temperature. The other two devices appear to be thermal fuses. They simply cut power if they sense too high a temperature. They are there for safety reasons, in the event that the main sensor fails.

One part that is not visible in this coffee maker is a one-way valve. This valve is either in the hole in the bucket or in the aluminum heating pipe. If there were no one-way valve, then the boiling water would be just as likely to flow back into the bucket as to rise up the black tube. The one-way valve lets cold water into the aluminum tube, but forces the bubbles of boiling water to flow up the black tube. If you blow on the tube leading into this value, the valve should be open. If you inhale through the tube, the one-way valve should block any air.

Toasters

For lots of people, the toaster is a daily part of breakfast (and lunch and maybe even dinner). A toaster is a machine for toasting food such as sliced bread and bagels. Toasted bread is called toast. Other toastable products may be described as toaster pastry.

A typical toaster uses infrared radiation to heat a piece of bread. The heat is usually produced by conducting electricity through nichrome wires (Joule heating). The toasting process consists of reducing the bread's water content (originally ~35% of total weight), raising its temperature, and slightly charring and caramelising its surface. The caramelisation process is a chemical reaction in which the complex starch molecules break apart into simpler sugar molecules upon heating. That is why toast is usually sweeter than normal bread.

Figure 7. Toaster

Toaster ovens perform toasting functions of a pop-up toaster, however, the heating elements are positioned horizontally. A toaster oven usually has a glass door and a pull out tray upon which the object to be toasted is placed. Because of its design, a toaster oven can also perform some of the functions provided by a regular oven, but on a somewhat smaller scale. Toaster ovens are freestanding units, commonly placed on countertops or hung from cupboards (kitchen cabinets).

How Toaster Works

The basic idea behind any toaster is simple. A toaster uses infrared radiation to heat a piece of bread. When you put your bread in and see the coils glow red, the coils are producing infrared radiation. The radiation gently dries and chars the surface of the bread.

The most common way for a toaster to create the infrared radiation is to use nichrome wire wrapped back and forth across a mica sheet. Toaster heating element, nichrome wire on mica sheet. Nichrome wire is an alloy of nickel and chromium. It has two features that make it a good producer of heat:

— Nichrome wire has a fairly high electrical resistance compared to something like copper wire, so even a short length of it has enough resistance to get quite hot.

— The nichrome alloy does not oxidise when heated. Iron wire would rust very quickly at the temperatures seen in a toaster.

The very simplest toaster would have two mica sheets wrapped in nichrome wire, and they would be spaced to form a slot about an inch (2.5 cm) wide. The nichrome wires would connect directly to a plug. To make toast:

— You would drop a piece of bread into the slot.

— You would then plug in the toaster and watch the bread.

— When the bread became dark enough, you would unplug the toaster.

— Then you would tip the toaster upside down to get the toast out!

Most people don't have this sort of patience, nor do they like crumbs all over the counter. So a toaster normally has two other features:

— A spring-loaded tray pops the toast out. This keeps you from having to turn the toaster upside down.

— A timer turns the toaster off automatically and at the same time releases the tray so the toast pops up.

11

PRESSURE COOKERS

Pressure cooking is a method of cooking in a sealed vessel that does not permit air or liquids to escape below a preset pressure. Because water's boiling point increases as the pressure increases, the pressure built up inside the cooker allows the liquid in the pot to rise to a temperature higher than 100 °C (212 °F) before boiling. The higher temperature causes the food to cook faster. Cooking times can be reduced by a factor of three or four. For example, shredded cabbage is cooked in one minute, fresh green beans take about five, small to medium-sized potatoes (up to 200 g) may be ready in five minutes or so and a whole chicken takes no more than twenty-five minutes. It is often used to simulate the effects of long braising or simmering in shorter periods of time.

A safety valve releases steam when the pressure exceeds the safety limit for the cooker; usually the steam pressure lifts a weighted stopper allowing excess pressure to escape. There is usually a backup pressure release mechanism, in the form of a hole in the lid blocked by a plug of low melting-point alloy. If internal temperature (and hence pressure) gets too high, the metal plug will melt, resulting in a release of the pressure.

A pressure cooker is often used by mountain climbers to compensate for the low atmospheric pressure at a very high altitude. A larger scale version of a pressure cooker, used by laboratories and hospitals to sterilise biological waste materials, surgical instruments etc. is known as an autoclave.

Pressure cookers create healthier, tastier meals and yet have remained an enigma to American cuisine and cooks. Because food cooks faster at higher temperatures, this cooking utensil works its magic by creating the necessary pressure to increase the temperature without burning the food. For example, water boils under pressure when the temperature is 30-50° higher than normal. The food cooks thoroughly and evenly, the nutrients stay in the food, and you get risotto in 7 minutes, artichokes in 10 minutes, beef stew in 15 minutes, cheese cake in 30 minutes.

Food properly cooked in a pressure cooker is safer, because it is cooked at higher temperatures that do a better job of killing microorganisms.

Figure 1. Pressure Cooker

A few very important pointers when cooking under pressure:

— Only fill the cooker to the recommended fill line, usually no more than 3/4 full. This allows room for the pressure to build and for excess steam to escape.

— Cook only foods that do not froth, foam or sputter, to prevent blockage of any of the relief valves.

— As with all cooking utensils, cleanliness is next to godliness.

— Replace any worn parts over time, like gaskets.

An early pressure cooker, called a 'steam digester', was invented by Denis Papin, a French physicist, in 1679. It was a large cast iron vessel with a lid that locked. It successfully raised cooking temperatures by 15% over boiling, and accordingly, reduced cooking time. Unfortunately, it also reduced the life span of some of the cooks who got in the way of the steam and building temperatures and became as one with the incurring explosions.

One hundred and twenty years later, Napoleon Bonaparte offered twelve thousand francs to anyone who could find a way to preserve food for his hungry troops. In 1809, the prize went to Parisian Nicholas Appert who utilized an early version of the pressure cooker to vacuum seal foods in clean jars. This led to the eventual development of the canning industry. His nephew, Raymond Chevallier-Appert, improved upon the design by inventing and patenting a sterilizer that provided more consistent results.

Early pressure cookers were huge industrial-size canners. In 1905 they were known as "canner retorts," and were manufactured by National Presto, then called Northwestern Iron and Steel Works. Soon fifty-gallon capacity pressure vessels for industrial use were developed and subsequently, thirty-gallon canners for hotel use. Soon thereafter, the ten-gallon models, more suitable for home canning, were also developed. In 1915 the term "pressure cooker" first appeared in print and National Presto installed an aluminum foundry for the specific purpose of manufacturing large-size pressure canners for home use.

Lightweight aluminum was used in manufacturing the canners for home use to promote canning as a means of preserving food in the days before refrigeration. In 1917, the United States Department of Agriculture determined that pressure canning was the only safe method of preserving low-acid foods without risk of food poisoning. In 1938 at a New York City Trade Show, Alfred Vischler introduced his *Flex-Seal Speed Cooker,* the very first pressure cooker designed for home use. His creation was so successful that it wasn't long before other manufacturers in America and Europe were producing many brands of pressure cookers in order to keep up with their growing popularity.

As people migrated from the country and a farming life-style to the cities and suburban living they craved all the comfort foods that Mom used to make in the big pressure canner back home. Housewives wanted a smaller, more convenient size and so the new *pressure saucepan* was developed. Smaller than the big farm-sized canning kettles, the new cookers were perfect for smaller families and the modern kitchen of the time.

The production of pressure cookers by eleven major manufacturers was tightly regulated during World War II, as aluminum was needed for the war effort. Many cooks held onto their pre-war cookers and often several families shared a single cooker. In a time when fuel and food were carefully rationed and shortages were commonplace, the pressure cooker became a necessity rather than a convenience. In 1945, with the war ending, the pressure was on for more pressure cookers. Soon there were eighty-five manufacturers and because of the overwhelming competition, production methods favoured quantity and not quality. These inferior cookers flooded the market from the late 1940s through the 50s. Cooks suddenly found exploding bombs in their kitchens and word quickly spread about accidents, resulting in a decline in their use.

Marked with a bad reputation, pressure cooker usage seemed doomed, and coupled with newer, modern cooking methods such as the arrival of the microwave oven, the art of pressure cookery nearly disappeared in the United States.

While American cooks were storing their pressure cookers in basements and attics, Europeans were content with their old prewar cookers and never experienced the problems of their American counterparts. European and Asian manufacturers developed new valve systems, safety features and improved pressure release methods. Americans soon began to adapt the new designs, although the jiggle top still remains the standard. Millions of European and Asian cooks continue to rely heavily on pressure cookers. In countries where the cost of fuel, natural gas, propane and electricity is very high, they have become an economic necessity in every home. India, Japan, Spain, Switzerland and Germany manufacture several brands of pressure cookers that are exported daily to the United States.

New pressure cookers, with their multiple safety features and improved vent systems, are once more catching on in The United States. These vessels offer a choice of a quick-release option, taking even less time to finish that meal and without the need for the water to cool down. Busy cooks with hectic schedules, demanding jobs, an active family and little spare time are looking for fast, economical ways for preparing home-cooked, nutritious meals. Television ads market overpriced cookers with fancy new names, touting the "latest, greatest new invention" to cooks who would never have considered buying a pressure cooker. Wide spread advertising has brought with it a resurgence of interest in pressure cookery, and now this old fashioned cooking method is suddenly new again!

The moral of the story is a moot one indeed. If you get a used pressure cooker, it is crucial to make sure that the gaskets (rubber seals) are still in the top of the pressure cooker. You must also make sure that the steam vent works properly. If you opt to buy a new cooker, keep in mind that the 6-quart size is the standard for most recipes. Select a cooker with a detachable pressure regulator that can adjust the pressure to low, medium and high. The higher the pressure, the higher the internal temperature and the less cooking time required. The safety valve automatically vents steam. Choose a pot with heat resistant handles, a locking lid that is easy to manoeuvre and a heavy bottom of stainless steel construction so that the same pot can be used to do preparatory sauteing.

Operating a Home Pressure Cooker

Do not place plastic items in a pressure cooker unless you want to end up with a gooey glob. A home pressure cooker consists of the following parts.

— Pot

— A Lid that has lugs built into its edge so that it can be screwed onto the pot.

— A release stem or nozzle that points up vertically in the lid. Make sure that this is not dented or damaged.

— A weight that sits on the release nozzle that is fitted into the lid. Weights come in many different shapes, and some have multiple settings.

— A rubber gasket, which is usually fitted into the edge of the lid. Make sure that this gasket is not cracked. If so, you will need to get a new one from a kitchen supply store.

— An emergency release plug, which is also in the lid.

— An interior support rack.

Make sure that all of the parts are present and in good condition. All parts must be in good condition because once heated, the contents will be at high pressure. Before beginning, make sure that you have the right size pot (or correct size containers) so that everything will fit. Usually cookers of 8 quarts or larger accommodate bottles and multiple layers of things rather well.

— Add approximately 1 inch (2 cm) of water into the pot. Then place the supporting rack in.

— Next add/stack the items you wish to sterilise into the pot. If you must sterilise things that should be dry, you will have to improvise with higher supporting racks.

— Affix the top to the pot, but do NOT place the weight on the steam release stem.

— Turn on the heat to high. Soon the water at the bottom of the pot will begin boiling and the water vapor will displace the air inside the unit. You want to expell all the air, so wait until a good jet of stem is spewing from the nozzle before going to the next step.

— Place the weight on the nozzle such that it is on 15 (1 atm). These weights are especially sized such that when the steam pressure inside the device reaches 15 psi (1 atm), it will be able to barely lift the weight and steam will escape.

— Turn down the heat about halfway. You want the escaping steam to jiggle the weight so that about 10 hisses per minute are emitted. If you keep the heat too high, you will boil away all the water inside the pot and "burn" the pot. If no steam is escaping from under the weight, the pressure is too low, and sterilisation will not be occurring.

— When the timer "dings", turn off the heat, and allow the device to remain sitting there. As it sits, it cools and the pressure slowly drops over the next 15 to 30 minutes. Do NOT remove the weight! Doing so when there is pressure inside will form a hot guyser that will coat your ceiling with all sorts of gooey stuff. And you will probably have widespread burns on your body!

— When you think that the pressure might be back to that of room pressure (ambient pressure), use a fork or spoon and very slightly lift the weight a millimeter - no more!. If you hear hissing, lower the weight back into place, and wait longer. If no hissing, then you may lift the weight off and set it aside.

— Carefully unscrew the lid and lift it off such that when you first start lifting it make sure that the rear edge of the lid lifts off the pot first. This makes the steam escape away from you. Of course, you may prefer having a face that looks like a blistered freshly boiled lobster, and hair that is in total disarray.

— If you have items inside that must be removed immediately - such as flasks of agar solutions that are going to be used to pour petri plates, you will have to cope with that situation without scalding yourself. Oven mitts usually work well as they protect your knuckles. Otherwise, it would be wise for you just to let the whole works cool off.

— Once you have emptied the pot of your supplies, dump the residual water into a sink, and leave the pot inverted to drain and dry. Once all the parts are dry, put the rack and weight into the pot and set the top in place.

Common Mistakes in Pressure Cookery

Whether you're a beginner or an experienced pressure cooker user, incorrect timing is the most common mistake made in pressure cooking, with most foods being overcooked. All too often pressure cooker users fail to follow recipe directions, or use someone's "heirloom" recipe that started off with the wrong cooking time, or they don't even use a recipe and just take a wild guess at the cooking time. Another mistake is the false assumption many users have in thinking that they must submerge everything underwater and boil it in the pressure cooker. Users of the "jiggle top" style pressure cookers often make the mistake of cooking with too high a heat once the pressure cooker has come to pressure.

Overcooking

Always use a recipe, especially if you are a novice. Even experienced p-cooker users should refer to the Cooking Time Charts for best results. Overcooking not only produces mushy foods, but a loss of nutrition. All the good stuff you want your family to have is cooked away and you cheat them of the very things they need for growth and good health. Overcooking also wastes energy, which is money out of your pocket that you needlessly 'give' to the utility company, not just for longer cooking times but the additional energy needed to cool down a hot kitchen. Most importantly, overcooking wastes your own valuable time when you might be doing something other than cooking.

Many cooks rely on heirloom recipes handed down from their mother or grandmother, and all too often these recipes were "homemade" and never followed the correct cooking times in the first place. Take a look at the cooking times of your old favourites and compare them to the timing charts or the cooking times used in similar pressure cooking recipes of a more current date.

Many pressure cooker users have a tendency to throw everything in the cooker at one time, but most combination dishes cannot be cooked at the same time. When making beef stew for example, the beef takes 15 minutes to cook, but the vegetables need only 5 minutes. The correct method is to partially cook the meat for 10 minutes first, using the phased cooking method, Use the quick or cold water release to open the lid and then add the vegetables to the cooker. Return to pressure for the last 5 minutes needed to cook the vegetables and use the natural release method.

Always use a recipe with accurate cooking times. Don't guess on the time, while a couple of extra minutes added to a tough roast that cooks for 25 minutes will not change the results that much, even just a minute more than necessary for shorter cooking foods like vegetables can result in soft or mushy food, great for babies but not exactly what you want for supper.

If you are an experienced pressure cooker user and do not need to use a recipe, refer to the Timing Charts to double check the cooking times for the ingredients used. Become familiar with different cooking methods as well, read about Interrupted Cooking, and Tiered Cooking are methods used in pressure cooking to achieve the best results with combination dishes or foods with different cooking times.

It is important to use some kind of a timer that will alert you when to turn off the heat, use the timer on your stove, or one of those inexpensive bell timers so you won't forget. Try one of the new digital timers that you can wear around your neck, that way you can leave the kitchen and still be reminded.

Longer cooking times will affect the final result of the foods you cook by changing the taste, appearance and texture, producing an unsatisfactory and disappointing final dish. Meats especially, can become dried out from over cooking when using a pressure cooker. This true of standard p-cookers using 15psi, and even more so if you are using a non standard model using less than 15psi because it takes longer to finish cooking. This also applies to electrics that are notorious for cooking at temps that are too high, and when users of jiggle top pressure cookers let the pressure rise so that the regulator weight is spinning rapidly.

To avoid overcooking, test for doneness by using the interrupted cooking method near the end of the cooking time stated in the recipe. Use the quick (best method) or cold water (2nd best method) to release pressure. Then use a meat thermometer to check the temperature. For example; at 160°F (71°C), a roast will be cooked to medium. At this temperature, some of the tougher connective tissue breaks down to gelatin, which helps "lubricate" and tenderise the meat.

Overheating

Understand how your cooker works. Many pressure cooker owners cook with the heat too high. Foods may be scorched or burned. Overheating shortens the life of gaskets and rubber parts and you will have the added expense of replacing them more often. Overheating can cause heat tint on stainless steel, leaving a permanent, iridescent blue discoloration, and while this doesn't damage the cookware it is unsightly.

Overheating is a problem for novices as well as many longtime pressure cooker users who make the mistake of cooking with too high a heat after the pressure cooker comes to pressure. Overheating results in over-pressure, and that could trigger the safety release methods on your cooker.

A 2nd generation cooker has a pressure indicator to show when pressure is reached. Overheating and the resulting over pressure is almost impossible with the new 2nd generation cookers. High heat triggers the first stage safety release and alerts you to the problem so you can lower the heat. Overheating is a common error for users of the "jiggle top" style pressure cookers. Once pressure is up and you have correctly lowered the heat, the pressure regulator should rock only 3-5 times a minute . If your "jiggler" is constantly in motion, rocking franticly, it's trying to reduce that over pressure before the blow-out plug pops.

Incorrect Pressure Release Methods

Use the correct method of releasing pressure for best results. All pressure cooker recipes should state the best way for dropping the pressure for that particular dish. Understand the three methods of pressure release, and follow the directions for best results. Your cooker will remain hot for a long time, and foods will continue cooking inside the pot until the heat has diminished. While this is excellent for finishing large cuts of meat and soups for-example, delicate foods like fish or tender-crisp veggies will be overcooked and do best when the cold water release method is used to stop the cooking process immediately. This is one of the major drawbacks facing owners of electric pressure cooker who have no means of stopping the cooking any faster than the time it takes for the electric heating elements to cool.

Incorrect Cooking Method

Many people are surprised learn there are several different methods used in pressure cookery. Most users only learn one method and never fully utilise the full potential of their cooker. The pressure cooker cooks with steam heat where a small amount of water is used to generate steam which produced pressure to rapidly cook food, this is the method used most often in pressure cooker recipes. Some users mistakenly "boil" everything, drowning foods under water results loss of nutrients and vitamins, and lengthier the cooking times as well as increased fuel costs.

Using Incorrect Amount of Liquid

All pressure cookers must have a minimum amount of liquid to build pressure. Check your owner's manual to see the amount recommended by the manufacturer. In general, a jiggle top model requires 1 cup, and a spring valve model uses 1/2 cup. These amounts are sufficient for about the first 15 minutes of cooking time, beyond that the cooker will require more liquid. Use the Test Drive to determine how much water your cooker uses. Using more than the recommended amount will result in longer times for the cooker to come to pressure and destroys more nutrients and increases fuel costs.

It is not necessary to drown meats or vegetables in water or other liquids unless you are using the infusion cooking method. In pressure cookery, we generally want to use the active steam under pressure to cook foods because it preserves the most vitamins and nutrients. That's not only good nutrition, but it's also economical.

Improper Food Preparation

A pressure cooker is a wonderful appliance, and a great addition to any kitchen, but foods must be properly prepared for the best results. Most meats should be at least partially thawed and browned first. To have mixed foods finish cooking at the same time they must have the same cooking times. To cook mixed foods that have slightly different cooking times you can 'fudge' a little by varying the size of the pieces- larger pieces for the quicker cooking foods and smaller pieces for the foods needing a little longer cooking times. Use the Interrupted Cooking Method for foods that have very different cooking times.

Over-Filling the Pressure Cooker

The pressure cooker should only be filled 2/3 full for most cooking purposes. The remaining space is need to generate steam to build pressure. When cooking foods that they froth or foam, such as dried beans, fruits like apples or rhubarb, or pasta, only fill the pressure cooker half-full. Using 1 tbsp. of light cooking oil will help minimise foaming. When cooking liquids, such as stocks, broths, soups or beverages the cooker should only be half-full.

Some pressure cookers have a max fill mark etched on the inside of the pot and this is a great asset, but unfortunately most don't have this feature. You can determine the 2/3 fill of your cooker by filling it with water and then equally dividing that water into 3 containers. Now pour 2 of the containers back into the cooker and note the measurement of the water level inside your cooker using a ruler. Empty the water and dry the cooker. For a simple way to mark the maximum fill level use a Sharpie or other indelible marker. Make a small line on the inside of the cooker at the waterline measurement and your cooker will stay marked for a while before the line fades and needs to be redone.

12

Refrigerators

Refrigeration and freezing are probably the most popular forms of food preservation in use today. In the case of refrigeration, the idea is to slow bacterial action to a crawl so that it takes food much longer to spoil. In the case of freezing, the idea is to stop bacterial action altogether. Frozen bacteria are completely inactive.

Refrigeration and freezing are used on almost all foods: meats, fruits, vegetables, beverages, etc. In general, refrigeration has no effect on a food's taste or texture. Freezing has no effect on the taste or texture of most meats, has minimal effects on vegetables, but often completely changes fruits. Refrigeration's minimal effects account for its wide popularity.

The fundamental reason for having a refrigerator is to keep food cold. Cold temperatures help food stay fresh longer. The basic idea behind refrigeration is to slow down the activity of bacteria so that it takes longer for the bacteria to spoil the food. For example, bacteria will spoil milk in two or three hours if the milk is left out on the kitchen counter at room temperature. However, by reducing the temperature of the milk, it will stay fresh for a week or two — the cold temperature inside the refrigerator decreases the activity of the bacteria that much. By freezing the milk you can stop the bacteria altogether, and the milk can last for months. Refrigeration and freezing are two of the most common forms of food preservation used today.

There are many options to choose from when shopping for a new refrigerator. Choices include a variety of models and styles that have new convenience and energy-saving features. Before purchasing a refrigerator, it is a good idea to measure the space available for the new refrigerator as well as door and hallway clearances. These measurements can be compared to the refrigerator's outside dimensions to make sure it will fit into the kitchen. When deciding what size of refrigerator to purchase, a rule-of-thumb is a minimum of 12 cubic feet for the first two persons in the household, plus 2 more cubic feet for each additional person.

General Features of a Refrigerator

A refrigerator (often shortened to fridge) or freezer is an electrical appliance that uses refrigeration to help preserve food. A domestic refrigerator is present in 99.5% of American homes. It works using phase change heat pumps operating in a refrigeration cycle. An industrial refrigerator or industrial freezer is simply a refrigerator used in an industrial setting, usually in a restaurant or supermarket.

They may consist of either a cooling compartment only (a larger refrigerator) or a freezing compartment only (a freezer) or contain both. The dual compartment was introduced commercially by General Electric in 1939. Some refrigerators are now divided into four zones for the storage of different types of food:

— -18 °C (0 °F) (freezer)

— 0 °C (32 °F) (meats)

— 4 °C (40 °F) (refrigerator)

Some newer refrigerators may feature:

— An LCD suggesting what types of food should be stored at what temperatures and the expiration date of the food stored.

— Filter Status Indicator tells you when it's time for a change.

— An in-door ice caddie, which relocates the icemaker storage to the freezer door and saves approximately 2 cubic feet (60 L) of usable freezer space. It is also removable, and helps to prevent icemaker clogging. In-door ice caddies are exclusive to side-by-side refrigerators.

— A cooling zone in the refigerator door shelves. Air from the freezer section is diverted to the refrigerator door, helping to keep milk or juice in the door shelf colder.

— A power failure warning, alerting the user to the failure, usually by flashing the temperature display. The maximum temperature reached during the power failure may be displayed, along with information on whether the frozen food has defrosted or may contain harmful bacteria.

— Frost-free operation. Over time atmospheric water vapour condenses onto the cooling coils as ice, which can eventually build up into a layer several centimetres thick. This can be removed by emptying the refrigerator and turning it off so that the ice melts. In a refrigerator equipped for frost-free operation, a heater and a thermostat are fitted around the cooling coils. Every six hours (varies between 6 to 24 hours depending on model) the cooling is switched off and the heater turned on until the temperature around the coils slightly exceeds the freezing point of water when normal cooling is restored. This melts any ice which has collected around the coils and prevents it from building up.

An increasingly important environmental concern is the disposal of old refrigerators - initially because of the freon coolant damaging the ozone layer, but as the older generation of refrigerators disappears it is the destruction of CFC-bearing insulation which causes concern. Modern refrigerators usually use a refrigerant called HFC-134a (1,2,2,2-tetrafluoroethane) instead of freon, which has no ozone layer depleting properties.

Disposal of discarded refrigerators is very often strictly regulated by municipalities, by mandating the removal of doors, as many children playing hide-and-seek had been asphixyated while hiding inside a discarded refrigerator.

Parts of a Refrigerator

The basic idea behind a refrigerator is very simple: It uses the evaporation of a liquid to absorb heat. You probably know that when you put water on your skin it makes you feel cool. As the water evaporates, it absorbs heat, creating that cool feeling. Rubbing alcohol feels even cooler because it evaporates at a lower temperature. The liquid, or refrigerant, used in a refrigerator evaporates at an extremely low temperature, so it can create freezing temperatures inside the refrigerator. If you place your refrigerator's refrigerant on your skin, it will freeze your skin as it evaporates.

There are five basic parts to any refrigerator:

- Compressor
- Heat-exchanging pipes - serpentine or coiled set of pipes outside the unit
- Expansion valve
- Heat-exchanging pipes - serpentine or coiled set of pipes inside the unit

— Refrigerant - liquid that evaporates inside the refrigerator to create the cold temperatures

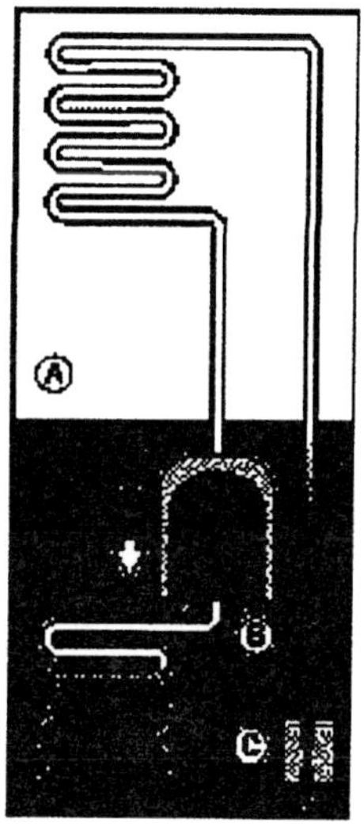

A. Inside the Refrigerator

B. Compressor

C. Expansion valve

Figure 1. Major parts of a refrigerator

Many industrial installations use pure ammonia as the refrigerant. Pure ammonia evaporates at -27 degrees Fahrenheit (-32 degrees Celsius).

The basic mechanism of a refrigerator works like this:

— The compressor compresses the refrigerant gas. This raises the refrigerant's pressure and temperature, so the heat-exchanging coils outside the refrigerator allow the refrigerant to dissipate the heat of pressurisation.

— As it cools, the refrigerant condenses into liquid form and flows through the expansion valve.

— When it flows through the expansion valve, the liquid refrigerant is allowed to move from a high-pressure zone to a low-pressure zone, so it expands and evaporates. In evaporating, it absorbs heat, making it cold.

— The coils inside the refrigerator allow the refrigerant to absorb heat, making the inside of the refrigerator cold. The cycle then repeats.

Types of Refrigerator

— Freestanding

— Counter/cabinet depth: a refrigerator can be approximately 30 inches deep as opposed to approximately 35 inches deep like a normal refrigerator. This allows the unit to be more flush with surrounding cabinets.

— Built under: fridges and freezers which can be installed under the counter top.

— Integrated.

— In-Column fridges or freezers: these are built into a tall cabinet in your kitchen furniture. The appliance is built in to your kitchen so that it looks like a normal cupboard. Getting the right size fridge is very important when choosing integrated.

Door Situation

— Eye level freezer refrigerator (or top mount).

— Bottom freezer refrigerator. The freezer is generally bigger and the refrigerator has two independent motor-compressors.

— French door (or trio). Similar to bottom freezer, but the refrigerator (top) section has two doors that swing outward like a kitchen pantry.

- Side-by-side. The unit is divided into two tall compartments, with the freezer on the left and the refrigerator on the right.
- Wide-by-side. Similar to side-by-side, but the refrigerator compartment is wider at eye level and becomes narrow at the bottom. Allows the convenience of a side-by-side, but able to fit wider items in the refrigerator.
- Single door. Originally, most units featured only one door, with the freezer compartment located within the larger refrigerator compartment.

New Models of Refrigerators

Side-by-side Refrigerators

The newest *side-by-side refrigerators* are the three-door models. Some have upper freezers that allow easy access to frequently used items with a minimal loss of cold air as well as lower freezers for long-term frozen food storage. For families that require a lot of refrigerator space, there are the separate refrigerator and freezer units designed to be used together. These units can be as large as 30 cubic feet each.

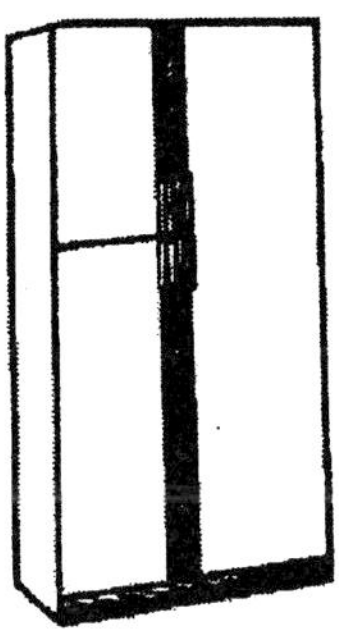

Figure 2. Side-by-side refrigerator

Built-in Refrigerators

Built-in refrigerators and freezers are made to be flush with surrounding cabinets. To create the built-in look, custom panels can be placed on doors to match cabinets. Unlike top-mounted refrigerator/freezer models, which are about 30 inches deep, built-ins are only 24 inches deep. Some of the built-in refrigerator/freezers are taller, as much as 19 inches higher than top-mounted refrigerator/freezers, and they are 5 inches wider.

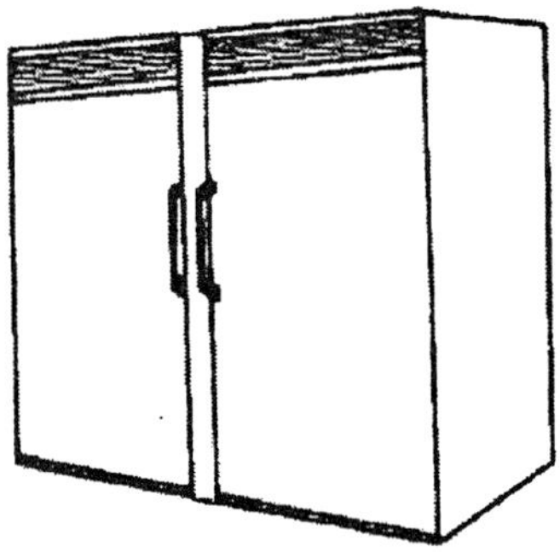

Figure 3. Separate Refrigerator and Freezer Units

Pull-down door or access door models

Pull-down door or access door models have small doors in the refrigerator that allow access to shelves inside the refrigerator. Frequently used items can be stored on those shelves and energy can be saved by opening only the small doors rather than the full refrigerator doors.

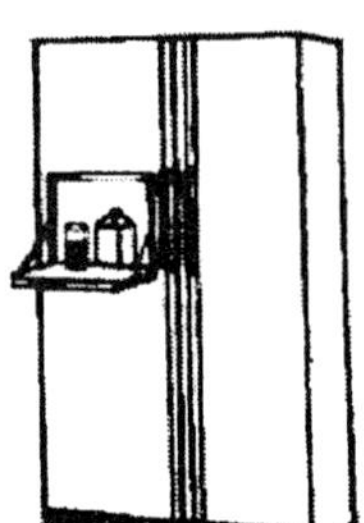

Figure 4. Pull-Down Door Refrigerator

Defrost systems

With manual-defrost systems, the removal of frost and condensation from both the fresh food and freezer compartments are entirely manual. In partial automatic or cycle defrost systems, only the fresh food compartment is defrosted automatically. The freezer compartment must be emptied and manually defrosted. In automatic or no-frost systems, frost is removed automatically in both the refrigerator and freezer compartments.

Efficiency of a Refrigerator

The efficiency of a refrigerator is an important consideration because it uses more energy than any other appliance in the kitchen. The total cost of a refrigerator is a combination of the purchase price and what it costs to operate and maintain over its lifetime. High-efficiency models may carry a higher price tag but they may pay for themselves with lower operating costs. Operating costs depend on the efficiency of the condenser and motor, the type and amount of insulation, additional design features, and the daily use of the refrigerator such as the number of door openings per month. Larger models and those with ice makers generally use more electricity. Models with automatic defrost systems use more electricity than those with partial or manual defrost. A manual defrost unit can use considerable energy if frost is allowed to build up over inch.

The bright-yellow energy guide labels displayed on the fronts of appliances in stores can be helpful when comparing energy costs of different refrigerators.

The label will give the certified cubic foot volume, average annual energy consumption in kilowatt hours, and average annual cost of operation in dollars and cents. The costs vary from model to model along with the capacities, freezer sizes, temperature settings, and type of defrost systems. Make sure to compare units of the same size and with the same features.

Gas Absorption refrigerator

The absorption refrigerator is a refrigerator that utilizes a heat source to provide the energy needed to drive the cooling system rather than being dependent on electricity to run a compressor. These refrigerators are popular where electricity is unreliable, costly, or unavailable.

In the developing world gas absorption refrigerators running on kerosene are very valuable where there is no reliable electricity supply. Besides the obvious advantages for food preservation, they supply safe storage of vaccines and drugs.

In the developed world, including the United States, absorption refrigerators are most often used for camping and in recreational vehicles, though some are used in remote areas or in off grid homes. The heat source that powers the refrigeration cycle is most often a propane burner, though other fuel gases such as butane and natural gas are sometimes used instead in areas where these are more readily available. Electricity can provide the heat for an absorption refrigerator and many camping versions can be switched to use it. In extremely remote areas, kerosene is used.

The cooling components of absorption refrigerators can be constructed without moving parts and with no reliance on electricity. However, most new units have thermostats, ignition systems, safety pilot controls, and lights that introduce some moving parts and reliance on a nominal amount of electricity — little enough to be supplied by a dry cell or battery. These refrigerators have the disadvantage of using a lethal gas, ammonia, although it is contained within a closed system; and if they are being run using an open flame then attention has to be paid to its safety and to maintaining the flame at an appropriate size.

The basic principle of how these refrigerators cool their interior is the same as in conventional compression refrigerators. Both use refrigerant liquids that boil at low temperatures to achieve cooling. A large amount of energy is needed to turn the liquid into gas, and this is absorbed from the surroundings, cooling them. The difference is in how the gas is turned back to liquid to use it again for more cooling. A conventional electric refrigerator uses a pump to compress the gas back to liquid, a gas absorption refrigerator uses another liquid to absorb the gas and then has extra stages to separate the pure refrigerant liquid out again for re-use, this extra part being where the heat source is involved.

Variations exist, but the usual pattern of gas absorption refrigerator uses ammonia as the refrigerant and water as the absorber, with hydrogen gas included to adjust the pressure in the system. The exact mixture and pressure has to be correct to give proper cooling at normal temperatures.

The cooling system consists of four main parts: the evaporator, absorber, generator and condenser. The evaporator is where chilling happens as the liquid ammonia evaporates, absorbing heat from its surroundings to enable the liquid to turn to gas. The ammonia gas passes on to the absorber, where it dissolves in water. The solution flows down to the generator where the external heat source is used to bubble the ammonia out again. This gas is purified by condensing out water vapour before rising to the main condenser. The condenser has big fins on the outside which let air cool it sufficiently for the ammonia to flow out of the bottom as a liquid again, down into the evaporator.

The hydrogen plays an interesting part in making this cycle work. Why does the ammonia which turned to liquid in the condenser then evaporate at essentially the same temperature and pressure in the evaporator? Because the evaporator also contains hydrogen gas, and the partial pressures exerted by the two gases mean that the ammonia liquid will evaporate. The hydrogen is present in the absorber too, but is not absorbed as it does not dissolve in the water. The ammonia, water and hydrogen system is closed. The water in the absorber is actually a weak solution of ammonia carried out of the generator when the ammonia bubbles out by a "bubble pump" like the pipe of a coffee percolator. There is no other pump in the system, liquids flowing back down under gravity and the gas pressure being the same throughout the system.

There are other gas absorption refrigerators which use only ammonia and water with a heat source applied intermittently, possibly just once a day. These have a pressure valve between the condenser and evaporator so that the generator and condenser are pressurised when the generator is heated. The liquid ammonia is forced slowly through the valve from the high pressure side into the evaporator where it evaporates in the lower pressure. The pressure differential will last for some time after the heat source is removed, so active cooling occurs for longer than the time the heat is applied. When the pressures have equalised, the ammonia solution from the absorber can flow back into the generator ready for the cycle to start again. Gas absorption cooling principles can be applied at other temperatures, notably for air-conditioning where water may be the refrigerant, evaporated at low pressure and absorbed into a salt solution.

Electric Coolers

You may have seen the new coolers that don't use ice, plugging into your car's cigarette lighter instead. These coolers rely on a process known as the Peltier effect, or thermoelectric effect, to produce cold temperatures electronically. You can create the Peltier effect with a battery, two pieces of copper wire and a piece of bismuth or iron wire. Just connect the copper wires to the two poles of the battery, and then connect the bismuth or iron wire between the two pieces of copper wire. The bismuth/iron and copper must touch — it is this junction that causes the Peltier effect.

The junction where current flows from copper to bismuth will get hot, and the junction where current flows from bismuth to copper the junction will get cold. The maximum temperature drop is about 40 F from the ambient temperature where the hot junction is located. To create a Peltier cooler, the hot junction is placed outside the refrigerator, and the cold junction is placed inside. Normally, you create a module containing many junctions to amplify the effect.

Cold Packs

Speaking of refrigeration and coldness, have you ever used one of those "instant cold packs" that looks like a plastic bag filled with liquid. You hit it, shake it up and it gets extremely cold. What's going on here? The liquid inside the cold pack is water. In the water is another plastic bag or tube containing ammonium-nitrate fertilizer. When you hit the cold pack, it breaks the tube so that the water mixes with the fertilizer. This mixture creates an endothermic reaction — it absorbs heat. The temperature of the solution falls to about 35 F for 10 to 15 minutes.

13

DISHWASHERS

The term dishwashing is used for cleaning, eating and cooking utensils, not just dishes. Dishes may be washed with a dishwashing machine or by hand. The right way to wash dishes by hand is typically a tradition passed directly from parent to child; the procedures used, like many cultural practices, are traditions that vary from country to country and within country, from family to family.

When dishwashing, a common kitchen sponge and nylon greenback scourer works well. This is really a matter of personal taste as is the choice of dishwashing detergent ("washing up liquid"). In some countries (such as the Netherlands) dishwashing is usually done with a brush instead of a sponge. Collect all of your cutlery into a pile. Remove food scraps and stack the plates and bowls neatly. Find all the coffee mugs, wine glasses, and what-have-you, and group them next to the sink. Arrange your dishes so that they are all in easy reach for when you are standing over the sink. Empty all glasses or other containers before filling the sink.

In some European countries the dishes are always washed in a separate tub placed inside the sink. This was a matter of hygiene, as the kitchen sink was the only sink available for all the household water. The clothes were washed in the sink; the water used to wash the floor went down the sink, and so it made sense to separate the dishwater from the sink. There were two other possible reasons. Kitchen sinks tended to be very large in a time when heating water was considered to be a major household expense — a tub used less water. Also kitchen sinks were usually made of hard ceramic; any contact between the sink and plates was liable to cause chips, but a tub could be made of more forgiving material. Using a separate washing-up bowl in the sink also provides a place (down the gap between bowl and sink) to dispose of unfinished drink, soaking-water, etc.

Washing up gloves may be worn when washing dishes. Also, modern devices which consist of a sponge mounted on a hollow plastic handle may also be used. The handle is filled with soap, which impregnates the sponge and is gradually released as the dishes are washed. This precludes the necessity of filling a sink or tub with soapy water, which eventually gets dirty.

There are two basic guiding principles in dishwashing. Principle one is "Clean Before Dirty" (CBD), and Principle two is "Small Before Large" (SBL). CBD means you wash the cleanest — e.g. the least dirty dishes — before the most dirty ones. For example: always do the glassware first while the water is clean. That way you will not get greasy smears on the glasses. Then move on to the plasticware, cups, bowls and plates, and finally the pots and pans. SBL is aimed at making stacking easier. Place all the small items underneath and the large items stacked on top. Place everything upside down to aid draining.

In cases where dishes are to be shared among many, such as restaurants, sanitising may be desirable. These are some steps to sanitise dishes.

— Scrape and rinse to remove visible food particles.

— Soak items briefly in soapy warm water, scrub, sponge.

— Rinse in clean water to remove soap.

— Rinse in dilute bleach solution (50-100 parts per million chlorine; about 2ml of 5% bleach per litre of water, approximately one capful bleach per gallon water).

— Allow to air dry.

Most institutions have a dishwashing machine which sanitises dishes by a final rinse in either very hot water or a chemical sanitising solution. Dishes are placed on large trays and fed onto rollers through the machine.

The use of bleach is critical to sanitation when large groups are involved. While toxic to the environment and not to be used more than necessary, it evaporates completely, is cheap, and kills almost everything. Cabinets, refrigerators, countertops and anything else touched by people in a large group setting should be periodically wiped or sprayed with a dilute bleach solution after being washed with soapy water and rinsed in clean water. Soap and water gets it clean, bleach solution sanitises it.

Hand Dishwashing

Hand dishwashing is probably subject to more variables than any other household clean-up job. In theory at least, any detergent or soap can be used for hand dishwashing, except an automatic dishwasher detergent. However, soap has become almost extinct as a dishwashing product and many laundry detergents are not very acceptable. Laundry detergents, may leave spots and streaks, the powders may not completely dissolve, or may discolour certain metals with soaking.

A light-duty liquid hand dishwashing detergent is the best choice. Regardless of brand, certain characteristics are important in a hand dishwashing liquid: lasting suds, effective cleaning performance, mildness to hands, safety for dishes and other washables, storage stability, pleasant fragrance and appearance, convenient packaging and dispensing. In formulating a product to meet these criteria, manufacturers, in general, use certain basic ingredients. Surfactants or surface active agents are the primary ingredients in a liquid hand dishwashing detergent. Often a combination of surfactants is used to produce good grease cutting capability and soil suspension, mildness in water of varying degrees of hardness, and a high, stable suds level. All surfactants in these detergents are biodegradable. Stability and Dispensing Aids are added to keep the product homogeneous under varying storage conditions, and to provide desirable dispensing characteristics.

Alcohols, hydrotropes, and salts are often used. Fragrance and Colour Additives are what give a product its "personality," and are important, though present in extremely small amounts. Mildness Additives may include moisturising agents, certain oils and emollients, certain protein compounds, or other neutralising or beneficial ingredients. Preservatives are added, if needed, in small quantities to help prevent any microbiological growth in the product which could cause colour or odour change, poor performance and separation of the ingredients.

Antibacterial Agents are sometimes added to provide antibacterial protection for the hands. Hand dishwashing liquids are relatively easy for consumers to compare. Users can experiment by trying various brands and deciding which product features are important to them: performance, price, sudsing, fragrance and "feel," or perhaps the packaging. Usage is often based on the amount it takes to produce a rich, thick layer of suds.

Though detergents are not as affected by water hardness as soap is, some additional product may be necessary in very hard water. An important difference in the quantity of liquid hand dishwashing detergent required is the concentration of the surfactants vs. water in a product. More concentrated products are more efficient and may be more economical to use than the more dilute ones. Grease removal is more effective in warm water than in cold water.

Mechanical Dishwasher

The term dishwasher can represent either a person who washes (cleans) dishes (a term commonly used in the food service industry) or a machine that performs a similar function. A dishwasher is a mechanical device for cleaning food utensils for preparation, keeping, serving and eating and drinking. They are found in restaurants and also in many kitchens of homes.

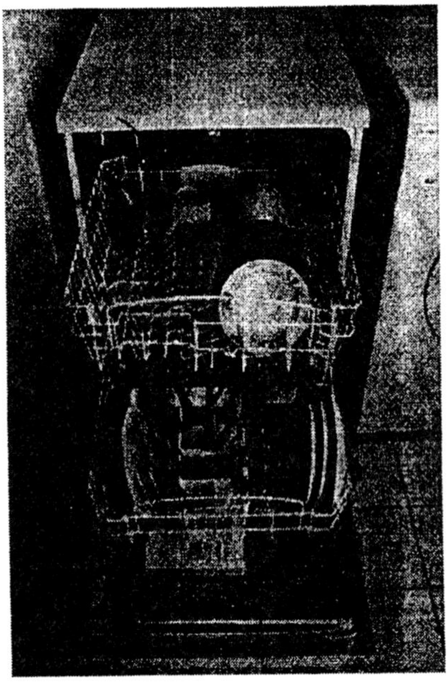

Figure 1. Mechanical dishwashing device

Unlike manual dishwashing, which relies largely on mechanical action to remove soiling, mechanical dishwashers use the circulation of quite hot (55-65 degrees Celsius or 130-150 degrees Fahrenheit) water (usually, but not always heated or brought up to temperature by an element) and very strong detergents (most far too alkaline for habitual exposure to the skin) to achieve its cleaning effect. The dishwasher therefore is mainly a device for spraying water on the dishes - first detergent-added water for cleaning purposes, then clean water (though sometimes with a rinsing aid added) to remove the detergent residue. Some dishwashers also contain a heating element to achieve fast drying of the dishes. The first reports of a mechanical dishwashing device are of an 1850 patent by Joel Houghton of a hand-powered device.

Modern dishwashers are descended from the 1886 invention of Josephine Cochrane, also hand-powered, which she unveiled at the 1893 Chicago World's Fair. Cochrane was quite wealthy and was the granddaughter of John Fitch, the inventor of the steam boat. She never washed dishes herself and only invented the dishwasher as her servants were chipping her fine china.

Models installed with permanent plumbing arrived in 1920s, and electric drying elements were added in 1940. Adoption was greatest at first in commercial environments, but by the 1970s dishwashers had become commonplace in domestic situations. In today's kitchens, an automatic dishwasher is no longer a luxury. Automatic dishwashers use less water and sanitise dishes far better than hand washing.

New Models

The built-in models are designed to fit into a 24-inch-wide space between cabinets and underneath the countertop. A few small-capacity models fit into an 18-inch space.

Built-ins can be finished or panelled to match kitchen cabinets. The convertible-portable models are essentially the same size as built-ins but have finished sides and tops, drain and fill hoses with a faucet connector, and casters for easy rolling to the sink. They are designed for families who move often or cannot remodel to include a built-in dishwasher. An advantage of the convertible-portable dishwashers is that they can be installed later as built-ins if desired.

The under-sink model is designed to save space in smaller kitchens. It fits under a specially designed sink or under a special double sink with a disposer under the second bowl.

Figure 2. Under-sink dishwasher

Electronic Touch Controls

A new feature found in dishwashers is electronic touch controls. Touch controls offer options previously unavailable, such as delay-start and diagnostic features. The delay-start option allows the dishwashing cycle to begin anywhere from 10 minutes to 9 hours after programming. With this feature owners can take advantage of offpeak electric rates, run the dishwasher when there isn't a high demand for hot water or simply when it is most convenient. The diagnostic feature allows a service technician to instantly check various functions of the dishwasher's operation.

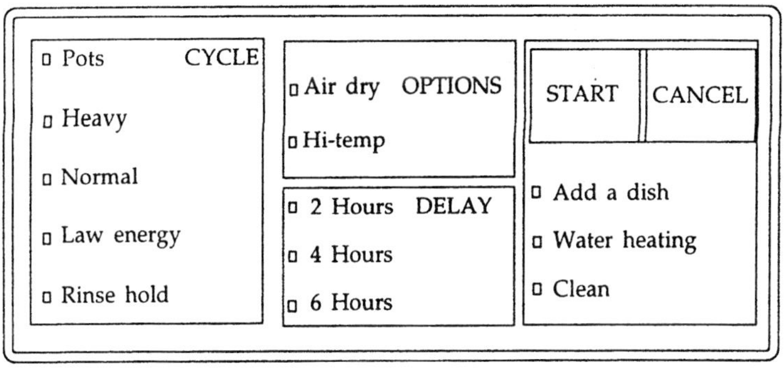

Figure 3. Electronic Touch Controls

Washing Options

Washing options may include a low-energy option for moderate to lightly soiled loads, a regular wash for normal loads, a rinse-and-hold wash option, a china-crystal option, and a pots-and-pans option. The rinse-and-hold option rinses the dishes off after each partial loading and then holds until a full load is collected. The china-crystal option is usually shorter than the regular wash and may have reduced spray force. The pots-and-pans option is for heavily-soiled dishes, pots, pans, and utensils.

Cycle times and water consumption vary considerably among different makes and models of dishwashers. Cycle times and water consumption can be checked by asking to see a machine's specification sheet, the instruction manual, or the model's use-and-care booklet. A normal or heavy duty cycle, including drying, can run anywhere from an hour to an hour and a-half. Short cycles vary from 35 minutes to more than an hour. Water consumption varies as well. For some machines, the water usage is from

8 to 14 gallons depending on the cycle, on others from 6 to 11 gallons.

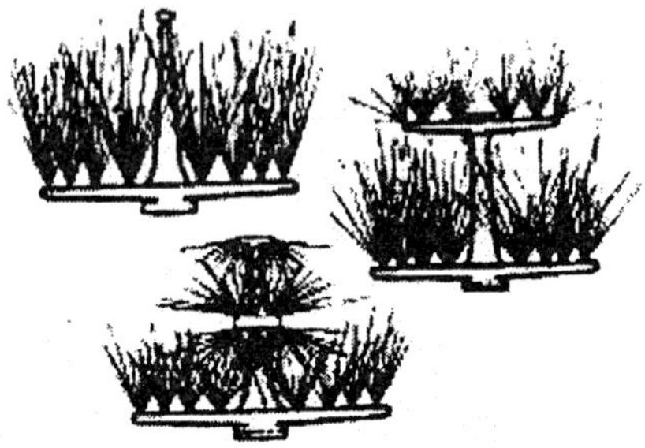

Figure 4. Water spray actions in three dishwashers

To improve washing action and reduce hot-water usage, spray arms and nozzles have been added in a variety of locations. More water sources mean better water distribution. The sizes and number of holes in spray arms are a good indication of a dishwasher's cleaning efficiency. Small holes create more vigorous washing action to remove stubborn food deposits. Holes that are closer to the size of a toothpick rather than the size of a pencil will produce better washing action.

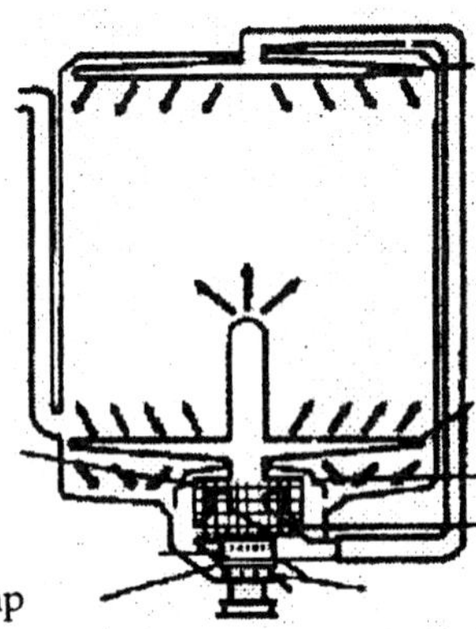

Figure 5. Dishwasher filtering system

A good water filtering system will trap the smallest food particles and prevents them from recirculating with the water and redepositing on dishes. Self-cleaning filters eliminate the need to remove the filter from the dishwasher for cleaning. Three different filtering systems used in dishwashers are the strainer, flusher, and small disposal systems. The strainer system works by collecting food particles so they are not redeposited onto the dishes. The flusher system works by flushing water and food particles down the drain. The disposal system is designed to collect food particles, grind them up, then flush them down the drain.

Water Heating Options

A water temperature booster checks the temperature of the incoming water and heats the water to the desired temperature. If the water is not hot enough it is heated automatically to provide good washing results. A temperature of 140 degrees F is needed to dissolve dishwashing detergents and to provide effective cleaning. The water temperature booster feature is especially important if a household often runs out of hot water or if the water heater is set at a low temperature to save energy. A sanitary cycle has a built-in heating element that maintains or increases the temperature of the water used in washing, during the last rinse, or both. In addition, the drying temperature may be increased. In some models, the rinse or drying temperature reaches 180 degrees F, which is recommended for sanitising by the U. S. Public Health Service. The sanitary cycle can be effective in reducing or preventing illness in the home because high temperatures kill disease-carrying organisms.

Drying Options

After the final rinse, the dishes are dried by either radiant heat or forced air. With the forced-air system, heated air is circulated through the dishwasher by a fan. With the radiantconvection system, a heating element is used to dry dishes. To conserve electricity, the consumer should select a dishwasher with an "Energy Saver" setting that allows dishes to air dry without the use of the heating element.

Racking Capacity

Most new dishwashers have more racking capacity. The purpose of racking is to separate dishes and hold them securely so they receive the maximum exposure to water action. Load the dishwasher according to instructions. Not all dishwashers should be loaded the same.

Adjustable upper racks can be raised or lowered on one or both sides to accommodate tall items above or bulky items below. There are also flip-down racks that provide an extra level for cups and oblong items. They fold back, out of the way, to make room for larger items.

Some dishwashers have racks with high sides to stabilise dinner plates and other large items. Shoppers with unusual-sized dishes will find it helpful to shop with "plate in hand." Some models have a silverware basket that slides into the door. This allows for more interior loading space.

Additional Features

Built-in dishwashers often come with colour panels that permit changing the colour of the dishwasher for decorating flexibility. Dishwashers also come with different types of tubs and door liners. Tubs and door liners are generally made of porcelain enamel, stainless steel, or molded plastic. Stainless steel is the most expensive of the three, followed by porcelain enamel and molded plastic. The hot, alkaline dish washing solution necessitates a tough tub lining in dishwashers. Purchase a finish that resists chipping, cracking, or peeling.

Energy Efficiency of Dishwashers

New dishwashers are 54 percent more energy-efficient than the older models. Energy savings are achieved because cycles use less hot water, less energy, and require less time to complete the washing action.

The consumer needs to carefully compare the energy-cost estimates on dishwashers energy guide labels. Energy guide labels will provide the approximate annual operating cost based on the number of loads washed per week and the local utility rates for gas and electricity for heating water. These figures are based on specific-use cycles established as a standard test for all dishwashers. Check the actual capacity and features, as these vary from model to model. The more energy-efficient models have higher price tags, but the money saved on the electric bill may make it economical as a long-range investment.

Characterisation

Capacity

The capacity of a dishwasher according to international standards is measured in standard place settings. Dishes or plates of irregular sizes may not fit properly in a dishwasher's cleaning compartment, so it is advisable to check for compatability before buying a dishwasher.

Size

Dishwashers that are installed into standard kitchen cabinets have a standard width and depth of 60 cm (Europe) or 24 inches (US), and most dishwashers must be installed into a hole a mininum of 86 cm (Europe) or 34 inches (US) tall. Portable dishwashers exist in 45 and 60 cm (Europe) 18 and 24 inch (US) widths, with castors and attached countertops. Dishwashers may come in standard or tall tub designs; standard tub dishwashers have a service kickplate beneath the dishwasher door that allows for simpler maintenance and installation, but tall tub dishwashers have approximately 20% more capacity and better sound dampening from having a continuous front door.

Features

The inside of a dishwasher, called the tub, can be composed of plastic or stainless steel. Stainless steel tubs resist hard water, provide better sound dampening, and preserve heat to dry dishes faster. They also come at a price premium.

Mid-to-higher end North American dishwashers often come with hard food disposal units, which behave like miniature garbage (waste) disposal units that eliminate large pieces of food waste from the wash water. One manufacturer that is known for omitting hard food disposals is Bosch, a German brand; however, Bosch does so in order to reduce noise. Pre-rinsing is not necessary even without integrated waste disposal units - all that is required is for the larger items of food waste to be removed before placing in the dishwasher. Pre-rinsing under a running tap beforehand simply wastes water.

Many newer dishwashers feature microprocessor-controlled, sensor-assisted wash cycles that adjust the wash duration to the quantity of dirty dishes or the amount of dirt in the rinse water. This can save water and energy if the user runs a partial load. In such dishwashers the electromechanical rotary switch often used to control the washing cycle is replaced by a microprocessor but most sensors and valves are still required to be present. However, pressure switches are not required in most microprocessor controlled dishwashers as they use the motor and sometimes a rotational position sensor to sense the resistance of water, when it senses there is no cavitation it knows it has the optimal amount of water.

Sound dampening

Using blankets, panels, and sound-absorbing materials in various configurations, dishwashers can achieve sound dampening levels down to 44 decibels or so. Undampened, low-end dishwashers generally output noise levels of anywhere from 65-70 decibels. Manufacturers generally use their own nomenclature with sound dampening, i.e. QuietGuard (Kenmore), QuietPartner (Whirlpool), Whisper Package (Maytag), followed by a number. Higher numbers usually indicate higher sound dampening and thus less noise output. Thus, a QuietPartner 1 or QuietGuard 2 dishwasher, despite the "Quiet" designation, may not actually be quiet at all. Sound dampening is the primary factor that determines the cost of a standard built-in dishwasher.

Hazing of Glassware

Glassware that is washed by dishwashing machines often develops a white haze on the surface over time. This may be caused by any or all of the below processes, only one of which is reversible:

— *Limescale deposit*: If the dishwasher has run out of the salt that recharges the ion exchange resin that softens the water, and the water supply is 'hard', limescale deposits can appear on all items, but are especially visible on glassware. It can be removed by cleaning with vinegar or lemon juice, or a proprietary limescale removal agent. The dishwasher should either be recharged with salt, adjusted appropriately for the hardness of the supply water - or possibly this is a symptom of failure of the ion exchange resin in the water softener (which is one of the more expensive components). The resin may have stopped working because it has be poisoned by iron or manganese salts in the supply water.

— *Silicate filming/etching/accelerated crack corrosion:* This film starts as an iridescence or 'oil-film' effect on glassware, and progresses into a 'milky' or 'cloudy' appearance that cannot be polished off or removed like limescale. It is formed because the detergent is strongly alkaline and glass dissolves slowly in alkaline aqueous solution. It becomes more soluble in the presence of silicates in the water. In certain cases, the etching will primarily be seen in areas that have microscopic surface cracks as a result of the items' manufacturing.

— *Physical abrasion*: Glassware placed such that it is physically touching can abrade and produce a milky surface.

Lead crystal should not be cleaned in a dishwasher as the corrosive effect of dishwasher detergent is high on such types of glass - that is, it will quickly go 'cloudy'. In addition, the lead in the crystal glass can be converted into a soluble form, which is not good for the health of subsequent users.

Level of Sterilisation

Domestic dishwashers do not sterilise the utensils, as proper sterilisation requires autoclaving at 121°C with pressurised wet steam for at least 15 minutes. Dishwashers do not do this. Commercial dishwashers can use one of two types of sanitisation methods. One is to use hot water sanitising, using final rinse water at a temperature of at least 83°C. The other method is a chemical sanitisation method, that many commercial low temperature machines use, using chlorine injected in the final rinse water.

Commercial Dishwashers

Much larger heavy-duty dishwashers with a high output are available for use in catering and commerical establishments where a large number of dishes are to be washed and sanitised. Commercial machines are capable of washing a rack of dishes in just a few minutes or less using a wash water temp of usually 120-140 degrees for a low temperature sanitising machine or 150 minimum wash temp for a hot water sanitising machine. Hot water sanitising requires a rinse temperature of at least 180 degrees. There are many types of commercial dishwashers including undercounter, single tank, conveyor, Flight type, and carousel machines.

How a Dishwasher Works

An automatic dishwasher produces clean dishes, keeps the kitchen free of clutter before and after meals, generally uses less water than hand dishwashing, reduces breakage, helps control germs and frees time for other activities. Automatic dishwashers vary from brand to brand, model to model, but all clean by the action of hot detergent solution that is circulated by spray arms and towers. Water temperature, detergent concentration, and proper loading of the racks are all important to good results.

For the best cleaning results, be sure water temperature in the dishwasher is hot. Most new dishwashers heat the water right in the tub to compensate for low temperature hot water supplies. If the dishwasher does not have a heat booster, run the hot water at the kitchen sink for a few minutes to clear the line of cool water before turning on the dishwasher.

Prerinsing dishes and glassware should not be necessary. An automatic dishwasher detergent and a properly installed and operating dishwasher of reasonably current vintage will do a thorough job with just a scraping off of large food particles. If dishes are loaded into the dishwasher and washed later, the "rinse-hold" cycle can be used; but experience may show that even this is not necessary. Extra heavily soiled cookware may need a rinse, soak or a prewash.

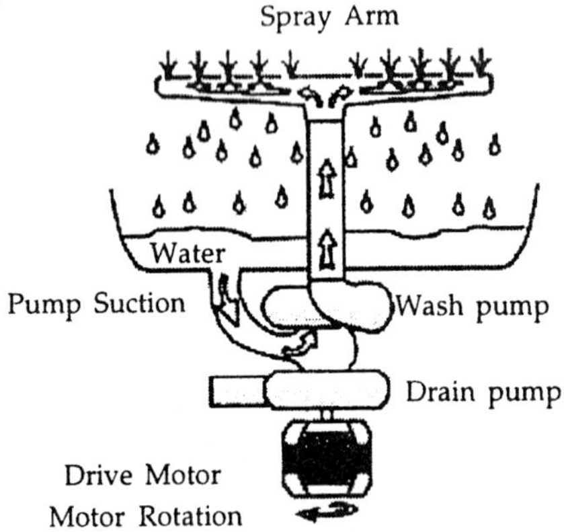

Figure 6. Dishwasher in wash mode

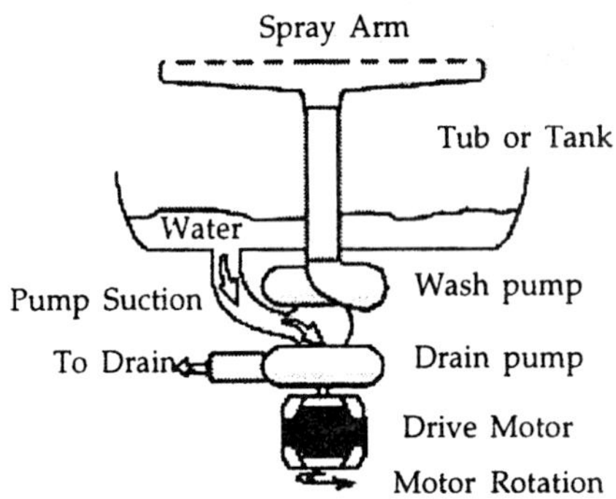

Figure 7. Dishwasher in drain mode

Put simply, the dishwasher takes in cold water and heats it to a temperature far higher than possible for hand washing - usually above 130°F. The dishwasher does not use a great deal of water, as it does not actually fill up. The water enters through a resin-based water softener, usually in the base of the machine. The water softener uses granular salt to maintain its efficiency and will require topping up regularly. Pumps force the water at high temperature into rotating arms containing spray jets. It is the force of the water that rotates the arms and enables the water and detergent to reach all parts of the load. After the programmed cycle of washing and rinsing is complete, heating elements dry the dishes, or they are left to drain dry, dependent on the programme you've chosen.

Loading

Scrape off as much surface food as possible and place larger and dirtier items on the bottom rack with cups, glasses and less soiled items on the top rack. Load plates and glasses so they aren't touching and put cutlery in the special basket, handles facing downwards. These items can be washed in a dishwasher, with the following guidelines:

— *Glassware*: Any ordinary glassware and ovenware such as Pyrex. Do not wash lead crystal glasses unless they carry a "dishwasher safe" label.

— *Tableware*: Most everyday crockery is safe. Bone china usually has under-glaze decoration and should be safe. Avoid antique or hand-painted and over-glaze decorated items. If in doubt, check with the manufacturer.

— *Cutlery*: Stainless steel and silver cutlery are normally suitable for machine washing, but it pays to rinse off any acidic food before loading to prevent any corrosion and, if possible remove the cutlery immediately after the cycle, to avoid prolonged exposure in a humid atmosphere. Do not mix steel and silver cutlery in the same basket and wash bone or wooden-handled items by hand.

— *Plastics*: Check whether they are dishwasher safe and do not place in the lower rack, where the heating element may affect the plastic during drying.

— *Pans*: Stainless steel is ideal for dishwashers. Aluminium can be washed in the machine, but may discolour during the rinsing.

Use of Water Softner

If the water is soft, the detergent will work more effectively and there will be less streaking on dishes. Hard water can also block the washer jets with lime scale and cause deposits on heating elements, which will reduce the cleaning efficiency, increase electricity costs and shorten the life of the machine. All dishwasher manufacturers and detergent suppliers want you to get the best results from the machine - and soft water is one of the most important factors in achieving this. The way to ensure water remains soft is to regularly top up the reservoir with granular salt.

Three in one salt tablets do not activate the water softener. For optimum results, the reservoir should be topped up with granular salt. Three-in-one and 'salt action' tablets do not top up the reservoir and should be used in conjunction with granular salt for optimum results.

Using granular salt will mean that you won't need to use as much detergent and rinse-aid - saving you money!

Your machine may have a float indicator or a warning light to tell you when salt needs adding to the water softener. Often float indicators are difficult to see, and there is no accurate guide as to how much salt you need to add. Quite simply, just add granular salt to the reservoir until it won't take any more!

The softener will use the salt to replenish itself each time you wash. As an approximate guide, you should do a full top up about once a month. If your machine doesn't have a warning light, a good way to remember to check and / or top up is to do it on a regular day of the month.

Granular salt is the only type of salt that should be used to regenerate the softener. Be aware that some varieties of 'dishwasher salt' use Dead Sea salt. This variety may contain minute insoluble organic matter that may adversely affect the resin within your softener over time. If you are in doubt about the origins of the salt, ask the retailer or manufacturer.

Cloudy Glassware

You can determine the cause of cloudy glassware by soaking a glass in vinegar for 5 minutes. If the cloudiness is removed it is due to hard water deposits; make sure the salt reservoir is topped up. Do not worry about over-filling it.

If the cloudiness is not removed, it is a permanent condition known as etching. In this situation, use less detergent and stop pre-washing. Dishwashing detergent needs a bit of soil to work on, otherwise it will tend to foam up.

Adding Detergent

Use only a product made specifically for automatic dishwashers. Any other type will cause oversudsing and possible damage to the dishwasher. Use the amount recommended on the detergent container and in the user's manual, adjusting it to the amount of soil, water hardness and load size. Some detergent dispensers have lines to indicate the amount of detergent to add.

In hard water, it is particularly important to use detergent as recommended by the dishwasher manufacturer. In general, the harder the water, the more detergent is required. In soft water, less detergent can be used. Add the detergent to the dispenser cup(s) after the dishwasher is loaded and is ready to be operated. Be sure the dispenser is dry and clean before adding detergent to maintain optimum performance. This also helps prevent powder detergents from becoming caked in the dispenser. Also, be sure to close the dispenser cup lid. Don't sprinkle or pour detergent on flatware or other metals; spotting and pitting may occur.

Dishwashing detergent contains:

— *Phosphates*: Solublises calcium and magnesium ions to prevent 'hard-water' type limescale deposits.

— *Oxygen-based bleaching agents*: Breaks up and bleaches organic deposits.

— *Non-ionic surfactants*: Lowers the surface tension of the water, emulsifies oil, lipid and fat food deposits, prevents droplet spotting on drying.

— *Enzymes*: Breaks up and solublises protein-based food deposits, and possibly oil, lipid and fat deposits.

— *Anti-corrosion agents*: Often sodium silicate, prevents corrosion of dishwasher components.

It may also contain:

— *Anti-foaming agents*: Used as foam decreases the effectiveness of the washing action.

— Additives to slow down the removal of glaze & patterns from glazed ceramics

— Perfumes

— Anti-caking agents (in granular detergent)

— Starches (in tablet based detergents)

— Gelling agents (in liquid/gel based detergents)

All modern dishwasher detergents are formulated to work specifically in dishwashers. On no occasion should ordinary washing up liquid be used, as it will cause excess foam, which can result in a leak. If it is accidentally used, sprinkle ordinary salt into the chamber to disperse the resulting suds. Then rinse away the excess salt before using.

There are 3 main types of dishwasher detergent - Powder, liquid or gel and tablets. Which one you choose will be down to personal preference, but most people find tablets very convenient, although using powder is usually more economical and liquids are less abrasive on more delicate items.

Rinse aid

Rinse Aid is added to a special compartment in the machine and a very small amount is released during the final hot rinse cycle, to reduce the formation of water droplets on crockery etc. and so ensures that the water dries away properly and evenly to avoid leaving smears.

Dual action detergent

Dual action detergent usually contains rinse aid, which is released at a different rate to the cleaning agent and so helps reduce smearing etc without the need to add separate rinse aid. Some 3-in-1 tablets contain an ingredient, which has a 'salt action', which also helps to improve cleaning, but note this is not a substitute for adding salt to the water softener.

The salt action takes place in the cleaning chamber of the machine, but does not actually replenish the water softener. Research has shown that whilst 3-in-1 detergents do clean dishes effectively, their performance is improved by adding salt to the water softener reservoir.

As the performance of machines can vary, as can local water conditions, it is always best to follow your manufacturer's advice. Some manufacturers advise that if you have unsatisfactory cleaning performance e.g. white powder residue, poor drying or dirty dishes, then you should return to using three separate products i.e. detergent, rinse aid and granular salt. Be aware that if you have not been filling the salt reservoir and relying on the salt in 3-in-1 tablets, then it may take a few cycles to re-generate the softener.

Depending on the model, various cycles are available to the user. They may vary by the number of washes and rinses, type of load, degree of soil, and type of drying (air or heated). For most full loads, the regular or "normal" cycle will do the job well, but consider all the options and use any of the features the dishwasher offers. Special "energy-saving" cycles may be offered. Don't shorten the normal wash time just to save energy; the washing action itself takes very little power. A too-short cycle may be a waste of hot water and detergent if results are poor.

Unloading Dishes

When dry and cool, a load of dishes can be left in the dishwasher until needed. Most users agree that unloading should be done before starting to prepare the next meal. To avoid the doubt about "clean or dirty," leave the door latched until all clean dishes are put away. Some newer models have a signal device to indicate the dishwasher has been run. The forceful action, hot water and alkaline detergent in a dishwasher can be harmful to some items. Always check the dishwasher manufacturer's instructions about washing.

Bibliography

Bryan, Mary and Etta Howes Handy. *Furnishings and equipment for residence halls.* New York city: Teachers college Columbia university, 1933.

Boomer, Lucius Messenger. *Hotel management; principles and practice.* New York: Harper, 1938.

Bradley, Alice. *Cooking for profit; catering and food service management.* Chicago: American school of home economics, 1922.

Dahl, J. O. *Food standards handbook for quantity cookery; buying guide, portion sizes, weightsmeasures.* Stamford Conn: The Dahls, 1939.

_______________., *Kitchen management, construction, planning, administration.* New York, London: Harper & Brothers, 1928.

Dana, Arthur W. *Kitchen planning for quality food service.* New York: Harper, 1949.

Maury, Sarah Webb and Lena L. Tachau. *A penny lunch, its equipment, menus and management.* Louisville Ky: The Standard printing co. incorporated, 1915.

Segeler, Curt George, J. Stanford Setchell, and American Gas Association. *Commercial kitchens: a guide to better performance.* New York: American Gas Association, 1948.

Thomas, Orpha Mae Huffman. *A scientific basis for the design of institution kitchens.* n. p., 1947.

Turner, E. *A catering business of your own; teashop, cafe & restaurant management.* London: Practical Press Ltd., 1949.

Vehling, Joseph Dommers et al. *Cooking, or, Practical and economical training for those who are to be* servants, wives, and mothers: management of the kitchen, plain cooking, bread-making, baking, brewing, *pickling, etc.* London: J. Masters, 1854.

Wendehack, Clifford Charles. *Golf & country clubs; a survey of the requirement of planning construction and equipment of the modern club house.* New York: W. Helburn inc., 1929.

INDEX